Ukraine's Outpost

Dnipropetrovsk and the Russian-Ukrainian War

EDITED BY

TARAS KUZIO, SERGEI I. ZHUK AND PAUL D'ANIERI

E-INTERNATIONAL
RELATIONS
PUBLISHING

E-International Relations
Bristol, England
2022

ISBN 978-1-910814-60-4

This book is published under a Creative Commons CC BY-NC 4.0 license. You are free to:

- **Share** – copy and redistribute the material in any medium or format.

- **Adapt** – remix, transform, and build upon the material.

Under the following terms:

- **Attribution** – You must give appropriate credit to the author(s) and publisher, provide a link to the license and indicate if changes were made. You may do so in any reasonable manner, but not in any way that suggests the licensor endorses you or your use.

- **Non-Commercial** – You may not use the material for commercial purposes.

Any of the above conditions can be waived if you get permission. Please contact info@e-ir.info for any such enquiries, including for licensing and translation requests. Other than the terms noted above, there are no restrictions placed on the use and dissemination of this book for student learning materials or scholarly use.

Production: Michael Tang
Cover Image: Taras Kuzio

The photos featured in this book taken from the exhibition section "The achievements of civil society in Dnipropetrovsk during the ATO" / Museum of the ATO are used with permission from the administration of the D. I. Yavornytskyy Dnipropetrovsk national historical museum. Images featuring the work of Valerii Kolor (Zdes Roy) and FreeDnipro.TV are used with permission.

A catalogue record for this book is available from the British Library.

E-International Relations

Editor-in-Chief and Publisher: Stephen McGlinchey
Books Editor: Bill Kakenmaster
Editorial Assistance: Sabrina Beaver, Jason Reynado

E-International Relations is the world's leading International Relations website. Our daily publications feature expert articles, reviews and interviews – as well as student learning resources. The website is run by a non-profit organisation based in Bristol, England and staffed by an all-volunteer team of students and academics. In addition to our website content, E-International Relations publishes a range of books. As E-International Relations is committed to open access in the fullest sense, free electronic versions of our books, including this one, are available on our website.

Find out more at https://www.e-ir.info/

Abstract

This is the first book to analyse the Russian-Ukrainian war from a regional perspective considering the role played by the Dnipropetrovsk region as the country's forpost (outpost) in Russia's war against Ukraine. In the Soviet Union, Dnipropetrovsk was a closed city due to its large military industrial complex, and it was the world's biggest producer of nuclear missiles. This book analyses how a city that was once the pride of Soviet power became a bastion of Ukrainian patriotism in the face of Russian military aggression in 2014 and thereafter. Led by Jewish-Ukrainian Russian speakers, the city of Dnipro and the region of Dnipropetrovsk prevented the spread of the Kremlin's so-called 'New Russia' project beyond the Donbas into the heart of Ukraine. This pathbreaking study challenges Russian disinformation and Western stereotypes of Ukraine which portray it as a regionally divided country with the military conflict as a 'civil war' between Russian and Ukrainian speakers.

Contents

INTRODUCTION
Paul D'Anieri   1

1. COMMUNIST PARTY POLITICS, ROCKETS AND KOMSOMOL BUSINESS IN SOVIET DNIPROPETROVSK
Sergei I. Zhuk   10

2. 'EASTERN UKRAINE' IS NO MORE: WAR AND IDENTITY IN POST-EUROMAIDAN DNIPROPETROVSK
Taras Kuzio   28

3. THE REVIVAL OF THE DNIPROPETROVSK AND DNIPRO JEWISH COMMUNITY IN UKRAINE
Olena Ishchenko   65

4. MEMORY POLITICS IN DNIPROPETROVSK, 1991–2015
Oleh Repan   90

5. THE OUTPOST OF UKRAINE: THE ROLE OF DNIPRO IN THE WAR IN THE DONBAS
Nicholas Kyle Kupensky and Olena Andriushchenko   107

6. DECOMMUNISATION IN DNIPROPETROVSK AND DNIPRO IN 2014–2019
Ihor Kocherhin   144

7. DO NATIONAL AND GEOPOLITICAL IDENTITIES EXPLAIN ATTITUDES TO DECOMMUNISATION? A COMPARISON OF DNIPRO AND KHARKIV
Oleksiy Musiyezdov   164

8. IDPS AND THE MEDIA: WHAT SHAPES THE NARRATIVES ON INTERNALLY DISPLACED PEOPLE IN DNIPRO MEDIA?
Kostyantyn Mezentsev and Eugenia Kuznetsova   191

NOTE ON INDEXING   213

Editors and Contributors

Olena Andriushchenko is an award-winning international journalist from Dnipro, Ukraine, where she wrote for the newspaper *Dnepr vechernii* and was the director of the press centre and anchor of the talk show *The Press Centre Reports* at Open TV Media. She is currently the director of EA Global Media, where she produces the social media talk show *The Ukrainian Dream* and has contributed to Voice of America, *Ukrainian People*, and multiple regional and national Ukrainian news outlets.

Paul D'Anieri is Professor of Political Science and Public Policy at the University of California, Riverside. His most recent book is *Ukraine and Russia: From Civilized Divorce to Uncivil War* (Cambridge University Press, 2019).

Olena Ishchenko is a Researcher at the Museum of Jewish Memory and Holocaust in Ukraine in Dnipro. In 1992–2017 she worked as a professorial assistant in the Department of the History of Ukraine, O. Honchar Dnipropetrovsk National University. Her academic research covers interethnic relations in Soviet Ukraine, Joseph Stalin's anti-Semitic policies in post-war USSR, and Jewish education and upbringing.

Nicholas Kyle Kupensky is an Assistant Professor in the Department of Foreign Languages at the United States Air Force Academy, where he teaches Russian and Foreign Area Studies. His research focuses on the aesthetics of industrial landscapes in Soviet Ukraine, and his work has appeared in *Harvard Ukrainian Studies*, *Nationalities Papers*, *Ukrayina moderna*, *Muzeinyi vistnik*, *Slovo*, and *H-Ukraine*.

Ihor Kucheriv is Professor of History and Political Theory at the National Technical University 'Dnipro Polytechnic'. Since 2019 he has served as head of Southern and Eastern Department of the Ukrainian Institute of National Remembrance. His research interests focus on the history of Southern Ukraine, local History in Dnipropetrovsk, the nobility, and genealogy.

Taras Kuzio is a Research Fellow at the Henry Jackson Society in London, and Professor of Political Science at the National University of Kyiv Mohyla Academy. He is the author, co-author, and editor of 21 books, including *Russian Nationalism and the Russian-Ukrainian War* (Routledge 2022), 6 think tank monographs, and 165 scholarly articles and book chapters on Ukrainian and Eurasian politics, nationalism, and European studies.

Eugenia Kuznetsova is a media researcher with a background in applied journalism research in societies afflicted by conflict and a research fellow at the Kyiv School of Economics. She works as a consultant for several international organisations, focusing on the fields of impartiality, balanced views, and conflict-sensitive reporting.

Kostyantyn Mezentsev is Professor and Head of the Department of Economic and Social Geography at Taras Shevchenko National University of Kyiv. His recent research examines the transformation of post-Soviet urban regions and cities, suburban spaces, migration, urban geopolitics, and IDPs issues. He is co-editor of the book *Urban Ukraine: In the Epicentre of the Spatial Changes* (2017).

Oleksiy Musiyezdov is a Professor at V.N.Karazin Kharkiv National University. He is the author of *Urban Identity in a (Post)Contemporary Megapolis: The Ukrainian Experience* (2016).

Oleh Repan is an Associate Professor in the Department of History of Ukraine, O. Honchar Dnipropetrovsk National University. In 2021 he was appointed Director of the Museum of the History of Dnipro. He has published 58 academic articles and 2 books. His academic interests are the history of Ukrainian Cossacks, local history, and social history.

Sergei I. Zhuk is Professor of History at Ball State University, Indiana, USA. His research interests are international relations (especially US-Russia), knowledge production, cultural consumption, religion, popular culture, and identity in a history of imperial Russia, Ukraine, and the Soviet Union. His latest book is *KGB operations against the USA and Canada in Soviet Ukraine, 1953–1991* (Routledge 2022).

Introduction

PAUL D'ANIERI

The literature on regionalism in Ukraine is extensive (see Arel and Khmelko 1996; Barrington 1997; Barrington and Faranda 2009; D'Anieri 2007; Hale 2008; Kubicek, 2000; Kulyk 2016; O'Loughlin 2001; Sasse 2010; Wolczuk, 2007). Scholars have debated the sources of regional differences from a variety of factors. They have debated the best way of defining regions, with some using a simple East/West dichotomy, others using a quadripartite East/South/Central/West, and still others identifying even more regions (see Barrington and Herron 2004). Particular attention has been paid to the political consequences of regionalism, and Russia's seizure of Crimea and intervention in Eastern Ukraine has raised the stakes in these discussions. Some see the conflict in Eastern Ukraine as a manifestation of Ukraine's regionalism, rather than of external intervention.

While the literature on regionalism is immense, the literature on regions themselves is much smaller, and is highly concentrated on a few prominent cases such as Crimea, Donbas (Donetsk and Luhansk *oblasts* – 'oblast' denotes an administrative division or region), and Galicia. Central Ukraine is treated largely as a residual category of Kyiv, while parts of the east outside the Donbas are given relatively little attention, as are parts of the south beyond Crimea. The concentration of these essays on Dnipropetrovsk oblast and the city of Dnipropetrovsk (from 2016 renamed Dnipro), which in the standard quadripartite scheme are usually considered part of the East but are sometimes placed in the South (and which Taras Kuzio's chapter argues has moved towards the centre), is therefore unusual and particularly valuable. Lowell Barrington and Erik S. Herron (2004) place Dnipropetrovsk oblast in the East of a four-region scheme while Olga Onuch and Henry E. Hale (2018) place it in the South.

The city of Dnipro, known from 1926 to 2016 as Dnipropetrovsk and before 1926 as Yekaterinoslav, is Ukraine's fourth largest city (see Zhuk 2010). The Dnipro River, sometimes seen as defining the heart of Ukraine and sometimes seen as the border between East and West, runs through it. While not receiving as much attention as some other cities and regions, Dnipro is far from obscure. In the Soviet Union, Dnipropetrovsk nurtured Leonid Brezhnev, who ran the USSR for 18 years between 1964–1982, and rivalled Leningrad for influence. From 1994 until the 2004 Orange Revolution, a reinvigorated Dnipropetrovsk clan, centred on Leonid Kuchma, held a powerful position in Ukrainian politics before being eclipsed by the rise of the Donetsk-based Party of Regions from 2005 to 2014.

Dnipro is the administrative centre of the region still known (since 1932) as Dnipropetrovsk. Because regional names are written in Ukraine's constitution, changing them is more complicated, and while the Constitutional Court has ruled the change constitutional, parliamentary approval was still needed at the time of writing. Therefore, in this collection of essays, authors generally refer to the oblast centre city as Dnipro, and to the region as Dnipropetrovsk.

Beyond a focus on this city and surrounding region, the chapters in this book are not constrained by a particular thematic, methodological, or theoretical orientation. While most of the essays are written by academics and reflect scholarly disciplines, the authors also include activists and public intellectuals, whose work is defined less in disciplinary terms. Rather they embody the notion that there is much to be gained examining a common topic through a diversity of approaches. Sergei Zhuk provides an important overview of the Soviet history of Dnipropetrovsk. Kuzio's chapter analyses the bigger picture, arguing that because of war in Eastern Ukraine, Dnipro city and Dnipropetrovsk region have effectively reidentified, such that they are now better thought of as part of Central Ukraine than as part of Eastern Ukraine. Olena Ishchenko examines the rise of Dnipropetrovsk's Jewish community since 1991. Nicholas Kyle Kupensky and Olena Andriushchenko investigate the impact of war with Russia in Dnipropetrovsk and Dnipro. Oleh Repan and Ihor Kocherhin analyse the process of decommunisation from 1991 to the present and competing identities and memory politics in Dnipropetrovsk. Oleksiy Musiyezdov compares attitudes to decommunisation in Dnipropetrovsk and Kharkiv, another important Eastern Ukrainian oblast and city. Kostyantyn Mezentsev and Eugenia Kuznetsova investigate the Dnipropetrovsk and Dnipro media's coverage of internally displaced persons (IDPs).

Zhuk's essay provides a broad overview of the pre-Soviet and Soviet history of Dnipropetrovsk. He stresses Dnipropetrovsk's rise to Union-wide significance in the post-World War II era due to two factors, the rise of the 'Brezhnev clan' in Soviet politics and the establishment of what came to be the *Pivdenmash* (*Yuzhmash*) missile factory in Dnipropetrovsk. *Pivdenmash* and the oblast centre's university drew some of the most talented engineers from throughout the Soviet Union and became not only a source of intercontinental ballistic missiles, but also rockets and satellites for the Soviet space programme. Facilities all over the Soviet Union reported to *Pivdenmash* leaders. While the rocket industry made Dnipropetrovsk prominent across the Soviet Union, it also meant it was closed to foreign visitors.

As a result of its Union-level prominence and Brezhnev's patronage, Dnipropetrovsk also became a dominant city in Ukraine, with over 50 per cent of Ukrainian SSR officials in the 1980s hailing from the region. Dnipropetrovsk's power meant that it had a large degree of autonomy from Kyiv.

Kuzio examines Dnipropetrovsk and Dnipro since 2014 and engages the vibrant debate about political reidentification in Ukraine. Several authors have argued that the Euromaidan Revolution (also known as the Revolution of Dignity) and Russian military aggression have led to a strengthening of Ukrainian identity in Ukraine, and Kuzio supports that argument by looking at events in this city and region. Dnipropetrovsk and Dnipro, Kuzio contends, became a crucial bulwark against the spread of Russian hybrid warfare in 2014, blocking its spread and containing it to Donetsk and Luhansk. This role accentuates the differences Kuzio finds between Dnipropetrovsk, on the one hand, and Donetsk and Luhansk, on the other. He links the opposition to Russian moves in the region with the strength of Ukrainian civic, rather than ethnic identity, pointing out that the three leaders of this resistance were not ethnic Ukrainians (1 was Russian and 2 were Jews).

Kuzio makes the more provocative argument, first aired by Tatyana Zhurzhenko (2015) that Ukraine's 'East' no longer exists. He argues that Dnipropetrovsk and Dnipro's identification with the Donbas was always tenuous, and the conflict there spurred a strengthening of identification with Central (or East-Central) Ukraine at the expense of its identification with the 'East.' This reidentification occurred in three neighbouring oblasts (Zaporizhzhya, Kherson, Mykolayiv) as well, with the result that the old pro-Russian 'East' consists now only of those parts of Donetsk and Luhansk that are occupied by Russian forces and their Ukrainian proxies. Pro-Russian sentiments and Soviet nostalgia have all but disappeared from these other four oblasts. This raises the deeper question of the validity of the macro regions scholars impose upon Ukraine.

Ishchenko analyses the revival of the Jewish community in Dnipro since independence. Jews experienced discrimination under the Soviets, and assimilation reduced the number of self-identified Jews, although the Soviet practice of recording people's nationality helped maintain some people's

Jewish identity. Under Soviet leader Mikhail Gorbachev's thaw in 1985-1991, Jews in Dnipro began organising more openly, and groups from abroad provided support, beginning a renaissance. After the fall of the Soviet Union, emigration to places with less discrimination and more economic opportunity lowered numbers but strengthened ties with communities in Israel, the US, and Western Europe. Initially dependent on support from abroad, the financial success of some members of the community led to substantial support from within Ukraine. Over time, the community developed a range of Jewish educational institutions, secured the return of three synagogues, built new community centres, and built a museum focusing on the Jewish experience in the region.

The war with Russia has helped redefine the relationship between the Jewish community and Ukraine more broadly. Jews, Ishchenko points out, had little reason to be nostalgic for the Soviet Union, and their prominence in Dnipro, she says, helps explain how Dnipro pivoted from Soviet stronghold to supporter of Ukrainian statehood. The Dnipro-based oligarch Ihor Kolomoyskyy has been a major benefactor of Jewish causes in Ukraine. In 2014, Kolomoyskyy organised volunteer battalions to combat Russia-backed separatists. Ishchenko documents the broader role of Jews in the war against Russia. The creation of a Jewish militia company by former *Pravyy Sektor* (Right Sector) head Dmytro Yarosh is evidence that relations between Jews and Ukrainian nationalists are more complex than is sometimes portrayed.

Oleh Repan analyses memory politics in Dnipropetrovsk during Ukraine's independence until the adoption of the decommunisation laws in April 2015. The case is especially interesting, Repan says, because under the Soviets, Dnipropetrovsk was in some respects the quintessential Soviet city. Repan argues that both culturally and politically, Dnipro gradually became a more Ukrainian city after 1991, and he sees these trends as being connected, with memory politics helping to drive changes in voting behaviour. Repan pays particular attention to the Cossack period of Ukrainian history, which receives relatively little attention in many treatments of memory politics but has salience in Dnipropetrovsk, where pro-Russian and pro-Ukrainian Cossack groups vied for influence. Regarding the Imperial period, a prominent theme of the political establishment was the civilising influence of the Tsarist Russian Empire on the region. A battle over Tsarina Catherine the Great's legacy was at the heart of this debate.

Repan moves through history, reviewing Ukraine's memory politics in each era. Overall, Repan says, memory politics in Dnipro has been consistent with that elsewhere in Ukraine more broadly, with particular focus on local events and issues. The persistence of statues of Soviet leader Vladimir Lenin alongside commemoration of the *Holodomor* (death by hunger), which Repan finds 'absolutely absurd,' perhaps captures the complexity and hybridity of post-Soviet memory. Nonetheless, after 2014, narratives more liberal and more critical of Imperial and Soviet identities resonated much more effectively, and therefore became dominant.

Kupensky and Andriushchenko investigate the role of Dnipropetrovsk and Dnipro and of people from the region in the Russian-Ukrainian war in Eastern Ukraine. Kupensky and Andriushchenko argue that Dnipropetrovsk and Dnipro's identity has changed from the Soviet-era 'Rocket City' to a new *forpost* (outpost) of Dnipro, which they characterise as an advance guard, with both offensive and defensive connotations. Dnipropetrovsk and Dnipro was both an important location from which to stage resistance to aggression in Donbas as well as a refuge for those fleeing the conflict. Kupensky and Andriushchenko examine why this came about.

Prominent in this chapter are the many refugees, volunteer fighters and civic volunteers, some of whose stories Kupensky and Andriushchenko relate. They also dig deeply into the cultural production that has resulted from the conflict, stressing the role of artists and exhibitions in representing Dnipropetrovsk and Dnipro's new role and identity. They provide detailed analysis of the ways in which the conflict is being memorialised. While Kupensky and Andriushchenko do not stress this, the process they chronicle is immensely important in the study of the politics of memory, in the sense that the real-time representation of the conflict and its consequences becomes the first draft of historical memory.

Ihor Kocherhin examines decommunisation in Dnipropetrovsk and makes the case for decommunisation in general. To Kocherin, the question of decommunisation is one of whether Ukraine could move towards becoming a European state, or whether it would remain part of the Russian World. Framing the problem this way makes a crucial point: battles over Ukraine's past have been so bitter because they are struggling over Ukraine's future. Kocherin summarises the arguments against removing monuments and changing place names and finds them 'unworthy.' He sees removing monuments and changing place names as essential for showing that Dnipropetrovsk and Dnipro is part of Ukraine, not the Russian World.

Like many Ukrainian cities, Dnipropetrovsk still had a monument to Lenin in its central Lenin Square which was pulled down by Euromaidan Revolutionary protestors on 22 February, the day President Viktor Yanukovych fled Kyiv, part of the nationwide movement known as *Leninopad* (Lenin-fall). Kocherin details the sources of the many new toponyms, which totaled over 300 in

Dnipro, showing how they reflected the city's history and geography. Kocherin states that much of the physical work of decommunisation in Dnipro is complete but he believes changes in people's attitudes will take longer.

Oleksiy Musiyezdov compares attitudes to decommunisation in Dnipro and Kharkiv. These two cities have much in common. More importantly, this within-region comparison (if one puts Dnipro in the East) or South versus East comparison (if one puts Dnipro in the South) provides a valuable variation from the East versus West comparisons that dominate discussion of Ukraine. Dnipro and Kharkiv, the authors contend, differ from Luhansk and Donetsk in that mining and metallurgy, which dominate in Donbas, tend to generate a homogeneous working class, whereas the high-tech industries (aviation, rocketry, weaponry) that dominate Dnipro and Kharkiv made the population more differentiated and therefore harder to mobilise.

Musiyezdov finds that while most respondents in both cities oppose decommunisation, opposition is higher in Kharkiv, and they ask why. Surprisingly, they find that neither Ukrainian nor Russian identity correlates with views on decommunisation, but that European identity, which is held by fewer than 30 per cent of respondents, does. Attitudes toward decommunisation appear to correlate with geopolitical preferences, and with more in Dnipro supporting a pro-Western orientation than in Kharkiv, that might explain the cities' different levels of support for decommunisation. Attitudes on decommunisation also correlate with views of the Soviet era. It appears that since 2014, more identity change has taken place in Dnipro than in Kharkiv, a matter that Kuzio's chapter takes up.

Mezentsev and Kuznetsova analyse the vital question of IDPs in Dnipropetrovsk and Dnipro, focusing on how media representations of IDPs shape attitudes and therefore policies. There are roughly 33,000 IDPs in Dnipro, a third of whom are retired and 17 per cent children, according to Mezentsev and Kuznetsova. They make the crucial point that after six years of war and occupation, IDPs are experiencing 'permanent temporariness.' While there is some tendency for people to integrate into their new surroundings, they point out, Ukrainian society continues to stress people's displaced status, because of the desire to believe that the occupied territories will soon be returned.

They sample local TV programming to assess the attitudes being disseminated to Dnipro residents. Among their many interesting findings is that in relatively few of the stories are the IDPs able to speak for themselves, and in that sense, they are often rendered silent or passive. The effect is that IDPs are presented not as agents, but as recipients of aid.

While this edited book focuses on Dnipropetrovsk and Dnipro, it illustrates the broad value of region-focused, multi-disciplinary projects. We would learn a great deal by such regional analyses of other parts of Ukraine that do not fit into the standard 'East-West' or 'East-West-Kyiv' schemes. Kharkiv, for example, is lumped in with the Donbas, but is clearly distinct, both in its history and its current politics. Uzhhorod and Trans-Carpathian oblast, similarly, are seen as part of the West but are quite different from Galicia, not to mention the rest of Ukraine. With so much written about the salience of regionalism in Ukraine, this book provides a groundbreaking contribution towards a deeper and broader scholarly examination of an important region which has been traditionally ignored in academic literature.

Figures

0.1 – Map of Casualties of Ukrainian Security Forces by Oblast as of 26 March 2021. The region with by far the highest number of deaths of Ukrainian security force personnel is Dnipropetrovsk (479). Source: http://memorybook.org.ua/indexfile/statbirth.htm

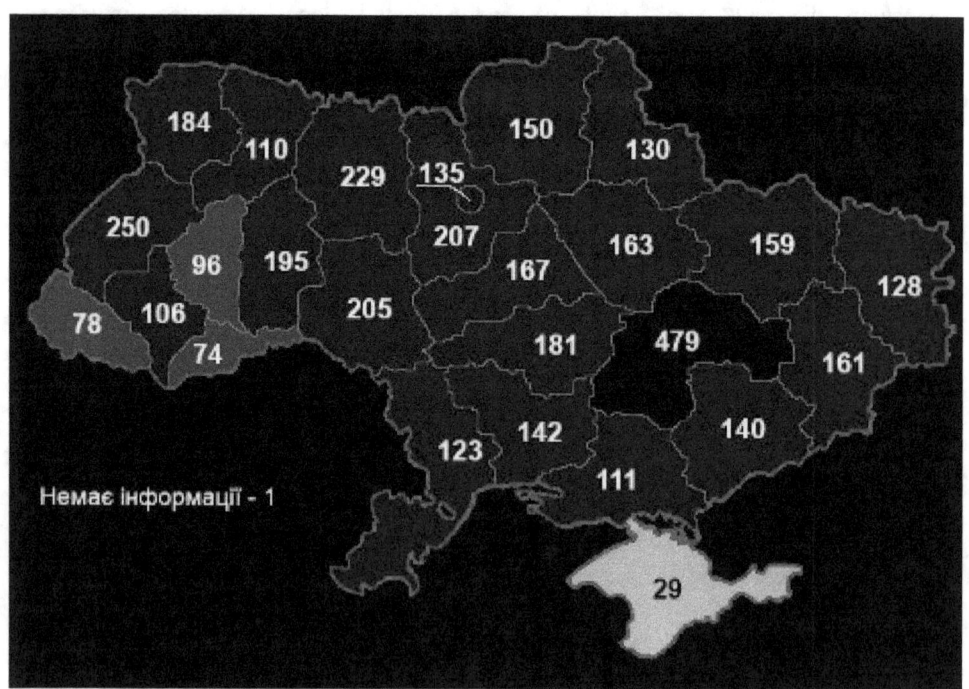

0.2 – Military Cemetery, Dnipro. Source: Taras Kuzio, 2019.

References

Arel, Dominique and Khmelko, Valeri. (1996). 'The Russian Factor and Territorial Polarization in Ukraine,' *Harriman Review*, 9, 1–2: 81-91.

Barrington, Lowell, B. (1997). 'The Geographic Component of Mass Attitudes in Ukraine,' *Post-Soviet Geography and Economics* 38, 10: 601–614.

Barrington, L. B. and Herron, Erik, S. (2004).'One Ukraine or Many? Regionalism in Ukraine and Its Political Consequences, *Nationalities Papers*, 32, 1: 53–86.

Barrington, L. and Faranda, Regina. (2009). 'Reexamining Region, Ethnicity, and Language in Ukraine,' *Post-Soviet Affairs* 25, 3: 232–256.

D'Anieri, Paul. (2007). 'Ethnic Tensions and State Strategies: Understanding the Survival of the Ukrainian State,' *Journal of Communist Studies and Transition Politics* 23, 1: 4–29.

Hale, Henry E. (2008). 'The Double-Edged Sword of Ethnofederalism: Ukraine and the USSR in Comparative Perspective,' *Comparative Politics* 40, 3: 293–312.

Kubicek, Paul. (2000). 'Regional Polarisation in Ukraine: Public Opinion, Voting and Legislative Behaviour,' *Europe-Asia Studies* 52, no. 2: 273–94.

Kulyk, Volodymyr. (2016). 'National Identity in Ukraine: Impact of Euromaidan and the War,' *Europe-Asia Studies* 68, 4: 588–608.

O'Loughlin, John. (2001). 'The Regional Factor in Contemporary Ukrainian Politics: Scale, Place, Space, or Bogus Effect?' *Post-Soviet Geography and Economics* 42, 1: 1–33.

Onuch, Onuch and Henry H.E. (2018). 'Capturing Ethnicity: The Case of Ukraine,' *Post-Soviet Affairs* 34, 2-3: 84–106.

Sasse, Gwendolyn. (2010). 'Ukraine: The Role of Regionalism,' *Journal of Democracy* 21, 3: 99–106.

Wylegałaa, Anna and Głowacka-Grajper, Małgorzata eds. (2020). *The Burden of the Past: History, Memory, and Identity in Contemporary Ukraine*, Bloomington: Indiana University Press.

Wolczuk, Kateryna. (2007). 'Whose Ukraine? Language and Regional Factors in the 2004 and 2006 Elections in Ukraine,' *European Yearbook of Minority Issues*, 5, 6: 521–547..

Zhuk, Sergei I. (2010). *Rock and Roll in the Rocket City: The West, Identity, and Ideology in Soviet Dniepropetrovsk, 1960–1985*, Baltimore: Johns Hopkins University Press.

Zhurzhenko, Tatiana. (2015). 'Ukraine's Eastern Borderlands: The End of Ambiguity?' In: Andrew Wilson ed., *What Does Ukraine Think?* London: European Council on Foreign Relations, 45–52. https://www.ecfr.eu/page/-/WHAT_DOES_UKRAINE_THINK_pdf.pdf

1

Communist Party Politics, Rockets and Komsomol Business in Soviet Dnipropetrovsk

SERGEI I. ZHUK

The Ukrainian city of Dnipropetrovsk (in 2016 the city was renamed Dnipro) was shown on a movie screen in the Soviet Union for the first time in 1981 as a 'Russian-speaking' city in Nikita Mikhalkov's feature film *Rodnia* (Relatives). A story of a Russian peasant woman who visited her daughter in the big industrial city was used by Mikhalkov in his movie to emphasise a growing crisis in Soviet family life during the Leonid Brezhnev era when former Russian peasants lost their Orthodox Christian identity during the process of socialist industrialisation and modernisation. Paradoxically, Mikhalkov completely ignored the real social and national problems of the city; instead choosing as the setting for his movie Russian peasants' adjustment to Soviet modernisation. Even now many Russians use this film as evidence of the 'Russian character' of Dnipropetrovsk ignoring the real demographic and social history of this Ukrainian region (Elberg-Wilson 2016).[1] Despite Mikhalkov's picture, the city of Dnipro and the Dnipropetrovsk region had a multi-national and multi-cultural character coupled with the strong influence of Ukrainian and Jewish culture.

Using various archival and published documents, this chapter will cover the social, economic and cultural development of the city and the region of Dnipropetrovsk through the period of late socialism after Stalin, showing the

---

[1] I used also numerous interviews conducted with my relatives, who are ethnic Ukrainians, but live in Moscow, Russia, who still support Russian President Vladimir Putin's anti-Ukrainian politics.

ties between the multi-national *Komsomol* (Communist Youth League) members and business ventures during *perestroika* and how this influenced the rise of oligarchic clans in post-Soviet Ukraine.

Emergence of Soviet Dnipropetrovsk

Paradoxically, from the early beginning, the founding of the 'city of Catherine's glory' (Ekaterinoslav in Russian) and its province in 1776 by the Russian imperial administration of Catherine the Second involved non-Russian ethnic groups, which shaped a historical demography of this region in Southern Ukraine. These ethnic groups included the local Ukrainian Orthodox Christian peasants and Cossacks, Jewish traders and artisans, Armenian Christians, and Tatar Muslim settlers. By the middle of the nineteenth century, thousands of German Protestant and Mennonite colonists also settled in the province. Moreover, by attracting foreign capital, the Russian imperial administration transformed this multi-ethnic and multi-religious region in the booming industrial centre of the Russian Empire by the beginning of twentieth century (Zhuk 2004, 33–96).

After the Russian Revolution and civil war, the province of Ekaterinoslav continued to play an important role in the industrial development of the Ukrainian Soviet Socialist Republic. In 1926 the Soviet administration decided to change the name of Ekaterinoslav which sounded too 'old fashioned' and 'imperial Russian.' The new name was a combination of the name of the Dnipro River with the last name of Grigorii Petrovskii, head of the All-Ukrainian Executive Committee of the Soviets, and well-known organiser of the working-class movement in the region of Ekaterinoslav before the Revolution. 'Dnipro-Petrovske' was later transformed into 'Dnipropetrovsk' (Bolebrukh 2001, 156).

Both the city and region of Dnipropetrovsk lived through the New Economic Policy (N.E.P.), industrialisation and the Stakhanovite movement. The region lost millions of human lives during collectivisation and the *dekulakisation* campaign, and especially during the Holodomor of 1932–33. During industrialisation, the Soviet government restored the industrial base of the region. Former metallurgical giants such as the *Petrovskii* (formerly *Brianskii*) plant, the *Chodoir* (formerly Vladimir Lenin) plant and others resumed production of pig iron and steel. During the 1930s, Dnipropetrovsk became an important centre for Soviet heavy industry. In 1932, Dnipropetrovsk regional metallurgical plants produced 20 per cent of the entire cast iron and 25 per cent of the steel manufactured in the Soviet Ukrainian Republic.

After the beginning of the campaign of 'Ukrainianisation' in 1923, the number of those who spoke Ukrainian grew, reaching 38.5 per cent in the city by the end of the 1920s. Between 1932 and 1939, the number of city dwellers in Dnipropetrovsk increased to over 500,662. The Dnipropetrovsk region became the most urbanised in Soviet Ukraine with more than 2,273,000 people living in the region (Vasiliev 1977, 55; Bolebrukh 2001, 159–164).

Dnipropetrovsk also became the cultural and educational centre of Soviet Ukraine. There were ten colleges, including the State University, 97 secondary schools and 19 vocational schools. The Soviet administration restored local drama and music theatres. During the 1930s, Dnipropetrovsk had 120 libraries, five museums, six movie-theatres, 30 clubs and palaces of culture (Bolebrukh 2001,159–164).

The Leonid Brezhnev Clan

Post-war Soviet modernisation influenced the careers of many young and ambitious *Komsomol* members in the region. One of them, Leonid Brezhnev, was born in 1906 in Kamenskoe, joined the Kommunystycheskaya Partyya Sovetskoho Soyuza (Communist party of the Soviet Union – KPSS) in 1931 and, after graduation from Dniprodzerzhinsk Metallurgical Institute was elected as a council deputy of the city of Dniprodzerzhinsk. The Stalinist purges of the 1930s removed many old Soviet and Communist officials from government positions who perished in prisons and the labour camps of the GULAG. Young people such as Brezhnev filled the void created by Stalinist repressions in the region. In 1938, the young Brezhnev was elected as a member of the regional committee of the Soviet Communist party of Ukraine (KPU) and head of the Department of Agitation and Propaganda. By the young age of 32, Brezhnev had become secretary of the KPU committee of the most important industrial region of Soviet Ukraine. His career was interrupted by the Great Patriotic War when Brezhnev joined the army as an ideological officer (see Mlechin 2005).

From August 1941 to October 1943, the Dnipropetrovsk region was occupied by the Nazis, and Soviet troops liberated the entire region by February 1944 (Berkhoff 2004, 11, 36, 49, 149–150, 152–153, 248–249). The Soviet administration restored the industrial base of Dnipropetrovsk, and by 1950 the main metallurgical and machine-building factories had reached their pre-war levels of industrial production and productivity.

During this period, Brezhnev began his political career as a talented and ambitious organiser of the industrial re-birth of Dnipropetrovsk. He was an experienced young army ideologist who had proved his loyalty to the Stalinist leadership during the war and was familiar with Dnipropetrovsk before 1941.

The Central Committee of the KPSS sent Brezhnev to Dnipropetrovsk in November 1947 when he was elected first secretary of the Dnipropetrovsk regional committee of the KPU, and he ruled the oblast until June 1950 (*Vosstanovlenie*). His successors were Andrei Kirilenko and Volodymyr Shcherbitskyy, both close friends. Two other young comrades of Brezhnev, Oleksiy Vatchenko and Yevhen Kachalovskii led the region respectively in 1965–1976 and 1976–1983 (Vasiliev 1977, 72; Bolebrukh 2001, 233; Mlechin 2005).

Brezhnev promoted the political career of his old friends, many of whom became prominent political figures in Kyiv and Moscow during his leadership of the KPSS. Both contemporaries and scholars who study the 'Brezhnev period' call this phenomenon the 'Dnipropetrovsk mafia' or rule of the 'Dnipropetrovsk Family' (Nahaylo 1999, 36, 69; Wilson 2000, 162). Since the rise of Brezhnev to the pinnacle of Soviet power, the ruling elites of Dnipropetrovsk influenced not only regional, but also republican and All-Union politics.

Dnipropetrovsk's transformation into an important centre of the Soviet military industrial complex was directly related to the sudden rise of Brezhnev to the pinnacle of Soviet power in October of 1964. Brezhnev promoted the political career of his compatriots from the Dnipropetrovsk military industrial complex. Brezhnev's friends and close colleagues from his post-war years in the Dnipropetrovsk region went to Moscow and became prominent political figures in the Soviet *nomenklatura* hierarchy during the 1960s and 1970s. Two main industries of the Soviet military industrial complex – metallurgy and missile-building – had important factories in Dnipropetrovsk and therefore provided the Brezhnev clan with new members from 1964 until 1982. Even after the downfall of the Brezhnev clan in Moscow in 1983, when Yurii Andropov began his struggle 'against corruption and nepotism' in the Soviet *nomenklatura*, members of this clan continued to play a prominent role in the political life of Soviet Ukraine.

Besides the Physical-Technical Department of Dnipropetrovsk State University, the Dnipropetrovsk Metallurgical Institute also assisted the political careers of many of Brezhnev's close friends who in the 1970s and 1980s became important members of the Kremlin *nomenklatura*. Nikolai Tikhonov, former head of Dnipropetrovsk *Sovnarkhoz* during the 1950s, was one of the deputies of the Soviet Prime Minister between 1966 and 1976, First Deputy of the Prime Minister from 1976 to 1980 and head of the USSR Council of Ministers from 1980 to 1985.[2] Nikolai Shcholokov was the Soviet Minister of

---

[2] *Sovnarkhoz* is abbreviated from Russian *Sovet narodnogo khoziaistva*, an economic department in the Soviet government during the early Stalin era and during Khrushchev's reforms.

Public Order in 1966–1968 and from 1968 to 1982 he was Soviet Minister of Interior. Georgii Tsynev was during 1971–1976 a member of the Central Revision Committee of the KPSS and a deputy head of the KGB from 1970 to 1982. In the KGB he was the 1st Deputy Chairman in 1982–1985 as well as a Candidate Member of the CPSU Central Committee in 1976–1981 and accordingly was a full Member of the said body in 1981–1986. Victor Chebrikov, who graduated from Dnipropetrovsk Metallurgical Institute in 1950, was one of the leaders of the city party organisation in Dnipropetrovsk from 1961 to 1971. In 1971 he became the head of the personnel department of the USSR KGB, First Deputy of the Head of this organisation and from 1982–1988 chairman of the KGB (Pikhovshek 1996, 11–12, 272–274).

Another of Brezhnev's close friends, Volodymyr Shcherbytskyy, promoted the careers of other people from the region of Dnipropetrovsk. With his support, Oleksii Vatchenko became the head of the Presidium of the Ukrainian Soviet Supreme Soviet from 1976 until 1984 with the assistance of another politician from Dnipropetrovsk, Valentyna Shevchenko. Aleksandr Kapto, who worked as a secretary of both the Dnipropetrovsk *Komsomol* organisation and the Soviet Ukrainian *Komsomol* in Kyiv in the 1960s, oversaw the Department of Culture in the Central Committee of the KPU; in 1979–1986 he was a Secretary of the Central Committee and accordingly was the main ideologist in Soviet Ukraine. Many other members of the 'Kyiv ruling class' under Shcherbytskyy were also linked to the Dnipropetrovsk metallurgical and military lobby. Shcherbytskyy's assistant from 1972 to 1984 was Konstantin Prodan who began his career in the *Komsomol* organisation of the city of Dnipropetrovsk (Pikhovshek 1996, 48–103). As a contemporary political analyst noted, 'Officially Prodan was put in charge of industrial production, though, according to insiders of the former KPU Central Committee, his principal function was 'maintaining' contact with Brezhnev's assistant Georgii Tsukanov in Moscow' (Pikhovshek 1996, 33–34).

Another important reason for the rise of the 'Brezhnev Clan' was the relative independence of Dnipropetrovsk's local administration from Kyiv. Because of the status of Dnipropetrovsk as a 'strategically important centre for military industry,' different branches of the local administration were under the direct supervision of Moscow, rather than Kyiv (Interviews with Tihipko, Markov and Bocharova).

The Military Industrial Complex and Ruling Elite of Dnipropetrovsk

The city of Dnipropetrovsk was the location of famous metallurgical and machine-building factories in pre-revolutionary Russia and the Soviet Union. Before 1941, Dnipropetrovsk became the most urbanised region of Soviet

Ukraine. Almost 53 per cent of this region's population lived in 16 cities and towns of the region (Vasiliev 1977, 55; Bolebrukh 2001, 159–164). In 1980, the industrial enterprises of Dnipropetrovsk manufactured a significant part of the industrial products and customer goods for the Soviet Ukrainian Republic. A total of 5.4 per cent of steel, 9 per cent of rolled iron, 28 per cent of pipes, 62 per cent of combine beet-harvesters, 27.9 per cent of television sets, and 8.5 per cent of knitted wear in Ukraine were produced in the city of Dnipropetrovsk (Bolebrukh 2001, 219).

After 1945, the main centre of economic and financial activities of the region and the city of Dnipropetrovsk became neither metallurgy nor mining. The new centre which changed the status of the region and of the city was a secret military factory in Dnipropetrovsk. The entire ideological and cultural situation in the region, and especially the city, depended on this one industrial plant which became the most important part of the Soviet military industrial complex. In July 1944, the State Committee of Defence in Moscow decided to build a large military machine-building factory in Dnipropetrovsk on the location of the pre-war aircraft plant. In December 1945, thousands of German prisoners of war began construction and built the first sections and shops of the new Dnipropetrovsk Automobile Factory (Markov, 1995). In 1947–1948 this factory produced its first cars and special military vehicles. However, on 9 May 1951 the USSR Council of Ministers decided to transform the main shops and sectors of this factory into 'secret production' which included not only special military vehicles, but also powerful rocket engines and different types of modern military aircraft. The former Dnipropetrovsk Automobile Factory was transferred to the Ministry of Armament of the USSR and received a new name – the State Union Plant #586 (Lukanov 1996, 12).

Stalin introduced the organisation of special secret training of highly qualified engineers and scientists who were to become rocket construction specialists. He recommended the introduction of a new college degree at Dnipropetrovsk State University which would be a Master of Sciences in rocket construction. In 1952 the university administration formed a new department with the name 'physical-technical faculty' which was the largest department at the university, admitting on average four hundred students each year. These students received better accommodation and a higher stipend payment than students from other departments and colleges; the lowest stipend for this department was 450 roubles, while the highest stipend at another prestigious school, the Dnipropetrovsk Medical Institute, was only 180 roubles. A special commission from Moscow selected talented undergraduate students studying physics from engineering schools all over the USSR and sent them to the physical-technical department at Dnipropetrovsk State University, where they resumed their studies as rocket engineers. Simultaneously, the university administration announced the admission of new freshmen students in this department. The promise of a good stipend and a 'romantic' career of rocket engineer attracted thousands of talented young people to this 'secret' department, which provided training specialists for only the Dnipropetrovsk Automobile Factory (Horbulin 1998, 9, 62–63).

In accordance with another decision of the Soviet government, in 1954 the administration of this automobile factory opened a secret design office with the name 'Southern Construction Bureau' (*konstruktorskoe biuro Yuzhnoe*). The main assignment of this office was to construct military missiles and rocket engines. Hundreds of talented physicists, engineers and machine designers moved from Moscow and other big cities in the Soviet Union to Dnipropetrovsk where they joined the *konstruktorskoe biuro Yuzhnoe (KBYu)*. In 1965, the secret Plant #586 was transferred to the Ministry of General Machine-Building of the USSR and the next year it changed its name into the 'Southern Machine-building Factory' (*Yuzhnyi mashino-stroitelnyi zavod*) or simply *Yuzhmash* (in Ukrainian *Pivdenmash*). The first 'General Constructor' and head of the 'Southern' design office was Mikhail Yangel, a prominent scientist and outstanding designer of space rockets who led the design office and factory from 1954 to 1971. Yangel designed the first powerful rockets and space military equipment for the Soviet Ministry of Defence. Yangel worked with talented engineers who later became the leaders of military production in Dnipropetrovsk and the official directors of *Pivdenmash*. Two close collaborators of Yangel were the *Pivdenmash* directors Leonid Smirnov (1952–1961) and Aleksandr Makarov (1961–1986). Makarov's successor was Leonid Kuchma, the Director General of *Pivdenmash* in 1986–1992, who later became one of the most prominent political leaders in independent Ukraine and was and still is the only President of Ukraine (1994–2005) elected twice (Strazheva; Platonov and Horbulin; Romanov and Gubarev; Baikonur; Baikonur, Korolev, Yangel).

In 1951 the Southern Machine-building Factory began manufacturing and testing new military rockets with an initial range of only 270 kilometres. By 1959 Soviet scientists and engineers developed new technologies, and as a result, the *KBYu* launched a new machine-building project producing ballistic missiles. Under Yangel, *KBYu* produced very powerful rocket engines which dramatically increased the range of ballistic missiles and from the 1960s, began to be used as launch vehicles for Soviet spaceships. *Pivdenmash* designed and manufactured four generations of missile complexes which included space launch vehicles *Kosmos, Interkosmos, Tsyklon-2, Tsyklon-3* and *Zenith*. The KBYu created a unique space-rocket system called *Energia-Buran* and manufactured 400 technical devices which were launched as artificial satellites (*Sputniks*).

For the first time in the world space industry, the Dnipropetrovsk missile plant produced space Sputniks. By the 1980s, *Pivdenmash* manufactured 67 different types of spaceships, 12 space research complexes and four defence space rocket systems. These systems were used not only for purely military purposes by the Ministry of Defence, but also for astronomical research, for global radio and television and for environmental monitoring. *Pivdenmash* initiated and sponsored the international space programme of Eastern European socialist countries, called *Interkosmos*. Twenty-two of the 25 automatic space *Sputniks* of this programme were designed, manufactured, and launched by engineers and workers from Dnipropetrovsk. *Pivdenmash* and *KBYu* became not only an important centre of the Soviet space industry and Soviet military industrial complex, but also the main rocket producer for the entire Soviet bloc. (Hall and Shayler 2001, 316ff; Siddiqi 2003, 97, 113, 114, 164, 177, 285) The military rocket systems manufactured in Dnipropetrovsk created the base for the Soviet Strategic Missile Forces (Dnepropetrovskii raketno 1994; Bolebrukh 2001, 209–211, 229; Lukanov 1996, 13).

On the eve of the disintegration of the Soviet Union, *KBYu* had nine regular and corresponding members of the Soviet Academy of Sciences, 33 full professors and 290 scientists holding a Ph.D. More than 50,000 people worked at *Pivdenmash*. *Pivdenmash* was 'a state' inside the Soviet state. In 1969, after a long competition with Moscow's V. Chelomei Centre of Rocket Construction, *Pivdenmash* rocket designs won, and from then leaders of the Soviet military industrial complex preferred only *Pivdenmash* models. The Soviet state provided billions of Soviet roubles to finance *Pivdenmash* projects (Horbulin 1998, 6, 24–31).

Officially, *Pivdenmash* also manufactured agricultural tractors and special kitchen equipment for everyday needs, such as mincing machines or juicers for Soviet households. In official reports and public information there were no details given about its production of rockets or spaceships. However, hundreds of thousands of workers and engineers in the city of Dnipropetrovsk were employees of this plant, and members of their families and therefore most local people knew about the 'real production' of *Pivdenmash*.

Dnipropetrovsk as a KGB "Testing Ground"

The Soviet government approved the KGB's proposal to introduce the highest level of secrecy over *Pivdenmash* and its products. According to the Soviet government's decision, the city of Dnipropetrovsk was officially closed to foreign visitors in 1959. No citizen of a foreign country (even Eastern European socialist) was allowed to visit the city or district of Dnipropetrovsk.

From the late 1950s, Soviet people called Dnipropetrovsk 'the rocket city' or 'closed city.' (Bolebrukh 2001, 211).

Members of the Brezhnev clan in the Moscow offices of the KGB and Ministry of Interior also contributed to centralised ideological control in Dnipropetrovsk, which especially influenced the KGB and security operations in the closed city. The local KGB office was always more Moscow-oriented, ignoring the interests of the authorities in Kyiv. At the same time, for Moscow officials who began their careers in Dnipropetrovsk, the city became the testing ground for many All-Union KGB campaigns which they attempted to initiate. Dnipropetrovsk KGB officers were 'pioneers' in the organisation of ideological campaigns which became 'models' for other 'closed' industrial Soviet cities. [This phrase – 'pioneers of ideological campaigns' – belongs to a local retired KGB officer. According to the KGB documents, Moscow's representatives in the Dnipropetrovsk clan always interfered in local KGB business, imposing their own practices on the local officers.] (Igor T.; DADO, f. 19, op. 52, spr. 72, ark. 1–18) As a result, the inhabitants of Dnipropetrovsk experienced more ideological limitations and more brutal anti-Western campaigns than people in many other Soviet cities. Facing direct Kremlin supervision, the local KGB and KPSS ideologists sought to prove their ideological reliability and occasionally exaggerated the 'threat from the capitalist West.'

KGB officers transformed one building in the Dnipropetrovsk Special Psychiatric Hospital (*psikhushka*), located in the town of Ihren (now a suburban district of Dnipro), into a special police facility for 'political dissidents.' All over the Soviet Union, Ihren's *psikhushka* (especially its Section 9) became notorious and known as the worst incarceration for political prisoners. The Dnipropetrovsk KGB tested various drugs on prisoners and performed different medical experiments, treating the most 'opinionated' political dissidents as mentally sick patients. Many religious and civil rights activists and 'bourgeois nationalists,' such as national communist dissident Leonid Plyushch, described the Dnipropetrovsk Psychiatric Hospital as 'mental hell' because of its police system of harsh treatment and everyday humiliation (Plyushch 1979, 304–326, 340–349). Meanwhile, local KGB officers explained their harsh treatment of dissidents such as Plyushch as an ideological necessity to protect a strategically important centre of the Soviet military industrial complex (Igor T).

Growth of the Population and Standards of Living in the Region

The new status of the city brought more state investments and contributed to the overall improvement of the standard of living of its inhabitants. During the 1950s, the main sponsor of city improvements and renovations was the metallurgical industry. During the 1960s and 1970s, the space rocket industry and its biggest factory, *Pivdenmash*, sponsored all major city programmes, renovations and new architectural projects which included the sports palace *Meteor* with a large indoor pool, football team *Dnipro*, city airport, city theatre of opera and ballet, historical museum of Yavornitskii, department store 'Children's World,' construction of thousands of modern apartments, libraries and movie-theatres, and celebrations of the 200th anniversary of the city of Dnipropetrovsk in 1976. (Bolebrukh 2001, 211–212).

Even the expansion and renovation of the Dnipropetrovsk Central Farmer's Market (known as *Oziorka*) was supported by *Pivdenmash* as part of its improvement of the city's life, and a reflection of the growth and strategic importance of the city. From 1958 to 1965 the city administration invested money in building a new covered location for the market and by 1970 they had re-built the entire neighbourhood transforming it into a modern and convenient place for the 'socialist consumption of goods and services.' (Lazebnik 2001, 167–185)

As a result, the missile factory, the centre of the Soviet military industrial complex, contributed to a new level of cultural consumption among not only the city's dwellers, but also among all guests of Dnipropetrovsk. Consequently, the pioneering efforts in the popularisation of new modern forms of Western music such as jazz and rock-n-roll also began among engineers and workers of *Pivdenmash* who contributed to the spread of new cultural forms and activities among those who lived in the city and region of Dnipropetrovsk.

The improving living conditions in Dnipropetrovsk led to an increase of the regional population from 2,339,800 people (with a 56 per cent urban population) in 1951 to 2,850,700 (with a 72 per cent urban population) in 1961. The larger salaries and better distribution of food and industrial goods also attracted young people from other regions of the Soviet Union to Dnipropetrovsk. From the 1950s onward, most of the Dnipropetrovsk population were people younger than 30 years old. In 1970 there were 3,343,000 people in the region (76 per cent of who lived in cities) which by 1984 had increased to 3,771,200 people (with 83 per cent urban population). The population of the city of Dnipropetrovsk grew from 660,800 people in 1959 to 1,066,000 in 1979 and more than 1,153,400 people in 1985 when Mikhail Gorbachev became Soviet leader (Glushkina 1985, 10, 11).

The Dnipropetrovsk region had a young multinational, predominantly Russian speaking population. Three major ethnic groups shaped the cultural development of the region – Ukrainians, Russians, and Jews. During the peak of 'international harmony and prosperity of developed socialism' in 1979, Ukrainians made up the overwhelming majority of the regional (72.8 per cent) and urban (68.5 per cent) population. Due to massive emigration from the Soviet Union, the Jewish population decreased from 2.7 per cent in 1959 to 1.7 per cent in 1979 and 1.3 per cent in 1989. The number of Russians in the region's population grew rapidly from 17.2 per cent in 1959, 20.9 per cent in 1970, 23 per cent in 1979 and 24.2 per cent in 1989 (O vozrastnoi structure 1971; Goskomstat USSR 1991, 100, 102). By 1985, more than a third of the population in the city of Dnipropetrovsk was ethnically Russian. If we add to this number the 3.2 per cent of Russian-speaking Jews and more than 33 per cent of Ukrainians who considered Russian their native language, we will have more than two thirds of the city's population who associated themselves with Russian rather than with Ukrainian culture. According to contemporaries, the high salaries and better conditions of living attracted representatives of various nationalities from different republics who also spoke Russian rather than the Ukrainian language in Dnipropetrovsk (Goskomstat USSR 1991, 106, 108, 119, 122; Prudchenko and Smolenska 2007).

Komsomol 'Business' During the Late Soviet Era

The regional economic activities of local 'businessmen and women' from the *Komsomol* during perestroika had their roots in the pre-perestroika era. They also strengthened trends for independence from Moscow which had earlier existed in Dnipropetrovsk. All the elements of their initial business had already been developed during the Brezhnev era when the cultural consumption of late socialism combined the structures of Soviet international tourism with the ideological efforts of *Komsomol* activists into one business network. Mass rock and discotheque music consumption among Soviet youth was delivered by *Komsomol* and trade union *apparatchiks*. International tourism and discotheque enthusiasts provided these *apparatchiks* with music and video material for their entertainment business. Without these relations it would be impossible to imagine the development of post-Soviet capitalism.

The first pioneers of organising *Komsomol* business in the region were two graduates of Dnipropetrovsk Metallurgical Institute, the Ukrainian-Moldovan Sergiy Tihipko, the First Secretary of the Dnipropetrovsk *Komsomol* regional organisation in 1986–91, and the Ukrainian Oleksandr Turchynov, who worked with Tihipko as head of the agitation and propaganda division in the same *Komsomol* regional organisation in 1987–90. Tihipko and Turchynov initiated and 'ideologically justified' the first *Komsomol* businesses in the region. Two other *Komsomol* members, who also graduated from the same institute as Tihipko and Turchynov, Kolomoyskyy and Viktor Pinchuk, both of Jewish origin, started their careers not in the official *Komsomol* business, but in the black market of Dnipropetrovsk, trading various goods, and using their financial and engineering skills for their own survival in the conditions of economic collapse of late socialism. Kolomoyskyy used his financial skills and connections with Tihipko to organise its own financial corporation *Privatbank*, which became the most successful bank in post-Soviet Ukraine. Pinchuk, using his engineering and managerial skills, founded his own metallurgical venture, entitled *Interpipe Company*. It is noteworthy that all four of those *Komsomol* members, two Ukrainian and two Jewish, used their personal connections through their friends and partners from *Pivdenmash*, including through its last director Leonid Kuchma, to start their first businesses in Dnipropetrovsk (see Golovko 2012).

In the mid-1980s, when *perestroika* (restructuring) created favourable conditions for the managerial skills of *Komsomol* activists, this system produced new activities for cultural consumption, such as video salons which brought their organisers more profits than traditional discotheque clubs. The video business used the same infrastructure and network of the discotheque movement; namely international tourism, *Komsomol* activists, trade union leaders and the 'discotheque mafia.'

This network contributed to the business career of two fans of Western popular music, Yulia Tymoshenko and her husband, Oleksandr (Popov, Milshtein, 55; Ponamarchuk). Yulia Grigian (Telegina) was the daughter of Armenian taxi-driver Grigian and Russian technical worker Telegina, a fan of British rock music. Yulia Grigian married Oleksandr Tymoshenko, son of a member of the city's KPU committee in the *Pivdenmash* administration. In 1978, Yulia Tymoshenko joined the student *Komsomol* organisation in the Department of the Economy at Dnipropetrovsk State University. This department was opened on the initiative of the *Pivdenmash* administration in 1977 to provide training for qualified economists in Dnipropetrovsk's growing military industrial complex.

Yulia Tymoshenko graduated with honours from the Department of Economy in 1984 and began her first job as an engineer-economist through the connections of her father-in-law, Hennadii Tymoshenko. For five years, she worked at the Lenin machine building plant, another factory which belonged to the Soviet military industrial complex. In 1979, she gave birth to her daughter Yevhenia, and until 1988 she and her husband enjoyed a typical Soviet upper-middle class life in their one-bedroom cooperative apartment. They continued to watch movies, listen to Western pop music, and occasionally visited and danced in well-known discotheque clubs in downtown Dnipropetrovsk (Popov and Milshtein 2006, 64–67; Suvorov 1991).

Perestroika changed the young Tymoshenko family. Hennadii Tymoshenko recommended his son and daughter-in-law to join the co-operative movement and promised his support through the city's KPU and Soviet administration. In 1988, the young Tymoshenkos used their old connections in the *Komsomol* discothèque world to open a public service enterprise, a video-rental shop in Dnipropetrovsk, with 5,000 borrowed Soviet roubles. The profits made from this first venture were used to open a chain of video rental stores. They used the experience of *Komsomol apparatchiks*, who brought their first VCRs in Dnipropetrovsk through *Sputnik*.

Contacts in the discotheque movement helped provide these *apparatchiks* with Western video tapes and an audience which was ready to consume new Western cultural products. Former discotheque enthusiasts tested these new business practices and proposed the idea of video salons, which had already become the most popular and fashionable form of entertainment in Moscow and the three Baltic republics. As a result, during *perestroika* both the *Komsomol* and 'discotheque mafia' provided infrastructure for these salons in Dnipropetrovsk.

When in 1987 the KGB opened the city of Dnipropetrovsk to foreigners, *Pivdenmash* imported thousands of VCRs using barter agreements with South Korean businessmen. As a regional KPU *apparatchik* who oversaw the distribution of movies throughout the Dnipropetrovsk region (*kinoprokat*), Yulia Tymoshenko's father-in-law had access not only to these Korean VCRs but also to local movie theatres which provided the first mass audience for video films.

The main base of a Tymoshenko's 'video enterprise' was the location of the former central *Komsomol* discotheque club of Dnipropetrovsk oblast – the Student Palace in the Taras Shevchenko Park of Culture and Relaxation in downtown Dnipropetrovsk (Popov and Milshtein 2006, 52–89; Ponamarchuk 2007). In 1989, she quit her old engineer-economist job and became the head of the *Terminal* co-operative. The same year, another participant in the 'discotheque mafia,' Serhiy Tihipko, was elected as the first secretary of the *Komsomol* organisation of Dnipropetrovsk oblast. He not only supported Tymoshenko's enterprise, but also brought his additional discotheque and *Sputnik* connections into *Terminal*. In this way, discotheque activists and *Komsomol* apparatchiks contributed to the growth and popularity of Tymoshenko's business (Tihipko).

In 1991 after the disintegration of the Soviet Union and Soviet state tourism, the representatives of the Brezhnev era *Komsomol* elite, such as Tymoshenko demonstrated again that a skilful adjustment of this network to the new economic situation was an important foundation for success in post-Soviet business activities. The initial capital of *Terminal*, the music and video *Komsomol* enterprise which Tymoshenko had launched during 'the discotheque era' of late socialism, became the foundation of her business and political career in post-Soviet Ukraine.

Epilogue: Dnipropetrovsk Komsomol Entrepreneurs and the Formation of Post-Soviet Oligarchs

Political corruption in the post-Soviet geopolitical space is rooted in cultural consumption during the Brezhnev era, especially in the so-called 'discotheque effect' on society during the era of 'mature socialism.' During this period of late socialism in the USSR, millions of Soviet young people, loyal members of the *Komsomol*, fell in love with the catchy sound of 'beat music' by the Beatles and hard rock by Deep Purple. Even ten years after the dissolution of the Soviet Union, the post-Soviet space was ruled by former Soviet hard rock fans, representatives of the so-called 'Deep Purple generation,' new post-Soviet politicians, such as former Russian Prime Minister and President Dmitri Medvedev, former Ukrainian Prime Minister Yulia Tymoshenko, former Ukranian President Petro Poroshenko and former Georgian President Mikheil Saakashvili.

Paradoxically, détente in the 1970s led to the influx of Western cultural products into the USSR, such as popular music and feature films. As a result, Soviet ideologists, including the *Komsomol*, attempted to control Soviet consumption of cultural products from the West using 'Komsomol discothèques' where Soviet young people could dance to 'ideologically permitted' Soviet and Western music. Contemporaries called these organisers 'disco mafia' in the industrial cities of Eastern Ukraine.

By the end of *perestroika* in 1991, more than 100 *Komsomol* businesses had emerged in industrial cities in Eastern Soviet Ukraine, of which more than ninety originated in the city of Dnipropetrovsk (Zhuk 2010, 301). Only a few of the most successful enterprises survived post-Soviet competition during the 1990s and created 'new business corporations' such as Yulia Tymoshenko's 'Gas Empire,' Kolomoyskyy's and Tihipko's *Privatbank*, Aleksandr Balashov's 'Trade Corporation' and Rinat Akhmetov's *Liuks*. The overwhelming majority of these post-Soviet successful businesses were organised by or directly connected to the 'disco mafia.' At the same time, the first Dnipropetrovsk 'capitalists' demonstrated a wide range of ethnic backgrounds, from the Ukrainian-Moldovan Tihipko, Armenian-Russian Tymoshenko, Russian Balashov and Jewish Kolomoyskyy contributing to the multi-national identity of the city of Dnipropetrovsk and Dnipro.

Some contemporaries noted how the business activities of *Komsomol* 'entrepreneurs' in the 1980s contributed to regional identity in Eastern Ukraine. Many of these 'entrepreneurs' who were not ethnic Ukrainians became active participants in the Ukrainian independence movement in 1988–1991 to protect their regional business interests rather than defending Ukrainian culture and language. In the 1990s, former members of the Soviet 'discotheque mafia' and their former KPU supervisors became an integral part of the business and political life of independent Ukraine. As leaders of oligarchic clans in Ukraine they have resisted Russian expansion into their 'spheres of influence.'

The case of Volodymyr Zelenskyy, elected in April 2019, whose entire career was generated inside the Soviet-based system of television entertainment, continues to demonstrate the connection between 'post-*Komsomol*' business and political careers. Zelenskyy began his acting career in *95-yi Kvartal*, which was a reference to a neighbourhood in Kryvyy Rih, where he had grown up and was inspired by the 1960s Soviet television show *KVN*. As we see, the Dnipropetrovsk and Dnipro elites, which are still rooted in their Soviet past, play a significant role in the development of independent Ukraine.

References

Berkhoff, Karel C., (2004). *Harvest of Despair: Life and Death in Ukraine under Nazi Rule.* Cambridge, MA: Harvard University Press.

Bolebrukh, Anatolii G. et al., eds., (2001). *Dnipropetrovsk: vikhy istorii.* Dnipropetrovsk: Grani.

Derzhavnyy arkhiv Dnipropetrovskoyi oblasti (hereafter – DADO), f. 19, op. 52, spr. 72.

Dnepropetrovskii raketno-kosmicheskii tsentr: Kratkii ocherk stanovlenia i razvitia. (1994). *DAZ-YuMZ-KBYu: Khronika dat i sobytii.* Dnipropetrovsk: YUMZ.

Glushkina, Liudmila G. ed. (1985). *Tsentral'noe Statisticheskoe Upravlenie Dnepropetrovskoi oblasti. Dnepropetrovshchina v tsifrakh. (K 40-letiu pobedy v Velikoi Otechestvennoi voine).* Dnipropetrovsk: Gosstat.

Golovko, Volodymyr. (2012). *Ukrainski finasovo-promyslovi grupy v modernizatsiinykh protsesakh 1991-2009.* Kyiv: Instytut istorii Ukrainy NAN Ukrainy.

Goskomstat USSR. Dnepropetrovskoe oblatnoe upravlenie statistiki. (1991). *Naselenie Dnepropetrovskoi oblasti po dannym Vsesoiuznoi perepisi naseleniia 1989 goda.* Dnepropetrovsk: Gosstat.

Hall, Rex, Shayler, David J. (2001). *The Rocket Men: Vostok and Voskhod, the First Soviet Manned Spaceflights.* Chichester, NJ: Springer.

Horbulin, Volodymyr P. et al. eds. (1998). *Zemni shlyakhy i zoryani orbity. Shtrykhy do portreta Leonida Kuchmy.* Kyiv: Druk.

Kuznetskii, Mikhail I., Stazheva, Irina V. eds. (1995). *Baikonur – chudo XX veka: Vospominania vevteranov Baikonura ob akademike Mikhaile Kuzmiche Yangele.* Moscow: Kosmos.

Kuznetskii, Mikhail I. ed. (1997). *Baikonur, Korolev, Yangel.* Voronezh: Kosmos.

Lazebnik, Valentina I. (2001). G. A. Efimenko ed., *Oziorka nasha: Istoricheskii ocherk o Dnepropetrovskom Tsentralnom rynke.* Dnipropetrovsk: Grani. 167–185.

Lukanov, Yuriy. (1996). *Tretii president: Politychnyi portret Leonida Kuchmy.* Kyiv: Taki Spravy.

Markov, Karlo A. (1995). 'Uchastie nemetskikh voennoplennykh i internirovannykh v vosstanovlenii narodnogo khoziaistva Dnepropetrovskoi oblastiv pervye polevoennye gody' In: Svetlana Bobyliova, ed., V*oprosy Germanskoi istorii: Ukrainsko-nemetskie sviazi v novoe i noveishee vremia. Mezhvuzovskii sbornik nauchnykh trudov,* Dnipropetrovsk: DDU, 158– 172.

Mlechin, Leonid M. (2005). *Brezhnev.* Moscow: Molodaia gvardia.

Nahaylo, Bohdan. (1999). *The Ukrainian Resurgence.* Toronto: Hurst.

O vozrastnoi structure, urovne obrazovania, natsional'nom sostave, iazykakh i istochnikakh sredstv sushchestvovania naselenia Dnepropetrovskoi oblasti po dannym Vsessoiuznoi perepisis naselenia na 15 ianvaria 1970 goda. (1971). *Dneprovskaia Pravda,* June 26.

Pikhovshek, Vyacheslav, et al., eds. (1996). *'Dnipropetrovska simya': Informatsia stanom na 25 lystopada 1996 roku.* Kyiv: Ukrainian Centre for Independent Political Research.

Pikhovshek, Vyacheslav et al. Eds. (1996). *Dnipropetrovsk vs. Security Service*. Kyiv: Lybed.

Platonov, Vitalii P. and Horbulin, Volodymyr.P. (1979). *Mykhaylo K. Yangel*. Kyiv: Nauka.

Plyushch, Leonid. (1979). *History's Carnival: A Dissident's Autobiography*. New York: Harcourt Brace Jovanovich.

Ponamarchuk, Dmytro. (2007). Prosto Yulia. *Izvestia*, September 20.

Popov, Dmitrii, and Milshtein, Ilia. (2006). *Oranzhevaia printsessa. Zagadka Yulii Timoshenko*. Moscow: Izdatel'stvo Ol'gi Morozovoi.

Romanov, Aleksandr P., Gubarev, Vladimir S. (1989). *Konstruktory*. Moscow: Molodaia gvardia.

Siddiqi, Asif A. (2003). *Sputnik and the Soviet Space Challenge*. Gainesville: University Press of Florida.

Elberg-Wilson, Eliot. (2016). 'Eduard Artem'iev and the Sonics of National Identity,' *Slovo*, 28, 2: 2–25.

Strazheva, Irina V. (1978). *Tiulpany s kosmodroma*. Moscow: Molodaia gvardia.

Vasiliev, I. V. et al. eds. (1977). *Istoria gorodov i sil Ukrainskoi SSR v 26-ti tomakh: Dnepropetrovskaia oblast*. Kyiv: Glavnaia redaktsia Ukrainskoi Sovestskoi Entsiklopedii.

Vosstanovlenie Pridneprovia (1946–1950). (1980). *Dokumenty i materially*. Kyiv: Nauka.

Wilson, Andrew. (2000). *The Ukrainians: Unexpected Nation*. New Haven, CT: Yale University Press.

Zhuk, Sergei. (2004). *Russia's Lost Reformation: Peasants, Millennialism and Radical Sects in Southern Russia and Ukraine, 1830–1917*. Baltimore, MD & Washington D.C: Johns Hopkins University Press and Woodrow Wilson Centre Press.

Zhuk, Sergei (2010). *Rock and Roll in the Rocket City: The West, Identity, and Ideology in Soviet Dniepropetrovsk, 1960–1985*. Baltimore, MD & Washington D.C: Johns Hopkins University Press and Woodrow Wilson Centre Press.

Interviews

Igor T., KGB officer, 15 May 1991, Dnipropetrovsk.
Karlo A. Markov, 12 April 1992, Dnipropetrovsk State University.
Mikhail Suvorov, 1 June 1991, Dnipropetrovsk.
Natalia V. Bocharova, 15 March 1993, Dnipropetrovsk State University.
Sergiy Tihipko, director of *Privatbank* in Dnipropetrovsk, 12 October 1993, Dnipropetrovsk.
Yevhen D. Prudchenko and Halyna V. Smolenska, 18 July 2007, Central Library of Dnipropetrovsk oblast, Dnipropetrovsk.

2

'Eastern Ukraine' is No More: War and Identity in Post-Euromaidan Dnipropetrovsk

TARAS KUZIO

'[Vladimir] Putin hates Ukraine. He hates every cell of it, I feel it...These are people who hate Ukraine. Who believe there is no such nation?'
– Deputy Governor of Dnipropetrovsk Hennadiy Korban (2014).

'I do not object to my vote for the law on decommunisation and de-nazification. This law is correct. It has a right to exist. But in addition to the general situation, we need to also consider the feelings of citizens, priorities, and the path which we are taking. We need to consider the specifics of the city.'
– Deputy Governor of Dnipropetrovsk Boris Filatov (Kasianov 2018, 181).

This chapter is a study of how Dnipropetrovsk halted the 'Russian Spring' and Russian President Vladimir Putin's 'New Russia' (*Novorossiya*) project in 2014–15 and became Ukraine's outpost (*Forpost*), preventing a breakthrough of Russian hybrid warfare into Central Ukraine, and Eastern Ukraine outside the Donbas region, which could have threatened Ukraine's independence. Dnipropetrovsk's fight back was an example of civic nationalism led by two Jewish-Ukrainian citizens of Ukraine, Dnipropropetrovsk oblast Governor Ihor Kolomoyskyy and Deputy Governor Hennadiy Korban, and by a Russian citizen of Ukraine Borys Filatov who was Deputy Governor of Dnipropetrovsk oblast and from 2015 mayor of Dnipro. The city of Dnipropetrovsk (from May 2016 renamed Dnipro) has a multi-national character which has been influenced by Ukrainian, Russian, and Jewish cultures (see the chapter by Zhuk). Since 1991, and especially since 2014, Ukrainian and Jewish identities have grown and Russian (and Soviet) have declined. Dnipropetrovsk Jewish activist Yevhen Hendin (2014) said 'Jews were always patriots of this country in which they live.'

The chapter is divided into two sections. The first analyses changes in Ukrainian identity since 2014 brought about by the Russian-Ukrainian war and makes two arguments. The first is that the balance which had characterised identity between the more 'Eastern' city of Dnipropetrovsk and more Central Ukrainian identity of small towns and villages in Dnipropetrovsk oblast has 'tipped' decidedly towards the latter. Since 2014, Dnipropetrovsk and Dnipro have become more ethno-culturally Ukrainian and more Central Ukrainian in its identity, helping to disintegrate the concept of 'Eastern Ukraine.'

The second is Ukraine's 'East' no longer exists (Zhurzhenko 2014, 2015). During wars it is impossible to continue sitting on the fence, and in the case of the Donbas war to straddle Ukrainian-Russian identities. Therefore 'post-Soviet ambiguities and tolerance of blurred identities and multiple loyalties has ended' (Zhurzhenko 2014). 2014 represented a 'new rupture in contemporary history, a point of crystallization for identities, discourses, and narratives for decades to come' (Zhurzhenko 2015, 52). Ukraine's fault line was no longer East versus West but Ukraine versus the Donbas (see Demchenko 2014; Fournier 2018).

Andriy Denysenko, head of Right Sector (*Pravyy Sektor*) political party in Dnipropetrovsk oblast, believes it was wrong to include his region as part of the 'East' because it always had a more Central Ukrainian identity. The Euromaidan Revolution was the straw that broke the camel's back, and many of its participants joined volunteer battalions or volunteer groups assisting Ukrainian security forces fighting Russian proxies and Russian invading forces (Reva 2020, 131, 196; see Poznyak-Khomenko 2020). Patriotism, a sense of injustice, Russia's annexation of Crimea, and what was seen as an attempt to drag Ukraine back to the Soviet Union (as one volunteer soldier put it 'They live in the Soviet Union' in the Donetsk Peoples Republic [Reva 2020, 142]) led many in Dnipropetrovsk to view the Russian-Ukrainian war as a continuation of the Euromaidan Revolution. 'Events in Dnipropetrovsk ended the so-called South-Eastern pro-communist and pro-Russian belt. And it disappeared *de facto* here. The breakthrough happened in Dnipropetrovsk…,' Denysenko said (Semyzhenko and Ostapovets 2014). Medical volunteer Natalya Zubchenko said 'We don't think of ourselves as East or West. We're Central' (Sindelar 2015). Because of its industrial power and size, Dnipropetrovsk's example led, Denysenko (Semyzhenko and Ostapovets 2014) believes, to a 'domino effect spreading to Zaporizhzhya,

Kherson, Mykolayiv and part of Odesa oblast.'[1] At the centre of Putin's 'New Russia' there is now a belt of four pro-Ukrainian oblasts lying between the Donbas in the East and Odesa to the West; Kharkiv, contrary to Putin's amateur history, was never part of the Tsarist Empire's 'New Russia.'

Ukraine's 'East' now consists of three groups of oblasts. The first, represented by Dnipropetrovsk, Zaporizhzhya, Kherson and Mykolayiv, has experienced the greatest degree of Ukrainianisation since 2014. The lowest support in Southern-Eastern Ukraine for the Russian World in 2014 was to be found in these four oblasts (O'Loughlin, Toal, Kolosov 2016, 760). Kharkiv and Odesa have also undergone changes but not to the same extent. The third consisting of two Donbas oblasts of Donetsk and Luhansk are all that is left of Ukraine's 'East.' The 60 per cent of the Donbas region which is controlled by Kyiv has experienced a growth of Ukrainian patriotism, and since 2014 a greater number of the region's population hold a Ukrainian over a regional identity. If Dnipropetrovsk has shifted westwards, the Western region of Donetsk controlled by Ukraine has shifted towards Dnipropetrovsk with which it has historically been connected. Ukrainian-controlled Donbas is undergoing Ukrainianisation while Russification and Sovietisation are taking place in the 40 per cent of the Donbas which is controlled by Russia in the so-called Donetsk People's Republic (DNR) and Luhansk People's Republic (LNR). Since 2014, 37 per cent in Donetsk declared Ukrainian to be their native language, 34 per cent were bilingual and 26 per cent gave Russian. 68 per cent agreed that all Ukrainian citizens should know the Ukrainian language, history, and culture with 26 per cent disagreeing (see Haran and Yakovlyev 2018; Haran, Yakovlyev and Zolkina 2019).

The second section analyses how the Dnipropetrovsk clan led by Governor Kolomoyskyy, Korban and Filatov together with civil society volunteers defended Dnipropetrovsk from Russian military aggression and transformed Dnipropetrovsk into Eastern Ukraine's Outpost (see Poznyak-Khomenko 2020). There are five factors why Dnipropetrovsk did not follow Donetsk (Semyzhenko and Ostapovets 2014). First, Dnipropetrovsk has no border with Russia, and Russian 'political tourists' were therefore fewer and any who arrived were dealt with more harshly. Second, there was no vacuum of power and more decisive leaders. Third, these leaders could rely on a large pro-Euromaidan and pro-Ukrainian constituency. Fourth, Russian media and information warfare had far less influence than in Crimea and the Donbas. Kolomoyskyy (1+1) and Viktor Pinchuk (ICTV, STB, New Channel) controlled pro-Euromaidan and pro-Ukrainian television channels. Finally, Jewish-Ukrainian patriotism and Jewish opposition to Russia and President Putin provided a further bulwark against separatism (see the chapter by Ishchenko).

---

[1] https://www.radiosvoboda.org/a/photo-megamarsh-vyshyvanok/31327623.html

War and Identities in Dnipropetrovsk

Scholarly studies of regionalism and national identity in Ukraine have traditionally focused on Lviv versus Donetsk with Kyiv straddling the middle, which exaggerated the country's East-West divisions (see Arel 1995a, 1995b; Arel and Khmelko 1996; Wilson 1997; Whitefield 2002). These works were heavily influenced by David D. Laitin's (1998) prediction of the emergence of bounded Russian speaking nationalities in Ukraine and other former Soviet republics which turned out to be wrong. These studies were increasingly challenged, especially since 2014, over their claims of bounded identities and the exaggerated influence of language on Ukrainian identity (see Kuzio 2001; Kulyk 2011; Kuzyk 2019; Bureiko and Moga 2019). Russian and Ukrainian speakers were never clearly delineated groups, language use was not static, and many Ukrainians were and remain bilingual. Therefore, 'it does not make sense to talk about bounded language groups' (Giuliano 2015, 517). Russophones in the former USSR – unlike Serbs in the former Yugoslavia – never showed a bounded identity (Kuzio 2007).

Prior to the 2014 crisis important Ukrainian cities, such as Dnipropetrovsk, Kharkiv and Odesa, were ignored in scholarly studies of Ukrainian regionalism. Until 2014, Dnipropetrovsk was included in sociological polls as part of Ukraine's 'East.' And yet, Dnipropetrovsk is more dissimilar to neighbouring Donetsk than Trans-Carpathia is to Lviv oblast. Sociological polls presented results which were biased towards the Russian-speaking city of Dnipropetrovsk, side-lining from the results the Ukrainian-speaking villages and small towns that gave Dnipropetrovsk oblast an identity that pulled it towards Central Ukraine.

Of the eight oblasts traditionally viewed as 'pro-Russian' four have stood out even more since 2014 as being different. When, for example, asked if the Ukrainian authorities were pushing out the Russian language since 2014, and since the adoption of the 2019 language law, only in Donetsk did a majority (65 per cent) believed this to be the case. In Odesa opinion was evenly split between 42 per cent who agreed and 46 per cent who did not. Kharkiv, in addition to the new group of Dnipropetrovsk, Zaporizhzhya, Mykolayiv and Kherson, did not agree (Assessment of vulnerabilities and resilience of residents of southern and eastern regions of Ukraine 2021). A Ukrainian-Estonian study found only Donetsk and Luhansk (which the authors classified as in their 'Red Zone') had a majority who believed the Ukrainian authorities were discriminating against the Russian language. Kharkiv and Odesa (which they defined as the 'Orange Zone') also exhibited some traces of this feeling. The study placed Dnipropetrovsk in the 'Green Zone' in its low levels of criticism of the central governments language policies and memory politics.

Dnipropetrovsk undertook the most radical decommunisation of any oblast in Southern-Eastern Ukraine (Oliinyk and Kuzio 2021, 813-815). The report found the following breakdown of Ukraine's Southern-Eastern regions in terms of their vulnerability to Russian disinformation on Ukraine controlled by Western governments and IMF (Ligacheva 2021):

- Red Zone: Donetsk and Luhansk had the highest level of vulnerability to Russian disinformation.
- Orange Zone: Kharkiv and Zaporizhzhya.
- Yellow Zone: Odesa, Mykolayiv, and Dnipropetrovsk have a high proportion of their populations who disagree with the Russian disinformation narrative of external control of Ukraine.
- Green Zone: Kherson had the lowest level of vulnerability.

The disappearance of the 'East' as a unified pro-Russian concept for Eastern Ukraine after the 2014 crisis and launch of the Russian-Ukrainian war was reflected in the publication of new scholarly studies of the weakness of separatism in Kharkiv (Stebelsky 2018) and Odesa (Richardson 2019) and the reasons for the failure of Putin's 'New Russia' project in 2014 (O'Loughlin, Toal, and Kolosov 2016, 2017; Kuzio 2019). Nevertheless, studies of the impact of the Russian-Ukrainian war on Dnipropetrovsk oblast continue to be rare (see Kulick 2019) and this chapter is a contribution to the gap in scholarly literature about an important city which in Soviet times was the home of the 'Leonid Brezhnev clan' and 'Dnipropetrovsk mafia.'

Dnipropetrovsk was both different to Donetsk on the one hand and Kharkiv and Odesa on the other. Dnipropetrovsk has no border with Russia (unlike Donetsk, Luhansk and Kharkiv) or Russian-controlled separatist region (Transniestria) next door to Odesa. The media environment in Dnipropetrovsk was less under the influence of Russia. Silviya Nitsova (2021) believes the following five factors prevented pro-Russian separatism from being successful in Kharkiv and Dnipropetrovsk in comparison to its success in the Donbas:

1. A well-organised Euromaidan movement.
2. Large numbers of young patriots among Kharkiv and Dnipropetrovsk football fans ('ultras') who aligned with the Euromaidan Revolution and civil society and joined volunteer battalions.
3. Alternative local elites and oligarchs to the Party of Regions.
4. Higher levels of Ukrainian national identity.
5. Pluralism in the business sector and support from small and medium business.

Dnipropetrovsk oblast had high levels of attachment to the Ukrainian language, culture, and history. In 2014, Dnipropetrovsk's oligarchs showed they were Ukrainian patriots; a statement which could not be said of the Donetsk clan (Kuzio 2017, 171–201). Dnipropetrovsk elites viewed Soviet and independent Ukraine as *their* country which *they* had a right to rule – as they did in the USSR. Finally, prior to 2014 Dnipropetrovsk was less reliant upon Russia for export markets and trade (Getmanchuk and Litra 2019).

Distinguishing Dnipropetrovsk from more urbanised Donetsk was the former's Ukrainian Cossack heritage and large number of Ukrainian speaking villages. This provided it with an identity closer to Central Ukrainian regions to its West. Dnipropetrovsk was an oblast with one foot in the 'East' and one foot in the 'Centre' of Ukraine. Central Ukrainian oblasts shared the Dnipro River, which is traditionally viewed as flowing through the 'middle' of Ukraine, with Dnipropetrovsk and Zaporizhzhya oblasts. The Russian-speaking city of Dnipropetrovsk co-existed with Ukrainian-speaking Dnipropetrovsk oblast.

Ukrainian-speaking villages in Dnipropetrovsk oblast were formed in Cossack times and the national memory of Cossacks has remained part of local legends, myths, and oral history (see the chapter by Repan). Cossack mythology experienced revivals during Soviet liberalisations in the 1960s and late 1980s and of course, in independent Ukraine. Cossack villages voted for Viktor Yushchenko in the 2004 presidential elections. There are other villages in Dnipropetrovsk oblast populated by the descendants of serfs who were brought from Central Russia during the Tsarist Empire who voted for Party of Regions leader Viktor Yanukovych.[2] Another important memory that survived was that of the 1933 Holodomor. Zubchenko's grandmother experienced the Holodomor in Zaporizhzhya and after moving to Dnipropetrovsk she was punished at school in 1963 for speaking in Ukrainian. Zubchenko's family history influenced the anti-Soviet views of her family, their support for the Euromaidan Revolution and volunteering to help Ukraine in its war with Russia (see Poznyak-Khomenko 2020).

Zaporizhzhya *and* Donetsk had industries with large proletariat bases. Dnipropetrovsk was more akin to Kharkiv in possessing high tech industrial plants and research establishments with technical and scientific elites servicing the economy and military industrial complex. Dnipropetrovsk and Kharkiv had large student bodies and a more middle class feel in contrast to more proletarian Zaporizhzhya and Donetsk.

Dnipropetrovsk was also different to Donetsk in its oligarchic pluralism. In the

---

[2] Interview with Ihor Kocherin, Ukrainian Institute of National Remembrance (UINP), Dnipro, 9 February 2020.

late 1990s, warring clans in Donetsk and Luhansk were pressured to integrate under the political *krysha* (roof [here meaning political protection]) of the Party of Regions (see Kuzio 2015). Such a unification of Dnipropetrovsk oligarchs never took place. Pavlo Lazarenko and Yulia Tymoshenko, Viktor Pinchuk, Serhiy Tihipko and Kolomoyskyy had different business interests, and often backed competing political interests and media groups.[3]

Oligarchic pluralism translated into media pluralism in Dnipropetrovsk which again made the *oblast* different to Donetsk. Russian television and information warfare in 2013-2014 had less influence on Dnipropetrovsk compared to that in the Donbas. 1+1 channel, one of Ukraine's biggest television channels owned by the Kolomoyskyy clan, broadcasts mainly in Ukrainian. Kolomoyskyy provided funding for *Ukraine Today* channel through 1+1 television channel for a counter-propaganda campaign to Russian information warfare which aired from August 2014 to April 2016 (and on-line until December 2016).

Since 1991, Dnipropetrovsk has always exhibited a high degree of attachment to the Ukrainian ethnos and the Ukrainian language. In the 2001 census, 79.30 per cent in the oblast and 56.9 per cent in the city of Dnipropetrovsk gave Ukrainian as their native language. In Dnipropetrovsk oblast, 17.6 per cent gave Russian as their native language. 67 per cent used Ukrainian as their first language in the oblast and 24.1 per cent in the city of Dnipropetrovsk, showing the difference between the former which was closer in identity to Central Ukraine and the latter which was closer to the 'East' (Piechal 2018).

Throughout Southern-Eastern Ukraine, Russian speakers were never a bounded group. As it became clear in 2014, Russian speakers who had given Ukrainian as their mother tongue in censuses might not use the Ukrainian language in their daily lives but nevertheless exhibited Ukrainian patriotism (Bureiko and Moga 2019). Denoting one's native language as Ukrainian in Soviet and Ukrainian censuses showed an emotional attachment to a language, culture and country that would come to the fore during times of crisis, as in 2014.

Speaking Ukrainian in public while using Russian at home did not reduce the level of Ukrainian patriotism (Osnovni Zasady ta Shlyakhy Formuvannya Spilnoyii Identychnosti Hromadyan Ukrayiny 2017, 25). Russian speaking Ukrainians and Russians volunteered to fight for Ukraine (see Poznyak-Khomenko 2020). Anatoliy Lebidyev, who was born in Russia and lived in Dnipropetrovsk, was scathing of Russia's 'open aggression' against Ukraine.

---

[3] Interview with Kocherin.

Artillery fired from Russia had killed his comrade-in-arms. Lebidyev said: 'I was born in Russia; all my family are Russian; so, because I was born there, I should act wrongly and say, 'I am also Russian' and go and fight against Ukraine?' Lebidyev said 'Before [2014] I used to be proud of being Russian.' As a citizen of Ukraine, Lebidyev had no hesitations or doubts about volunteering to serve in the Ukrainian army and defending Ukraine against Russia, the country in which he was born (Reva 2020, 240–241).

Deputy Governor of Dnipropetrovsk oblast Filatov recalled telling members of the Party of Slavic Unity that Ukrainians no longer viewed Russians as their 'brothers.' Filatov told them: 'tell me the name of the man who completely destroyed for centuries the very idea of Slavic unity and forced for the first time in the history of Russia and Ukraine, or even Russians and Ukrainians, to look at each other through the sights of a machine gun?' Filatov's pro-Russian guests were silent, and he continued telling them: 'I say this was not [US President Barack] Obama, [acting head of state Oleksandr] Turchynov, [Prime Minister Arseniy] Yatsenyuk, or not even [Right Sector nationalist leader Dmytro] Yarosh. This was your so to speak favourite [Putin]. That's right' (Semyzhenko and Ostapovets 2014, 9).

Those Ukrainians who had defined themselves prior to 2014 as 'ethnic Russian' were often from mixed marriages and in some cases held a Soviet identity. The core group which re-identified in Ukraine and especially since 2014 came from the 25.3 per cent of families with mixed (usually Russian and Ukrainian) parents. In the Ukrainian SSR, 59 per cent of Russians and 75 per cent of Jews married outside their ethnic group compared to only 18 per cent of Ukrainians. Ethnic intermarriage was especially prevalent in industrialised regions in Southern-Eastern Ukraine (Osnovni Zasady ta Shlyakhy Formuvannya Spilnoyii Identychnosti Hromadyan Ukrayiny 2017).

In the USSR, 'Russian' and 'Soviet' were understood interchangeably, signifying identity with the Soviet state, and Russian the language of Soviet power. Russian speaking and pro-Russian were not the same in Dnipropetrovsk as in Donetsk. Anna Fournier (2018, 35–36) describes how 'pro-Russianism' in different parts of Ukraine produces 'different Russian intensities' with the highest levels to be found in Crimea and Donbas. The impact of the war in 2014 was not unique and had its historical antecedents; Ivan Dzyuba (2018, 94), a native of Donetsk, points to Ukrainian nationalists in World War II who found common cause with Russian-speaking Ukrainians in Dnipropetrovsk and Donetsk.

In the 1989 Soviet census, Soviet Ukrainian citizens chose 'Russian' as their identities or were given 'Russian' by their parents. Re-identification from this arbitrary pressure of the Soviet state has been on-going since 1991 and has especially grown since 2014. Ukraine's first Defence Minister Konstyantyn Morozov was from the Donbas and was registered by his parents as 'Russian;' after 1991 he found out he was Ukrainian and re-identified himself. Leonid Kuchma was from Chernihiv but had spent most of his working life in Dnipropetrovsk. When he was elected to parliament in 1990, he declared his ethnicity to be 'Russian' but three years later upon becoming prime minister he re-identified himself as 'Ukrainian.'

Analysing trends in ethnic re-identification between the 1989 Soviet and 2001 Ukrainian censuses, Ihor Stebelsky (2009, 100) believed higher numbers declaring a Ukrainian identity 'are not surprising and are expected to continue.' This would especially come to the fore during times of dramatic change (1991) or crisis (2014) when identities would undergo radical re-definition. In 1990s Ukraine the number of 'real Russians' in Ukraine was estimated by Stephen Rapaway to be as low as 11 per cent, not 22 per cent as recorded in the 1989 Soviet census, because of high rates of inter-marriage and arbitrary registration as 'Russian.' In the 2001 census the share of Russians in Ukraine was 17.3 per cent, a decline from 22.1 per cent in the 1989 Soviet census (Kuzio 2003). By 2013, 82.9 per cent of the population declared themselves to be ethnic Ukrainian and 12.8 per cent ethnic Russian, a figure like Rapaway's estimate. Since then, this has changed to 88.6 per cent ethnic Ukrainian and 6.9 per cent ethnic Russian under the impact of the Russian-Ukrainian war (Bureiko and Moga 2019). These figures are like those recorded by the Razumkov Centre (Osnovni Zasady ta Shlyakhy Formuvannya Spilnoyi Identychnosti Hromadyan Ukrayiny 2017, 5) which found the number of ethnic Ukrainians to be 92 per cent and among 18–29-year-olds as high as 96 per cent. Nadiia Bureiko and Teodor Moga (2019) and the Razumkov Centre both found only 6 per cent of Ukraine's population declaring themselves to be 'ethnic Russian,' nearly a four-fold decline from 22 per cent in the 1989 census.

In 2014, mixed Russian-Ukrainian identities in Southern-Eastern Ukraine collapsed (O'Loughlin and Toal 2020, 318). In Dnipropetrovsk, those with mixed identities halved from 8.2 to 4.5 per cent and in Zaporizhzhya and Odesa mixed identities collapsed from 8.2 and 15.1 per cent to 2 and 2.3 per cent respectively. Mixed identities were never strong in Kherson and Mykolayiv where they have *de facto* disappeared, dropping to a statistically insignificant 0.6 per cent and 1.6 per cent respectively. Kharkiv registered the lowest decline from 12.4 to 7.7 per cent. These changes are what Zhurzhenko (2014, 2015) called the 'end of ambiguity' in Eastern Ukraine.

In the two decades prior to 2014, attitudes in Dnipropetrovsk towards hearing and using Ukrainian had already improved[4] and increasing numbers of the Ukrainian population had re-identified themselves as 'ethnic Ukrainian.' Prior to 2014, political entrepreneurs had artificially manipulated language questions and exaggerated alleged threats to Russian speakers to mobilise Russian speakers behind the Party of Regions. This strategy became redundant during the Euromaidan Revolution, and after the disintegration of the Party of Regions and Russian military aggression. Bureiko and Moga (2019) talked of the 'de-politicisation' of language issues during and after the Euromaidan Revolution.

In 2014, Russian claims that Russian speakers were threatened in Ukraine was not reflected in opinion polls. 87.6 per cent in Mykolayiv, 86.1 per cent in Kherson and 79.7 per cent in Dnipropetrovsk did not believe the rights of Russian speakers were being infringed; even in Kharkiv a high of 71.8 per cent did not see discrimination (Dumky ta Pohlyady Zhyteliv Pivdenno-Skhidnykh Oblastey Ukrayiny: kviten 2014). This is one factor why high majorities in Kherson (61.1 per cent), Dnipropetrovsk (65.6 per cent), and Mykolayiv (71.5 per cent) opposed Russia's claim to possess a right to protect Russian speakers in Southern-Eastern Ukraine (Dumky ta Pohlyady Zhyteliv Pivdenno-Skhidnykh Oblastey Ukrayiny: kviten 2014). This was also echoed in low average support in Southern-Eastern Ukraine (11.7 per cent) for the introduction of Russian troops into Ukraine; the lowest support was to be found in Kherson (4.7 per cent), Dnipropetrovsk (5.2 per cent), and Mykolayiv (6.5 per cent).

During the 2014 crisis the Ukrainian language remained important, but it was never the primary and only marker of attitudes towards the Euromaidan, national identity and patriotism. Different studies have shown the strength of Russian speaking Ukrainian patriotism in Dnipropetrovsk and Dnipro co-existing amicably with Ukrainian speaking patriotism under a common civic Ukrainian identity (Kasianov 2018, 220–221). In Southern-Eastern Ukraine, Dnipropetrovsk and Dnipro had the highest number of people (70.8 per cent) who celebrated Ukrainian Independence Day followed by Zaporizhzhya (71.9 per cent) with the number in Kharkiv far lower at 47.1 per cent (Kasianov 2018, 159).

Kolomoyskyy, Korban and Filatov are all Russian speakers. Ukraine's Jewish community is largely Russian speaking. Since 2014 there has been a growth of patriotism in Dnipropetrovsk, as seen in widespread military and civilian

---

[4] This author's personal experience in speaking Ukrainian in Dnipropetrovsk in 1996 and 2019–2020 were radically different. In the 1990s one still received funny looks when asking questions in Ukrainian; this is no longer the case.

volunteer work for the wounded and very long queues of people donating blood, an increase in the number of taught Ukrainian-language courses and greater demonstrative use of Ukrainian in public (see Poznyak-Khomenko 2020).[5] In 2013–2015, increased use of Ukrainian was recorded in sixteen Ukrainian oblasts.

Language was irrelevant during the implementation of the 2015 decommunisation laws by the Dnipropetrovsk authorities, Jewish community, and the Ukrainian institute of National Remembrance. The growth of anti-Russian attitudes, an active civil society, weak pro-Russian opposition, and disorientated public also played important roles. 330 toponyms were changed in Dnipropetrovsk oblast to new Jewish, Ukrainian and local names.[6] Dnipropetrovsk was the only region of Southern-Eastern Ukraine which renamed streets after Ukrainian nationalist figures, including nationalist ideological theorists Mykola Mikhnovskyy (born in what is now Poltava oblast but also associated with Kharkiv) and Dmytro Dontsov (born in what is now Zaporiozhzhya oblast), and nationalist leaders Symon Petlura, Vasyl Kuk (who led the OUN [Organisation of Ukrainian Nationalists] underground in Dnipropetrovsk during World War II), and Roman Shukhevych.

The 2014 crisis and Russian-Ukrainian war transformed on-going evolutionary into revolutionary changes in Ukrainian identity. Between 2013–2015, attitudes to the questions 'I love Ukraine' and 'I feel Ukrainian' in Dnipropetrovsk oblast grew from 88.8 to 92.8 per cent in the former and 85 to 90.1 per cent in the latter. Similar increases were found in Zaporizhzhya (81.1 to 94.4 per cent and 79.8 to 88.8 per cent), Mykolayiv (87.1 to 98.3 per cent and 90.3 to 94.6 per cent), and Kherson (90.2 to 92.2 per cent and 82.6 to 85.7 per cent) (Bureiko and Moga 2019, 151).

In Dnipropetrovsk the war brought the identities of the oblast centre and oblast towns and villages beyond the centre closer together with the former moving away from the 'East' towards Central Ukraine. If before 2014 the ratio between pro-Ukrainian and pro-Russian identities was 50:50 this has now shifted to 70:30.[7] Dnipropetrovsk (9.4 per cent) and Zaporizhzhya (10.4 per cent) had two of the lowest levels of support in Southern-Eastern Ukraine for the attractiveness of Russian culture (Dumky ta Pohlyady Zhyteliv Pivdenno-Skhidnykh Oblastey Ukrayiny: kviten 2014). Higher attractiveness to Russian culture in Kharkiv (18.3 per cent) and Odesa (18.5 per cent) than Donetsk (14.6 per cent) and Luhansk (7.7 per cent) reflected the former two as middle-class cities and the latter two as proletariat where universities were less

---

[5] Interview with volunteer Olha Volynska, Dnipro, 8 February 2020.
[6] Interview with Oleh Rostovtsev and I. Kocherin, Dnipro, 9 February 2020.
[7] Interview with Anatoliy Korniyenko, Dnipro, 8 February 2020

prominent and created more recently. Dnipropetrovsk had lower levels of Soviet identity (15.5 per cent) compared to Zaporizhzhya (25.6 per cent) and Kharkiv (23.3 per cent).

Surveys showed that the Donbas was different in its identity to the remainder of Southern-Eastern Ukraine while Dnipropetrovsk was the most Ukrainian in identity of what sociologists traditionally grouped together as the 'East.' In 2007 in Dnipropetrovsk, 73.1 per cent declared they were Ukrainian speakers or bilingual; the latter are important to include as they would not have had an antipathy towards the Ukrainian language. In Zaporizhzhya and Kharkiv, the figures were 68 per cent and 62.5 per cent respectively.

What also differentiated the Donbas was attitudes towards the Russian language because it was closely tied to allegiance to Soviet identity which remained high in the region. The 'Donbas cardinally differs in its attitude to the language question from the general mass opinion in east Ukrainian oblasts' (Formuvannya Spilnoyi Identychnosti Hromadyan Ukrayiny: Perspektyvy i Vyklyky 2007, 18). In Dnipropetrovsk, the Russian language came third in the allegiance of its population following Ukrainian and Ukrainian-Russian bilingual. In Zaporizhzhya, Russian came second while in Kharkiv it came first. Only in the Donbas was there a majority for the radical policy of elevating Russian to a second state language; and even in this region there were differences with Donetsk far more in support of this step than Luhansk. Northern Luhansk includes a large Ukrainian-speaking rural population which has more in common in identity with Kharkiv (see Donbas. Realii 2017). In 2014, local volunteers in Northern Luhansk rebuffed pro-Russian proxy forces. In Dnipropetrovsk, Zaporizhzhya and Kharkiv there was higher support for the more moderate policy of making Russian an official language. Dnipropetrovsk gave by far the lowest support for elevating Russian to a state language of only 16 per cent (Identychnist Hromadyan Ukrayiny v Novykh Umovakh 2016, 58–65).

Since 2014, Dnipropetrovsk has recorded the highest rates of allegiance to Ukrainian as their native language (50 per cent) and the lowest for bilingual (32 per cent) and Russian (15 per cent) in Southern-Eastern Ukraine. 41 per cent of Kharkiv gave Russian as a native language compared to 24 per cent for Ukrainian. The results for Zaporizhzhya lay between Kharkiv and Dnipropetrovsk. Taken together, a high of 82 per cent gave Ukrainian as their native language or were bilingual (and therefore held an attachment to Ukrainian) in Dnipropetrovsk.

Asked about cultural affiliation, Dnipropetrovsk gave the highest for Ukrainian in the 'East' (54.9 per cent). In the Donbas there were differences between

Donetsk where the most popular cultural affiliation was Soviet identity (37.1 per cent) and Luhansk where it came second after Ukrainian (24.5 per cent) (Formuvannya Spilnoyi Identychnosti Hromadyan Ukrayiny 2007). A decade later allegiance to Soviet (10 per cent) and Russian (3 per cent) cultural traditions in Dnipropetrovsk were the lowest in Southern-Eastern Ukraine. At the same time, Dnipropetrovsk exhibited the highest allegiance to Ukrainian (68 per cent) and European (11 per cent) cultural traditions (Identychnist Hromadyan Ukrayiny v Novykh Umovakh 2016, 58-65). Allegiance to Soviet cultural traditions remained the highest in Ukrainian-controlled Donetsk (28 per cent); although this had declined from being the most popular form of identity because of the growth of Ukrainian cultural traditions (32 per cent).

Dnipropetrovsk as an outlier on identity issues in the 'East' was evident in responses to whether to define the Ukrainian nation as civic, ethnic-civic, or purely ethnic. The two most popular identities in Dnipropetrovsk were ethnic-civic (32.4 per cent) and a surprisingly high ethnic (25.2 per cent); one might have assumed civic would be the most popular in Southern-Eastern Ukraine. Whereas 20 per cent supported a civic nation in Dnipropetrovsk (the lowest of the three categories), 48.1 per cent and 50.1 per cent gave their support to this category in Zaporizhzhya and Donetsk respectively (Identychnist Hromadyan Ukrayiny v Novykh Umovakh 2016, 58–65).

Changes in Ukrainian identity which had taken place prior to 2014 were evident in regional attitudes to the Euromaidan Revolution which — unlike the Orange Revolution — received support in Ukraine's 'East.' In Southern-Eastern Ukraine, 51 per cent were neutral, 15 per cent were hostile and 25 per cent supportive of the Euromaidan Revolution. The highest level of support (27 per cent) and lowest level of opposition (11 per cent) to the Euromaidan Revolution in Southern-Eastern Ukraine was in Dnipropetrovsk (Identychnist Hromadyan Ukrayiny v Novykh Umovakh 2016, 58–65). 83.7 per cent in Dniproptrovsk opposed the seizure of official buildings by pro-Russian rallies (Dumky ta Pohlyady Zhyteliv Pivdenno-Skhidnykh Oblastey Ukrayiny: kviten 2014).

Dnipropetrovsk at War: Patriots, Oligarchs, and Civil Society Volunteers

Patriots

In 2014–2015, Ukraine had not much of an army because it had been asset stripped during Yanukovych's kleptocratic presidency (see Kuzio 2012). Only Dnipropetrovsk and Kharkiv oblasti in Southern-Eastern Ukraine had military bases which became crucially important in the intense war of 2014-2015. Putin's senior adviser on the 'Russian Spring' Sergei Glazyev is caught on tape talking to Konstantin Zatulin (head of the pro-Putin Institute of the CIS) about attempts to block the 25th Separate Dnipropetrovsk Airborne Brigade from moving to Crimea (Shandra 2019). Donetsk, Luhansk and Zaporizhzhya had no military bases. The 25th Separate Airborne Brigade and 93rd Independent Kholodnyi Yar Mechanised Brigade based in Hvardsiiske and Cherkaske, Dnipropetrovsk oblast and the 92nd Mechanised Brigade based in Chuhuyiv, Kharkiv oblast were the closest Ukrainian forces to the frontline and took the brunt of much the initial stages of the fighting in 2014–2015.

Three factors were important in shaping developments and resistance to Russian hybrid warfare in 2014–2015. First, the disintegration of the Party of Regions, Ukraine's only political machine (see Kuzio 2015), unpopularity of the Communist Party of Ukraine (KPU) and removal of traditionally pro-Russian voters (see D'Anieri 2019) because of Russia's annexation of the Crimea and military control of 40 per cent of the Donbas had reduced pro-Russian influences in Ukraine. Pro-Russian political forces lost 16 per cent of voters who had traditionally voted for them. Second, regional elites, nationalist political forces, the Jewish community, and volunteer civil society viewed the defence of Dnipropetrovsk as their defensive outpost of Ukraine from Russian military aggression. A breakthrough by pro-Russian forces into Dnipropetrovsk would have opened the door into Central Ukraine and Kyiv. Third, the Soviet concept of three 'fraternal brothers' rested on a shared past (i.e., Kyiv Rus, 1654 Treaty of Pereyaslav, Great Patriotic War) and a shared future in the Russian World (see Fournier 2018). Russia's annexation of Crimea, Putin's territorial claim to 'New Russia,' promotion of himself as the 'protector' of Russian speakers, and Russian military aggression against Ukraine (particularly after August 2014 when Russian forces openly invaded Ukraine) crossed many red lines. Russians could not be viewed as 'brothers' if they stole your land, killed Ukrainian soldiers and forced two million civilians to flee from their homes. Russia's breaking of the Soviet 'contract' of 'brotherly peoples' helped to tip the balance of identity in Dnipropetrovsk and elsewhere in Southern-Eastern Ukraine. The death of the Soviet 'brotherhood of peoples' re-aligned most of Eastern with Western Ukrainians and thereby increased civic national integration.

In Western Ukraine and Kyiv, the Soviet concept of 'brotherly (Russian-Ukrainian) peoples' had never sunk roots. The greatest impact of the Russian-Ukrainian war has been on Ukraine's South and East and therefore on Ukraine's Russian speakers. Russia's invasion of Crimea and Russian military aggression in Eastern Ukraine led to a re-thinking of Ukrainian attitudes to Russia (see Aliyev 2019, 2020). Putin's military aggression had turned a large part of Ukraine's 'East' against Russia; two thirds of Ukrainians no longer viewed Russians as 'brothers' (Kulchytskyy and Mishchenko 2018, 192). The bulk of the fighting against Russian forces and Russian proxies was being undertaken by Southern-Eastern Ukrainians which is reflected in Dnipropetrovsk and Dnipro suffering the highest level of casualties of Ukrainian security forces (see figure 0.1).

Anatoliy Korniyenko, a 58-year-old resident of Dnipro, enlisted on 19 November 2014 after his 22-year-old son Yevhen had been killed in the war on 12 August 2014. The last time he had served in the military was in the Soviet army in 1976–1978. Korniyenko served five years on the Ukrainian-Russian front line. I asked him why he had enlisted, to which he replied, 'I wanted revenge.'[8] There are many Korniyenkos in Ukraine, particularly in the South and East, who have lost their loved ones to Russian military aggression or who have friends who have lost family members in the Russian-Ukrainian war.

The highest numbers who would offer armed resistance to a Russian invasion are to be found in the four oblasts of Kherson (36.9 per cent), Mykolayiv (31 per cent), Dnipropetrovsk (26 per cent) and Zaporizhzhya (25.9 per cent). The lowest numbers greeting Russian troops in Southern-Eastern Ukraine are to be found in Kherson (1.2 per cent), Dnipropetrovsk (2.2 per cent), Zaporizhzhya (2.5 per cent) and Mykolayiv (4.7 per cent) (Dumky ta Pohlyady Zhyteliv Pivdenno-Skhidnykh Oblastey Ukrayiny: kviten 2014).

The Russian-Ukrainian war is brought home to Ukraine by the fact 15 per cent of Ukrainian voters are veterans of the Donbas war or are family members of veterans. Ukraine's only Museum dedicated to the Russian-Ukrainian war (*Muzey ATO*, see figures 2.1, 2.2 and 2.3) is based in Dnipro which came into fruition in 2016–2017 with the support of the Fund in Defense of Ukraine.

In the centre of Dnipro, approximately 100 school children a day visit the *Muzey Alley* (Museum Alley, see figure 2.4) with graphical memorials to the war and headstones in different languages with the faces of soldiers who have been killed in action.[9]

72 per cent of Ukrainians believe there is a Russian-Ukrainian war, ranging from a high of 91 per cent in the 'West' to 62 per cent in the South and 47 per cent in the 'East.' Another poll found 71 per cent believed what was taking place in the Donbas is a Russian-Ukrainian war (Yak zminylasya dumka ukrayintsiv pro rosiysko-ukrayinsku viynu za dva roky prezydenstva Zelenskoho 2021).

---

[8]   Interview with Korniyenko.
[9]   Interview with volunteer Natalya Khazan, Dnipro, 8 February 2020.

In Ukrainian-controlled Donbas, views are evenly split between 39 per cent who believe a Russian-Ukrainian war is taking place and 40 per cent who do not (Poshuky Shlyakhiv Vidnovlennya Suverenitetu Ukrayiny Nad Okupovanym Donbasom: Stan Hromadskoyii Dumky Naperedodni Prezydentskykh Vyboriv 2019). Nevertheless, 76 per cent and 47 per cent of residents of Ukrainian-controlled Donetsk and Luhansk respectively believe Russia is a party to the conflict with 12 per cent and 31 per cent respectively disagreeing (Public Opinion in Donbas a Year After Presidential Elections 2020). Dnipropetrovsk and Zaporizhzhya have higher numbers of people who blame Russia (40–44 per cent) than Kharkiv (24 per cent) for the military aggression (Identychnist Hromadyan Ukrayiny v Novykh Umovakh 2016, 58–65).

44 per cent in Ukraine's 'South' and 'East' believe Russia's annexation of Crimea was illegal while a similar number (43 per cent) believe it was due to 'free will.' The oblasts with the highest views believing the annexation are illegal are the four new dissenting oblasts in the former 'East' - Mykolayiv (68.2 per cent), Dnipropetrovsk (61.1 per cent), Kherson (56.7 per cent) and Zaporizhzhya (53.6 per cent). Kharkiv (42.8 per cent) and Odesa (46.9 per cent) are close to the regional average while Donetsk (62.9 per cent) and Luhansk (58.1 per cent) gave very high support for the Russian view of 'free will' (Dumky ta Pohlyady Zhyteliv Pivdenno-Skhidnykh Oblastey Ukrayiny: kviten 2014).

Patriotic Oligarchs

In 2014, the 'Dnipropetrovsk mafia' was a battered political force. Lazarenko was fighting an extradition battle to Ukraine after being released from a US jail. Victorious Euromaidan Revolutionaries released Tymoshenko from jail. Pinchuk refused the offer of governor of Zaporizhzhya, while Tihipko was discredited after aligning with Yanukovych and failing to make a political come back in the October 2014 pre-term parliamentary elections. Kolomoyskyy returned from exile and agreed to the proposal from acting head of state Turchynov[10] to become governor of Dnipropetrovsk. In Donetsk, some leaders of the former Party of Regions and extreme left-wing allies became Russian proxies, while others fled to Russia with Yanukovych. Oligarch Rinat Akhmetov waited to see which way the wind was blowing and did not begin to support Ukraine until May 2014 when he brought his workers on to the streets of Mariupol who, together with the Azov volunteer battalion, liberated the city from Russian proxies. Akhmetov's neutrality during the crucial months of February–April 2014 lost Ukraine control over a major portion of Donetsk oblast.

---

[10] The offer was made in March 2014 when Ukraine had no president. Elections were held in May which Petro Poroshenko won.

Volodymyr Zelenskyy missed the war as well. He became a major television celebrity six months after Kolomoyskyy was removed as governor in March 2015 with the launch of Servant of the People television show on 1+1 television channel where he played the small-town schoolteacher Vasyl Holoborodko. The three series of Servant of the People running from October 2015-May 2019 complexly ignored Putin, annexation of Crimea and the Russian-Ukrainian war. Alexander Motyl (2019) writes, 'In its alternate universe, Crimea and Donbas are not occupied. There is no war. There are no deaths.' In the third season, bringing the show up to Zelenskyy's election as president, extremist nationalists stage a coup d'état and Ukraine disintegrates with regions breaking away.

Dnipropetrovsk oligarchs were never cut from the same cloth. Pinchuk and Tihipko were 'white collar' oligarchs who had cultivated a bourgeoise image for themselves; albeit tarnished in the case of the latter. Pinchuk was nowhere to be seen during the 2014–2015 war. Hendin (2014) explained that Pinchuk was less 'risk prone' in business affairs and more concerned about his international image. 'Pinchuk will for a thousand times contemplate and think over how Elton John, Paul McCartney, Bill Clinton and Madeleine Albright will react to him. He will compare these [reactions] with global cosmopolitan values and then make a decision' (Hendin 2014).

Pinchuk's cultivation of a bourgeoise image was no match for Russia's hybrid warfare and its weaponisation of organised crime. Kolomoyskyy was different with a thuggish reputation like that found among oligarchs in Donetsk (see Rojansky 2014).[11] Kolomoyskyy's thuggish character proved to be the perfect riposte to Putin's hybrid warfare (Kuzio 2019).

Political instability in Dnipropetrovsk in January-March 2014 reflected instability at the national level. During and after the Euromaidan Revolution, Korban and Filatov opposed the Party of Regions which was in retreat but at the same time ensconced in several Dnipropetrovsk cities. Their allies were patriotic Ukrainians, civil society, Euromaidan Revolutionaries, the influential Jewish community, and nationalist groups. Of Ukraine's eight Southern and Eastern oblasts, Mykolayiv (60.3 per cent) and Dnipropetrovsk (54.5 per cent) had the highest support for the view of the Euromaidan Revolution as a protest movement against a corrupt dictatorship (Dumky ta Pohlyady Zhyteliv Pivdenno-Skhidnykh Oblastey Ukrayiny: kviten 2014).

A local and national tipping point took place in Dnipropetrovsk. The local tipping point was widespread public anger at the beatings of Euromaidan

---

[11] Interview with political technologist Denis N. Semenov, Dnipropetrovsk, 26 May 2014.

Revolutionaries in Dnipropetrovsk on 26 January 2014 by vigilantes working with the police at the behest of Governor Oleksandr Vilkul, a Party of Regions hardliner. With Kolomoyskyy still in exile, Korban and Filatov mobilised pro-Ukrainian sentiments by replaying the Euromaidan Revolution live on Channel 5 broadcast on large plasma television screens in the centre of Dnipropetrovsk and flying Ukrainian and EU flags on official buildings. Of the 40 arrested during the violence outside the State Administration, Filatov recalls not a single person was a 'Banderite' (i.e., follower of nationalist leader Stepan Bandera) and all were local civic activists. Vilkul's use of vigilante violence came on top of four years of the Donetsk clan's kleptocracy during which they thought 'they had grabbed God by his beard' and would be in power forever (Semyzhenko and Ostapovets 2014). By February 2014, the population of Dnipropetrovsk had enough of Donetsk and its Kremlin supporters.

The national tipping point was the murder of protestors on the Euromaidan Revolution on 18-20 February 2014 followed by the disintegration of the Party of Regions after Yanukovych fled from Kyiv. In Dnipropetrovsk 65.1 per cent and in Mykolayiv 70 per cent disagreed with the use of deadly force by the Yanukovych regime against protestors (Dumky ta Pohlyady Zhyteliv Pivdenno-Skhidnykh Oblastey Ukrayiny: kviten 2014).

Both developments tipped the balance of power towards pro-Ukrainian forces in Dnipropetrovsk and sparked a spontaneous demolition of the main monument to Lenin in the centre of Dnipropetrovsk on 22 February 2014. Dnipropetrovsk was painted blue and yellow from 26 January and especially after 22 February 2014 when the Ukrainian national flag came to symbolise resistance against the Donetsk clan's authoritarian kleptocracy and Putin's military aggression against Ukraine. Hendin (2014, 20) explained that the flag and national hymn did not mean much to him until the Euromaidan Revolution but after became symbolic and touched his heart because of the wounding and murder of protestors. 'There has been serious suffering and deaths for this country' and 'That is why the hymn 'Plyve kache' is now mine' (Hendin 2014, 20), referring to a song in memory of the 'Heavenly Hundred' murdered during the Euromaidan Revolution.[12]

Blue and yellow became widespread colours painted on cars, balconies, bridges, and lamposts, as well as trade centres and shops owned by the Kolomoyskyy clan. The fence around the State Administration, where vigilantes had attacked Euromaidan Revolutionaries on 26 January, was painted blue and yellow. The Ukrainian national hymn was played over

---

[12] 'Plyve kacha. Pamyati Nebesnoyii sotni,' https://www.youtube.com/watch?v=3afvyGNbGoE

loudspeakers in the centre of Dnipropetrovsk. Even Red and Black (symbolising blood and soil) nationalist flags began to appear for the first time. Where the monument to Lenin had once stood was renamed the 'Heroes of the Euromaidan Revolution Square.' 'If a year ago you had shown someone here a blue-and-yellow flag, I don't think it would have meant anything special to them at all. But the *Maydan* roused people's sense of national identity' (Sindelar 2015).

The appointment of Kolomoyskyy after three months of instability and uncertainty 'felt good,' volunteer Natalya Khazan recalled.[13] She credited him with immediately standing up to Putin and eventually thwarting his 'New Russia' project. Jewish-Ukrainian Oleksandr Cherkasskyy, who volunteered for one of the Kolomoyskyy-funded battalions, credits the governor with playing a positive role in halting Russian aggression: 'If there had been no Kolomoyskyy there would be no Ukraine.'[14] Without the work of many people in Dnipropetrovsk, including civil society volunteers, Zubchenko believes Russian forces 'might have made it to Dnipropetrovsk, or even further into Ukraine' (Sindelar 2015).

Dnipropetrovsk welcomed 'any strong hand, Ukrainian or not' (Carroll 2015) with the arrival of Kolomoyskyy because it prevented the disintegration and chaos which they saw in the Donbas, and to a lesser extent in March-May 2014 in Kharkiv and Odesa. Importantly, Kolomoyskyy's team took control of the security forces and thus prevented defections to Russian proxy forces, as in the Donbas and Crimea (Kuzio 2012).

Kolomoyskyy played an important role beyond his home city in Kharkiv and Odesa. His influence in the leadership of the Jewish community in Ukraine persuaded Kharkiv Mayor Hennadiy Kernes, who had been a faithful Party of Regions official, to remain loyal to Ukraine. In February-March 2014, Kernes adopted a similar approach to Akhmetov of straddling pro-Ukrainian and pro-Russian fences. Kolomoyskyy's persuasion tilted him towards being pro-Ukrainian. Kolomoyskyy told Kernes 'he was risking everything by betting on the wrong horse' (Carroll 2015). Kernes visited Kolomoyskyy in Geneva in late February 2014, after which he returned to Kharkiv declaring himself a 'Ukrainian patriot.' Slowly, 'the separatist storm in Kharkiv – at one point the most violent in the land – began to dampen down' (Carroll 2015). In April 2014, pro-Russian *Oplot* (Bulwark) vigilantes probably undertook the assassination attempt on him because of his pro-Ukrainian stance.

In Odesa, Kolomoyskyy influenced the appointment of a new oblast Minister

---

[13] Interview with Khazan.
[14] Interview with Oleksandr Cherkasskyy, Dnipro, 9 February 2020.

of Interior and regional governor Ihor Palytsya on 4 and 6 May 2014 respectively. Kolomoyskyy, as with Kernes, neutralised another former Party of Regions mayor, Hennadiy Trukhanov, by 'persuading' him to support Ukraine. These appointments, coming after the death of 42 pro-Russian and 6 pro-Ukrainian activists on 2 May 2014 in Odesa, 'enabled the implementation of more expansive and coordinated control over security' (Richardson 2019, 293). Palytsya organised new volunteer groups and self-defence forces who jointly patrolled Odesa with the police until 23 March 2015. As in Dnipropetrovsk and Kharkiv, what was crucially important was ensuring control over the security forces, so they did not defect to Russian proxies.

In the following year's local elections, Filatov defeated former Party of Regions Dnipropetrovsk governor and Opposition Bloc deputy Oleksandr Vilkul for the position of mayor of Dnipropetrovsk. During the elections, Filatov had 'resorted to anti-separatist and pro-Ukrainian rhetoric, fiercely attacking politicians linked to the Opposition Bloc' (Piechal 2018). Filatov's coalition included former Party of Regions politicians, the *Ukrop* (nationalist) party funded by the Kolomoyskyy clan, Self-Reliance (*Samopomych*) party, civil society volunteers and Euromaidan Revolutionaries.

Security Forces and Volunteer Battalions

Control over the security forces was a crucial factor differentiating Dnipropetrovsk from the Donbas. The Security Service of Ukraine (SBU) were given direct orders by Governor Kolomoyskyy to deal toughly with pro-Russian protestors and groups. Criminal prosecutions were launched. Russian flags were banned. Courts blocked and seized the properties of Party of Regions defectors to Russian proxies, such as Oleg Tsaryov. A death threat was given to Tsaryov over the telephone by one of the Dnipropetrovsk clans (Kulick 2019, 383). For the Kolomoyskyy team, taking over Tsaryov's properties was an act of revenge for the theft of their own business interests in Crimea after its annexation by Russia.[15]

On 2 March 2014, Kolomoyskyy was appointed governor of Dnipropetrovsk. A Fund for the Defence of the Country was set up on 18 March by one of his senior advisers, Pavlo Khazan, to protect major installations and official buildings. On 17 April 2014, a bounty of $10,000 was announced for the capture of any Russian 'saboteurs.' Between April-May 2014, four volunteer battalions were established by the Kolomoyskyy clan through the Fund for the Defence of the Country and the Ministry of Defence – Donbas, Dnipro-1 (successor to the Regiment for the Defence of the Dnipropetrovsk region

---

[15] Interview with Volynska.

formed by Yuriy Bereza, a Ukrainian speaker from Luhansk) (Bukkvoll 2019, 301), Dnipro-2 and *Pravyy Sektor*. Most of the volunteers, such as *Pravyy Sektor* leader Yarosh and oblast leader Denysenko, were local activists.[16] The Kolomoyskyy clan financed and equipped the volunteer battalions with everything except weapons which were supplied by the military and Ministry of Internal Affairs (Korban 2014).

Filatov, an ethnic Russian citizen of Ukraine, coordinated Dnipropetrovsk-based volunteer battalions. At 58 *Komsomol* Street in the city of Dnipropetrovsk, the *Pravyy Sektor* nationalist volunteer battalion was based on the second floor, Sicheslav (old name for Dnipropetrovsk) volunteer battalion on the third, and Dnipropetrovsk Territorial Defence units on the fourth (Hladka, Hromakov, Myronova, Pluzhnyk, Pokalchuk, Rudych, Vasilisa, Shevchenko 2016, 181). With memory politics popularising them since the late 1980s, Cossacks (including some former *Berkut* riot police officers) from Dnipropetrovsk and Zaporizhzhya formed the Novokodatskyy, Verkhnodniprovska and Staro-Samarska platoons (*sotnyas*). A study of Dnipropetrovsk in the Russian-Ukrainian war analysed *Berkut* officers from Western Ukraine and Zaporizhzhya who fought for Ukraine (Reva 2020, 217, 225).

Countering the 'Russian Spring'

During the 2014 'Russian Spring' the three jewels in the crown of Putin's 'New Russia' project were Kharkiv, Dnipropetrovsk and Odesa. Thuggish 'political tourists' from Russia were the main initiators of violence against Euromaidan Revolutionaries and pro-Ukrainian forces on the streets of cities such as Donetsk and elsewhere. In Kharkiv and Odesa, Russian 'political tourists' travelled from Belgorod in Russia and Moldova's Transniestr region respectively.

The atmosphere in Southern-Eastern Ukraine was a mixture of disquiet at the unstable political situation and weak understanding of what would come next at a time when Putin's objectives were still unclear. In 2007, 61.8 per cent of Dnipropetrovsk disagreed with the view that regional differences were so acute in Ukraine that one could speak of two peoples, with Donetsk giving the lowest (48.4 per cent) support for this view (Formuvannya Spilnoyi Identychnosti Hromadyan Ukrayiny 2007). Sixty-nine per cent in Dnipropetrovsk (the highest in the 'East') disagreed with the statement that regional differences in Ukraine were so great one could call 'East' and 'West' two different peoples, a harbinger of a future base for national integration. In Kharkiv 49 per cent disagreed with this view (Identychnist Hromadyan

---

[16] Interview with D.N. Semenov.

Ukrayiny v Novykh Umovakh 2016, 58–65). With a regional average of 19.1 per cent, the lowest belief there would be 'civil war' was to be found in Dnipropetrovsk (10.6 per cent).

Dnipropetrovsk (17.1 per cent) was close to the regional average (16.9) of the fear of Russian invasion. Such sentiments produced a rallying around the flag and governor in Dnipropetrovsk. Not surprisingly, the highest fear was to be found in Kherson (45.3 per cent) and Mykolayiv (36.2 per cent) because they bordered or were close to Crimea (Dumky ta Pohlyady Zhyteliv Pivdenno-Skhidnykh Oblastey Ukrayiny: kviten 2014).

In Ukraine's 'East,' Zaporizhzhya (93 per cent) and Dnipropetrovsk (86.2 per cent) were the most opposed to separatism. In 2007, only in the Donbas did regional autonomy receive relatively high support of 39.7 per cent (Donetsk) and 33.6 per cent (Luhansk) (Formuvannya Spilnoyi Identychnosti Hromadyan Ukrayiny 2007). A decade later support for regional autonomy in the 'East' dropped to only 7 per cent in Dnipropetrovsk with a very high 79 per cent opposed (Identychnist Hromadyan Ukrayiny v Novykh Umovakh 2016, 58–65). These figures ensured a high level of Ukrainian patriotism and opposition to Putin's 'New Russia' project.

Federalism had always been a political football in Ukraine, raised at different times by Eastern Ukrainian political entrepreneurs and then quietly dropped. Russia's long-term policy has been to weaken the Ukrainian state by transforming it into a loose federation or even confederation of 'New Russia,' Ukraine ('Little Russia') and 'Galicia.' Support for federalism in Ukraine ranged between a high of 38.4 per cent in Donetsk and 41.9 per cent in Luhansk, where the Party of Regions had played with the idea, to a low of 6.9 per cent in Kherson, 10.7 per cent in Mykolayiv, 11.4 per cent in Dnipropetrovsk and 15.3 per cent in Zaporizhzhya. Kharkiv (32.2 per cent) was closer to the views of the Donbas on federalism (Dumky ta Pohlyady Zhyteliv Pivdenno-Skhidnykh Oblastey Ukrayiny: kviten 2014).

There was little belief in Russian political rhetoric and Russian information warfare and disinformation claiming Russian speakers were threatened by the rise of extremist nationalists. Mykolayiv (60.3 per cent and 78.2 per cent) and Kherson (60.4 per cent and 69.8 per cent) had similar results to Dnipropetrovsk in their opposition to the seizure of official buildings (55.7 per cent) and Russia's illegal interference in Ukrainian affairs and Russian support for separatist rallies (72 per cent) (Dumky ta Pohlyady Zhyteliv Pivdenno-Skhidnykh Oblastey Ukrayiny: kviten 2014).

Political forces formerly linked to Dnipropetrovsk oligarchs had never supported separatism or exhibited pro-Russian Soviet nostalgia. Pro-Russian crowds were never large and were countered by different actors. Communist Party of Ukraine members were mainly pensioners and were not adept at seizing official buildings or in street fights with young vigilantes. Communist Party members dominated the Union of Soviet Officers which was the main pro-Russian force in Dnipropetrovsk. In view of the influence of the Jewish community in Dnipropetrovsk it did not help the pro-Russian cause that the Union of Soviet Officers was anti-Semitic, with its leaders warning of the alleged threat of a 'World Zionist government' taking over the world (Hladka, Hromakov, Myronova, Pluzhnyk, Pokalchuk, Rudych, Vasilisa, Shevchenko 2016, 180). Hendin (2014) described how he had attended both the Euromaidan Revolution and anti-*Maydan* meetings and had only ever heard anti-Semitic rants about 'Jewish conspiracies led by Kolomoyskyy' at the latter (see Kuzio 2017, 118–140). Jews in Dnipropetrovsk associated anti-Semitism with pro-Russian forces in Crimea and the DNR and LNR and not with Ukrainian nationalists. They were happy to work with and finance *Pravyy Sektor*. Only 10.6 per cent in Dnipropetrovsk were concerned at the growth of Ukrainian extremist nationalism.

Opposed to pro-Russian forces in Southern-Eastern Ukraine were Ukrainian patriots who prevented local councils from adopting pro-Russian resolutions denouncing the 'fascist coup' in Kyiv, security forces which remained loyal and prevented their arms falling into the hands of pro-Russian forces, football *ultras* (extremist members of support clubs) and Kolomoyskyy's 'patriotic vigilantes' who confronted pro-Russian supporters on the streets. In Dnipropetrovsk the largest protest took place in May 2014 and attracted 200 people with only 32 attending the last rally on 22 June 2014. Asked if they would participate in pro-Russian rallies, 25 per cent said they would in the Donbas and 15 per cent in Kharkiv. In the remainder of Southern-Eastern Ukraine this dropped to between 3 and 7 per cent (Stebelsky 2018, 42–43). Pro-Russian Soviet nostalgia was again shown to be higher in Kharkiv and especially the Donbas than in Dnipropetrovsk or Odesa.

Pro-Russian rallies in Dnipropetrovsk and Zaporizhzhya were minimal compared to those in the Donbas, Kharkiv and Odesa. Only 5.9 per cent in Dnipropetrovsk (with similar figures in Mykolayiv [7.2 per cent] and Kherson [2.7 per cent]) supported rallies calling for their regions to join Russia. Low numbers backed the right of secessionist regions to join Russia ranging from 3.5 per cent in Kherson, 6.2 per cent in Zaporizhzhya, 6.9 per cent in Dnipropetrovsk to 7.2 per cent in Mykolayiv and Odesa (Dumky ta Pohlyady Zhyteliv Pivdenno-Skhidnykh Oblastey Ukrayiny: kviten 2014). In Dnipropetrovsk (4 per cent), Mykolayov (4.2 per cent) and Kherson (0.7 per cent) a miniscule number supported unification of Ukraine and Russia into one state (Dumky ta Pohlyady Zhyteliv Pivdenno-Skhidnykh Oblastey Ukrayiny: kviten 2014).

Union of Soviet Officers and Union of Afghan Veterans organised meetings wearing St. George ribbons and carrying Russian flags which made them unpopular in Dnipropetrovsk. The Russian flag had supporters in Donetsk and Luhansk but not in Dnipropetrovsk. On 1 March 2014, in coordination with other cities in Southern-Eastern Ukraine these pro-Russian forces planted Russian flags on the Dnipropetrovsk State Administration building. In Kharkiv and Dnipropetrovsk, Ministry of Interior special forces removed the flags.

Rumours of summary justice of pro-Russian activists have been hinted at by members of the Kolomoyskyy clan. Kolomoyskyy said 'We had a problem, we dealt with it, and thank God we did' (Carroll 2015). As a corporate raider, Kolomoyskyy had tough young 'sportsmen' at his disposal who could be quickly mobilised as vigilantes against a Russian threat to Dnipropetrovsk.

'Patriotic' vigilantes came to the small number of poorly attended pro-Russian meetings and broke them up. 'It just so happened that very active comrades when leaving pro-Russian meetings ended up in reanimation (hospital)' (Hladka, Hromakov, Myronova, Pluzhnyk, Pokalchuk, Rudych, Vasilisa, Shevchenko 2016, 210). In other cases, 'Some of them had their heads cracked at bus stops, some did not make it to the underpass, and the result was that they concluded it was better to not become involved in these activities' (Hladka, Hromakov, Myronova, Pluzhnyk, Pokalchuk, Rudych, Vasilisa, Shevchenko 2016, 210). Kolomoyskyy's clan never shied from using 'marches to the woods,' summary shootings, gang warfare' (Carroll 2015). Such claims, part of the urban legend of the outpost of Dnipropetrovsk in 2014, are widely believed but of course cannot be verified.

Korban does not shirk responsibility for his tough response to Russian proxies. The Kolomoysky clan took control of organised crime in the oblast and ensured they worked for Ukrainian interests – and not Russian hybrid warfare (Kulick 2019, 252). The Kolomoyskyy clan believed Ukraine was at war and therefore their rules of war applied to all types of combat. If they had not been tough with pro-Russian activists from the beginning Korban (2014) was 'sure we would have had Chechen mercenaries here long ago.' After pro-Russian activists were removed from official buildings they were taken to the woods where they received 'a stern lesson' in 'how to love Ukraine' (Kulick 2019, 377). Filatov (2014) also talked of 'separating the separatists' which he meant as sowing divisions within their ranks.

Civil Society Volunteer Movement

The city of Dnipropetrovsk and oblast played a crucial role in 2014–2015 in halting and reversing Russian military aggression and it could not have accomplished this without a large civil society volunteer movement. One volunteer recalled 'This is a part of the history of Ukraine' and 'Dnipro was the outpost' (Hladka, Hromakov, Myronova, Pluzhnyk, Pokalchuk, Rudych, Vasilisa, Shevchenko 2016, 230). 'If people did not support the war through volunteers, then the enemy who invaded our land would have not been halted' (Hrushko-Kolinko 2017, 7).

In 2014, pressure was intense on Ukrainian patriots in Dnipropetrovsk to become involved in fighting a war they did not at that stage fully comprehend. A volunteer recalled 'Every day, the intelligence services came to us and informed us that there was the possibility of the (separatist) fighters breaking through' (Hladka, Hromakov, Myronova, Pluzhnyk, Pokalchuk, Rudych, Vasilisa, Shevchenko 2016, 222). Svyatoslav Oliynyk recalls that the first goal of volunteers and volunteer battalions was to push Russian and separatist forces as far east as possible from the Dnipropetrovsk-Donetsk 'border', 'so that this epidemic did not spread' (Hladka, Hromakov, Myronova, Pluzhnyk, Pokalchuk, Rudych, Vasilisa, Shevchenko 2016, 183). The second goal was to ensure strategic buildings, such as the State Administration and Ministry of Internal Affairs were protected (Hladka, Hromakov, Myronova, Pluzhnyk, Pokalchuk, Rudych, Vasilisa, Shevchenko 2016, 227).

Dnipropetrovsk already had an active civil society movement that was galvanised by Yanukovych's kleptocratic authoritarian regime and the Euromaidan Revolution when human rights organisations had assisted prisoners with free legal advice and appeals to the ECHR. In Dnipropetrovsk, Kharkiv and Zaporizhzhya, 27–30 per cent were willing to participate in the volunteer movement, a high figure in a region where civil society had traditionally been less active than in Western Ukraine and the capital city of Kyiv (Identychnist Hromadyan Ukrayiny v Novykh Umovakh 2016, 58–65).

In 2014 *Forepost* (Outpost) and *Sich* NGOs emerged from these existing human rights groups with the purpose of legally defending prisoners-of-war and providing aid to soldiers. They produced Unbroken (*Nezlamnyy*), a documentary film about Ukrainian women illegally imprisoned in the DNR and LNR, Crimea and the Russian Federation.[17]

Volunteers 'defended' their land not with weapons but with 'mercy (*myloserdya*)'; they were 'crucial rear volunteers' (Hrushko-Kolinko 2017, 4). The Dnipro Volunteer Centre collected money, food, clothing, footwear, tea, coffee, soap, sleeping bags and blankets and bought bullet proof vests, night vision glasses, binoculars, uniforms, and other items. Women baked and cooked food which was freeze dried for transportation to the war zone.

---

[17] Interview with Volynska.

Children and school pupils wrote letters and painted pictures (Hrushko-Kolinko 2017, 21–22). They transported these products to Ukrainian military bases at Piske and Butivka near Donetsk airport on the front line. When they arrived 'our lads were already waiting for us' (Hrushko-Kolinko 2017, 9).

Women have played a disproportionate role in Ukraine's volunteer movement since 2014, providing expertise in the medical, psychological, catering, and educational fields. Hairdressers and dentists volunteered their services. A *Sestrynska sotnya* (Sister's platoon) of 100 women was created in the National Defence HQ in the State Administration (Hladka, Hromakov, Myronova, Pluzhnyk, Pokalchuk, Rudych, Vasilisa, Shevchenko 2016, 184). A 'culinary *sotnya*' prepared food packages which included freeze dried 'Dnipro borsch.' An 84-year-old grandmother brought food to the train station for soldiers. A 60-year-old pensioner came to the military hospital to wash the floors. People – especially women – volunteered with whatever help they could provide. Monks came to help Church chaplains in the military. Father Dmytro Povorotnyy of the Ukrainian Orthodox Church-Kyiv Patriarch became a local hero as a volunteer army chaplain. Most of these volunteers, especially from the older generation, had never before been involved in civil society work.

Volunteers dealt with the sudden and horrific flow of casualties from the war zone. 'This was a major trauma. All of the city remembers the sirens of ambulances and within each ambulance there was a human fate' (Hladka, Hromakov, Myronova, Pluzhnyk, Pokalchuk, Rudych, Vasilisa, Shevchenko 2016, 201). Tents had to be quickly put up at Dnipropetrovsk airport for the wounded. The main military hospital had to be prepared and equipped largely with donations and staffed by volunteers. Far greater numbers of Ukrainian wounded were brought to Dnipropetrovsk from the Donetsk war zone than to Kharkiv which took casualties from the Luhansk war zone.

Dnipropetrovsk Airport was a 'surreal' place converted from civilian to civilian-military purposes over-night. Wounded on the front line were first taken to stabilisation points at front-line hospitals where they were provided with emergency treatment. From there, helicopters (or if there was bad weather, trains) evacuated the wounded from the Donetsk war zone to Dnipropetrovsk Airport and from there they were taken by ambulance to be treated in hospitals in the city.[18]

'Most of us did not have any experience with field medicine or treating combat injuries. We weren't treating combat injuries. We weren't expecting a war. It took us about two months to get up to stuff,' recalled Zubchenko who together with her husband worked as anaesthesiologists in the front-line evacuation

---

[18] Interview with Khazan.

hospital in Dnipropetrovsk (Sindelar 2015). Hanna Teryanik, a resident of Dnipropetrovsk with her husband from Luhansk, recalled seeing numerous vehicles driving past her apartment window with wounded Ukrainian soldiers.

The volunteer movement expanded in number after the August 2014 Ilovaysk massacre of Ukrainian soldiers who had been given 'safe passage' by Putin but were attacked and shelled, killing over 300 and wounding many more. Teryanik recalled cancelling her June 2014 vacation because 'She had to do something.' She and others used any vehicles they could commandeer to drive to the Donetsk war zone and bring dead and wounded back to Dnipropetrovsk.[19] The Ilovaysk massacre and Russia's invasion of Ukraine was one of the many factors that buried the Soviet concept of Russian-Ukrainian 'brotherly peoples' (see Aliyev 2019, 2020).

Conclusion

This chapter has challenged the traditional concept of a unified Ukrainian 'East' by showing it had been mistaken to view eight Southern-Eastern Ukrainian oblasts in such a manner prior to the 2014 crisis, and with the impact of the Russian-Ukrainian war on Ukrainian national identity this is even more the case since then. A bounded Russian speaking nationality had never emerged in Ukraine prior to 2014 (Arel 1995a, 1995b; Arel and Khmelko 1996; Laitin 1998; Whitefield 2002). The Russian-Ukrainian war has tipped the balance between the more 'Eastern' identity of the city of Dnipropetrovsk and more Central Ukrainian identity of Dnipropetrovsk towns and villages towards the latter. Zaporizhzhya, Mykolayiv, and Kherson are similar to Dnipropetrovsk in moving since 2014 away from the 'East' towards a more Central Ukrainian identity.

Two major crises in 1991 and 2014 dramatically reduced the size of Ukraine's ethnic Russian population by three quarters from 22 per cent to 6 per cent. In Dnipropetrovsk, a large proportion of those who had defined themselves as 'Russians' or biethnic Ukrainian-Russian have re-identified as Ukrainian. In wars, such as that taking place since 2014 in Eastern Ukraine, sitting on the fence is no longer an option. Answers to survey questions about Dnipropetrovsk show how identities were changing in an evolutionary fashion prior to 2014 and since then have changed in a more revolutionary manner.

Dnipropetrovsk and Dnipro is historically analogous to Lviv in Western Ukraine which was a Ukrainian outpost in the fight with Poland over their border. Since 2014, Dnipropetrovsk and Dnipro are playing an analogous role

---

[19] Interview with Hanna Teryanik, ATO Museum, Dnipro, 3 November 2019.

as the outpost in the war with Russia over their border, as seen in the region having the highest rate of security force casualties of any Ukrainian region.

Kolomoyskyy is undoubtedly a controversial figure in Ukraine. Nevertheless, in 2014-2015 his clan played a positive role in leading, mobilising, organising, and financing volunteer battalions which successfully halted the 'Russian Spring' and Putin's 'New Russia' project. The Kolomoyskyy clan accomplished this together with Euromaidan Revolution activists, Ukrainian patriots, civil society volunteers and the Jewish community. Language played no role in Dnipropetrovsk in Ukrainian patriotism and was overshadowed by the civic Ukrainian patriotism of Jewish-Ukrainian and Russian governors and deputy governors (Bureiko and Moga 2019).

The defeat of Dnipropetrovsk would have opened a gateway for the spread of Russian hybrid warfare into Central Ukraine and ultimately becoming a threat to the capital city of Kyiv. This never came to pass as Putin's 'New Russia' project was halted in the outpost of Dnipropetrovsk. The Kremlin never expected pushback from Southern-Eastern Ukraine's Russian speakers and Jewish community because it never understood – and continues to not understand – the internal dynamics of identity and nation-building of a country, Ukraine, and people, Ukrainians, it denies exist.

Figures

2.1 – *Muzey ATO* (Museum of the ATO), Dnipro. Taras Kuzio, 2019.

2.2– *Muzey ATO* (Museum of the ATO), Dnipro, Taras Kuzio, 2019.

2.3 – *Muzey ATO* (Museum of the ATO), Dnipro, Taras Kuzio, 2019.

2.4 – *Muzey Alley* (Museum Alley), Dnipro, Taras Kuzio, 2019.

References

Aliyev, Huseyn. (2019). 'The Logic of Ethnic Responsibility and Pro-Government Mobilization in East Ukrainian Conflict.' *Comparative Political Studies*, 52, 8: 1200–1231.

Aliyev, H. (2020). 'When neighbourhood goes to war. Exploring the effect of belonging on violent mobilization in Ukraine.' *Eurasian Geography and Economics*, 62, 1: 21–45.

Arel, Dominique. (1995a) 'Language politics in independent Ukraine: Towards one or two state languages?' *Nationalities Papers*, 23, 3: 597–622.

Arel, D. (1995b) 'Ukraine: the temptation of the nationalizing state'. In Vladimir Tismaneanu ed., *Political Culture and Civic Society in the Former Soviet Union*. Armonk, NY: M.E. Sharpe, 157–188.

Arel, D. and Khmelko, Valerii. (1996) 'The Russian Factor and Territorial Polarization in. Ukraine,' *The Harriman Review*, 9, 1–2: 81–91.

Assessment of vulnerabilities and resilience of residents of southern and eastern regions of Ukraine. (2021). Kyiv: Democratic Initiatives Foundation, 12 May. https://dif.org.ua/en/article/assessment-of-vulnerability-and-resilience-of-residents-of-southern-and-eastern-regions-of-ukraine

Bukkvoll, Tor. (2019) 'Fighting on behalf of the state- the issue of pro-government militia autonomy in the Donbas war,' *Post-Soviet Affairs*, 35, 4: 293–307.

Bureiko, Nadiia and Moga, Teodor. L. (2019) 'The Ukrainian-Russian Linguistic Dyad and its Impact on National Identity in Ukraine,' *Europe-Asia Studies*, 71, 1: 137–155.

Carroll, Oliver. (2015) 'Star Wars in Ukraine: Poroshenko versus Kolomoisky,' *Politico*, 21 December. https://www.politico.eu/chapter/star-wars-in-ukraine-poroshenko-vs-kolomoisky/

D'Anieri, Paul. (2019) 'Gerrymandering Ukraine? Electoral Consequences of Occupation,' *East European Politics and Societies and Cultures*, 33, 1: 89–108.

Demchenko, Oleksandr. (2014) 'Pivdennoho Skhodu bilshe nemaye,' *Ukrayinska Pravda*, 22 April. https://www.pravda.com.ua/chapters/2014/04/22/7023182/

Donbas. Realii. (2017). Pochemu Svatovo udalos dat otpor separatyzmu? *Radio Svoboda*, 7 February. https://www.radiosvoboda.org/a/28316111.html

Hladka, Kateryna, Hromakov, Dmytro, Myronova, Veronika, Pluzhnyk, Olha, Pokalchuk, Oleh, Rudych, Ihor, Vasilisa, Trofymovych, and Shevchenko, Artem. (2016). *Dobrobaty*. Kharkiv: Folio.

Dumky ta Pohlyady Zhyteliv Pivdenno-Skhidnykh Oblastey Ukrayiny: kviten 2014 (2014). Kyiv International Institute of Sociological Studies. http://www.kiis.com.ua/?lang=ukr&cat=reports&id=302&page=1

Dzyuba, Ivan. (2018) 'Donetska rana Ukrayiny,' *Suspilno-Politychni Protsesy*, 3, 10: 37–159.

Formuvannya Spilnoyi Identychnosti Hromadyan Ukrayiny: Perspektyvy i Vyklyky. (2007) *Natsionalna Bezpeka i Oborona*, 9. http://razumkov.org.ua/uploads/journal/ukr/NSD93_2007_ukr.pdf

Fournier, Anna. (2018) 'From Frozen Conflict to Mobile Boundary: Youth Perception of Territoriality in War-Time Ukraine,' *East European Politics and Societies and Culture*, 32, 1: 23–55.

Getmanchuk, Alyona. and Litra, Leo. eds., (2019) *The European Map of Ukraine. Rating of European Integration of Regions*. Kyiv: New Europe Centre. http://neweurope.org.ua/wp-content/uploads/2019/05/Euromap-eng-web.pdf

Giuliano, Elise. (2015) 'The Social Bases of Support for Self-Determination in Eastern Ukraine,' *Ethnopolitics*, 14, 5: 513–522.

Haran, Oleksii and Yakovlyev, Maksym. eds., (2018) *Constructing a Political Nation: Changes in the Attitudes of Ukrainians during the War in the Donbas*. Kyiv: Stylos Publishing and Democratic Initiatives Foundation. https://dif.org.ua/en/chapter/constructing-a-political-nation-changes-in-the-attitudes-of-ukrainians-during-the-war-in-the-donbas

Haran, O., Yakovlyev, M. and Zolkina, Maria. (2019) 'Identity, war, and peace: public attitudes in the Ukraine-controlled Donbas,' *Eurasian Geography and Economics*, 60, 6: 684–708.

Hendin, Yevhen. (2014) 'Yak Dnipropetrovsk iz nevyraznoho milyonnyka stav shche odniyu stolytseyu Ukrayiny,' *Kray magazine*, 227, 17 June. https://gazeta.ua/chapters/events-journal/_istoriya-lazarenka--ne-taka-krivava-yak-ahmetova-tut-zavzhdi-vmili-dobazaryuvatisya/564714

Hrushko-Kolinko, Zinaiida. (2017) *Volonterski Budni. Dorozhni Spovidi-Opovidi*. Dnipro: Lira.

Identychnist Hromadyan Ukrayiny v Novykh Umovakh: Stan, Tendentsii, Rehionalni Osoblyvosti. (2016). *Natsionalna Bezpeka i Oborona*, 3-4. http://razumkov.org.ua/uploads/journal/ukr/NSD161-162_2016_ukr.pdf

Kasianov, Heorhii. ed., (2018) *Polityka i Pamyat. Dnipropetrovsk-Zaporozhzhya-Odesa-Kharkiv. 1990-x do syohodni*. Lviv: FOP Shumylovych.

Korban, Hennadiy. (2014) Interview. www.gazeta.ua, 14 June. https://gazeta.ua/chapters/events-journal/_vzyav-avtomat-i-kazhu-anu-suki-stavajte-do-stinki-doki-vi-nabivayete-kisheni-tam-lyudi-ginut/564393

Kramar, Oleksandr. (2019) The new multivectoral economy,' *Ukrainian Week*, 9 November. https://ukrainianweek.com/Economics/237529

Kulchytskyy, Stanislav, and Mishchenko, Mykhaylo. (2018) *Ukrayina na Porozi Obyednanoyi Yevropy*, Kyiv: Razumkov Centre. https://razumkov.org.ua/uploads/article/2018-Ukr_na_porozi...pdf

Kulick, Orysia. (2019) 'Dnipropetrovsk Oligarchs: Lynchpins of Sovereignty or Sources of Instability?' *The Soviet and Post-Soviet Review*, 46, 3: 352–386.

Kulyk, Volodymyr. (2011) 'Language identity, linguistic diversity and political cleavages: evidence from Ukraine,' *Nations and Nationalism*, 17, 3: 627–648.

Kuzio, Taras. (2001) 'Nationalising States' or Nation Building: A Review of the Theoretical Literature and Empirical Evidence'. *Nations and Nationalism*, 7, 2: 135–154.

Kuzio, T. (2003). 'Census: Ukraine, More Ukrainian', *Russia and Eurasia Review,* 4 February. https://jamestown.org/program/census-ukraine-more-ukrainian/

Kuzio, T. (2007) 'Russians and Russophones in the Former USSR and Serbs in Yugoslavia: A Comparative Study of Passivity and Mobilisation' in *Theoretical and Comparative Perspectives on Nationalism: New Directions in Cross-Cultural and Post-Communist Studies. Soviet and Post-Soviet Politics and Society series 71* Hannover: Ibidem-Verlag, 177–216.

Kuzio, T. (2012) 'Russianization of Ukrainian National Security Policy under Viktor Yanukovych,' *Journal of Slavic Military Studies*, 25, 4: 558–581.

Kuzio, T. (2015). 'The Rise and Fall of the Party of Regions Political Machine,' *Problems of Post-Communism*, 62, 3: 174–186.

Kuzio, T. (2017) *Putin's War Against Ukraine. Revolution, Nationalism, and Crime.* Toronto: Chair of Ukrainian Studies.

Kuzio, T. (2019) 'Russian Stereotypes and Myths of Ukraine and Ukrainians and Why Novorossiya Failed,' *Communist and Post-Communist Studies*, 52, 4: 297–309.

Kuzyk, Petro. (2019) 'Ukraine's national integration before and after 2014. Shifting 'East–West' polarization line and strengthening political community,' *Eurasian Geography and Economics*, 60:6: 709–735.

Laitin, David. D. (1998) *Identity in Formation. The Russian-Speaking Populations in the Near Abroad.* Ithaca, NY: Cornell University Press.

Ligacheva, Natalia. (2021). On the Side of the Screen. An analysis of media consumption and disinformation in the Ukrainian information environment, Kyiv: Detektor Media and Tallinn: Estonian Centre of Eastern Partnership. https://detector.media/doc/images/news/archive/2021/188115/Fin_On_the_other_side_DM_final_ENG_WEB%20(2).pdf

Motyl, Alexander.J. (2019) Ukraine's TV President Is Dangerously Pro-Russian, *Foreign Policy*, 1 April. https://foreignpolicy.com/2019/04/01/ukraines-tv-president-is-dangerously-pro-russian/

Olearchyk, Roman. (2019). 'Ukraine's workers abroad fuel property boom back home.' *Financial Times*, 26 August. https://www.ft.com/content/762a17b2-c3f0-11e9-a8e9-296ca66511c9

O'Loughlin, John., Toal, G. and Kolosov, V. (2016) 'Who identifies with the 'Russian World'? Geopolitical attitudes in southeastern Ukraine, Crimea, Abkhazia, South Ossetia, and Transistria' *Eurasian Geography and Economics*, 57, 6: 745–778.

O'Loughlin, J., Toal, Gerard., and Kolosov, Vladimir. (2017). 'The rise and fall of 'Novorossiya': examining support for a separatist geopolitical imaginary in southeast Ukraine.' *Post-Soviet Affairs*, 33, 2: 124–144.

O'Loughlin, J. and Toal, G., (2020) 'Does War Change Geopolitical Attitudes? A Comparative Analysis of 2014 Surveys in Southeast Ukraine,' *Problems of Post-Communism*, 67, 3: 303–318.

Osnovni Zasady ta Shlyakhy Formuvannya Spilnoyii Identychnosti Hromadyan Ukrayiny. (2017) *Natsionalna Bezpeka i Oborona*, 1–2. http://razumkov.org.ua/uploads/journal/ukr/NSD169-170_2017_ukr.pdf

Piechal, Tomasz. (2018) 'Dnipropetrovsk Oblast: new times, old rules,' *OSW Commentary 260*, 8 February. https://www.osw.waw.pl/en/publikacje/osw-commentary/2018-02-08/dnipropetrovsk-oblast-new-times-old-rules

Poshuky Shlyakhiv Vidnovlennya Suverenitetu Ukrayiny Nad Okupovanym Donbasom: Stan Hromadskoyii Dumky Naperedodni Prezydentskykh Vyboriv. (2019) Kyiv: Democratic Initiatives, 13 February. https://dif.org.ua/chapter/poshuki-shlyakhiv-vidnovlennya-suverenitetu-ukraini-nad-okupovanim-donbasom-stan-gromadskoi-dumky-naperedodni-prezidentskikh-viboriv

Poznyak-Khomenko, Natalka. (2020). ed., *Voluntery: syla nebayduzhykh*. Kyiv: Ukrainian Institute for National Remembrance. https://uinp.gov.ua/elektronni-vydannya/volontery-syla-nebayduzhyh

Public Opinion in Donbas a Year After Presidential Elections. (2020). Kyiv: Democratic Initiatives, 9 April. https://dif.org.ua/en/chapter/public-opinion-in-donbas-a-year-after-presidential-elections

Reva, Iryna. (2020). *Voyiny Dnipra. Tsinnosti, Motyvatsii, Smysly*. Kyiv: Ukrainian Institute of National Remembrance. https://uinp.gov.ua/elektronni-vydannya/voyiny-dnipra-cinnosti-motyvaciyi-smysly

Richardson, Tanya. (2019). 'The Regional Life of Geopolitical Conflict: The Caseof Odesa,' *The Soviet and Post-Soviet Review*, 46, 3: 263–303.

Rojansky, Matthew. A. (2014) 'Corporate Raiding in Ukraine: Causes, Methods and Consequences,' *Demokratizatsiya*, 22, 3: 411–443.

Semyzhenko, Anton. and Ostapovets, Halyna. (2014) 'Yak Dnipropetrovsk ne stav Donetskom' *Kray magazine*, 227, 17 June. https://gazeta.ua/chapters/events-journal/_my-separirovali-separatistov-etih-napravo-teh-nalevo-etim-chtoto-poobeschat-etih-napugat-no-v-pervuyu-ochered-ob-yasnyali/564700

Shandra, Alya. (2019) 'Glazyev tapes, continued: new details of Russian occupation of Crimea and attempts to dismember Ukraine,' *Euromaidan News*, 16 May. http://euromaidanpress.com/2019/05/16/glazyev-tapes-continued-ukraine-presents-new-details-of-russian-takeover-of-crimea-and-financing-of-separatism/

Sindelar, Daisy. (2015) 'We're nothing more than bargaining chips. What it means to be Ukrainian in wartime,' *The Guardian*, 23 January. https://www.theguardian.com/world/2015/jan/23/-sp-ukraine-russia-identity-wartime

Stebelsky, Ihor. (2009) 'Ethnic Self-Identification in Ukraine 1989–2001: Why More Ukrainians and Fewer Russians,' *Canadian Slavonic Papers*, 51, 1: 77–100.

Stebelsky, I. (2018) 'A tale of two regions: geopolitics, identities, narratives, and conflict in Kharkiv and Donbas,' *Eurasian Geography and Economics*, 59, 1: 42–43.

Ukrainian Jews rally to nation's cause in conflict with Russia (2014). *BBC Monitoring*, 11 November.

Whitefield, Stephen. (2002), 'Political Cleavages and Post-Communist Politics,' *Annual Review of Political Science*, 5: 181–200.

Wilson, Andrew. (1997) *Ukrainian nationalism in the 1990s, a minority faith*. Cambridge: Cambridge University Press.

Yak zminylasya dumka ukrayintsiv pro rosiysko-ukrayinsku viynu za dva roky prezydenstva Zelenskoho. (2021). Democratic Initiatives Foundation, 9 June. https://dif.org.ua/article/yak-zminilasya-dumka-ukraintsiv-pro-rosiysko-ukrainsku-viynu-za-dva-roki-prezidenstva-zelenskogo

Zhurzhenko, Tatiana. (2014) 'From Borderlands to Bloodlands,' paper presented at a conference at the University of Alberta, 16 October.

Zhurzhenko, T. (2015) 'Ukraine's Eastern Borderlands: The End of Ambiguity' In: A. Wilson ed., *What Does Ukraine Think?* London: European Council on Foreign Relations, 18 May, 45–52.

3

The Revival of the Dnipropetrovsk and Dnipro Jewish Community in Ukraine

OLENA ISHCHENKO

The Ekaterinoslav Jewish community was one of the first to receive official status in the Russian Empire. In 1791, by order of Catherine II 'On granting citizenship to Jews in the Katerynoslav governorate and the Tavriya region,' Jews received permission to settle in these territories. In less than a century, the urban Jewish population grew from a small group of 376 people in 1805 to a community of 41,240 Jews in the 1897 census or 36.3 per cent of the urban centres. Katerynoslav was a Jewish city and a centre of Zionism and Hasidism.[1] During the Soviet era, Judaism and the Dnipropetrovsk Jewish community were practically destroyed. Even in the short period of the introduction of the policy of indigenisation in the 1920s, Jewish culture was allowed to develop legally only within the narrow confines of a secular, acceptable version of communist ideology. Judaism and Hebrew were illegal. The Katerynoslav synagogues, which were the centres of Jewish communities and numbered more than fifty before the revolution, were closed in the 1920s (Loshak and Starostin 2019, 320). The process of revival endured for more than three decades, beginning in the late 1980s and continuing in independent Ukraine after the dissolution of the Soviet Union.

This chapter is divided into eight sections. The first two sections analyse Jews in the Soviet Union and the late 1980s during Mikhail Gorbachev's *perestroika* and *glasnost* as well as their coexistence with Soviet reality in Dnipropetrovsk. The third section surveys the revival of the Jewish community after 1991 in Dnipropetrovsk and Dnipro. The fourth and fifth analyse the

---

[1] Istoriya yevreyskogo Dniepropietrovska – novyie istoricheskiye otkrytiya i intieriesnyie fakty. https://djc-com-ua.translate.goog/news/view/new/?id=14835&_x_tr_sl=uk&_x_tr_tl=en&_x_tr_hl=en

creation of numerous Jewish educational institutions and the restitution of Jewish properties which had been confiscated by the Soviet regime in Dnipropetrovsk and Dnipro. The sixth investigates the importance of honouring the Jewish victims of the Holocaust by creating the Ukrainian Institute for Holocaust Studies 'Tkuma' and Museum of Jewish Memory and the Holocaust in Ukraine. The seventh and eighth sections survey the support given by the Jewish community in Dnipropetrovsk and Dnipro to the Euromaidan Revolution and Ukraine's fight against Russian military aggression and the role played in the Russian-Ukrainian war by Dnipropetrovsk Governor Ihor Kolomoyskyy in 2014–2015.

Jews in Soviet Dnipropetrovsk: Stagnation and Anti-Semitism

The last Soviet census in 1989 recorded 486,300 Jews in the Ukrainian SSR[2] of which 37,869 lived in Dnipropetrovsk (Bystriakov 2002, 91). Only 1,767 Jews in Dnipropetrovsk considered Yiddish to be their native language (Bystriakov 2002, 91). However, these official figures did not correspond to the real demographic situation. Since the Nazi occupation and throughout the post-war Soviet period, anti-Semitic policies, and the corresponding atmosphere in society, it became customary for Jews to conceal their nationality. The ethnic origin of each Soviet citizen was indicated in their internal passport. Any person born to two Jewish parents was registered as a person of Jewish nationality. Thus, the Soviet government helped preserve the identity of Soviet Jewry by individually labelling each Jew. Children born in mixed marriages were able to choose the ethnicity of one or another parent, and most of them preferred to choose Russian (Pryvalko 2014, 9).

Thus, taking into account both the 'core population' and marginal groups of mixed origin, it is estimated that at the end of the Soviet era in Dnipropetrovsk there were 100,000 Jews accounting for 10 per cent of the city's inhabitants.[3] The 1989 census revealed a high level of education of the Jewish population; for each 1,000 Jews over the age of 15, 351 had higher education; 26 had incomplete higher education; 252 had secondary special education; 189 had secondary education; 108 had incomplete secondary education; and 14 had primary education. 57 per cent of Jews worked in production, including industry (34.1 per cent); construction (8.5 per cent); transport and communications (5.6 per cent); agriculture (0.9 per cent); and trade (6.2 per cent). 41.7 per cent of Dnipropetrovsk Jews worked in the service sector, including medicine, sports, and social welfare (9.8 per cent); education,

---

[2] Iosef Zisels, Dinamika chislennosti yevreyskogo nasielieniya v Ukrainie. http://www.vaadua.org/analitika/dinamika-chislennosti-evreyskogo-naseleniya-ukrainy

[3] A. Bystriakov, 'Khronika zhyzni yevreyev Yekatierinoslava – Dniepropietrovska', *Yevrieyskaya starina*, 2 (85), 2015. https://berkovich--zametki-com.translate.goog/2015/Starina/Nomer2/Bystrjakov1.php?_x_tr_sl=uk&_x_tr_tl=en&_x_tr_hl=en

culture and the arts (13.7 per cent); and science (9.2 per cent) (Bystriakov 2002). By the early 2000s, most Jews in Dnipropetrovsk had emigrated. The 2001 Ukrainian Census recorded only 13,700 Jews in Dnipropetrovsk oblast accounting for 0.4 per cent of the population.[4]

In the Soviet era Jewish life in Dnipropetrovsk had gradually died because communist rule was hostile to the religious life of national communities and the authorities fanned anti-Zionism and anti-Semitism. From the 1970s, only one synagogue remained in the city, and its was the place of gathering of Jews during religious festivals. The Jewish community did not belong to any denominational branch. They were just Jews. Among them were former Zionists, atheists, former Komsomol members who no longer believed communist propaganda, real believers and those who just showed interest. In the late Soviet era, Arkady Shmist[5] notes that they were united by blood, love for their history and a lack of interaction.[6]

Jewish Revival in the Gorbachev Era

However, some positive changes in the situation of Soviet Jews occurred during Gorbachev's liberalisation during the second half of the 1980's when former dissidents convicted of Zionist activity created Jewish community organisations and press clubs, where Jews could study Yiddish and Hebrew. There were also people in the city administration (for example, Dnipropetrovsk city Mayor Valeriy Pustovoytenko and Deputy Mayor Valentina Talian) who were ready for a dialogue with the Jewish community. According to the Jewish elders, Pustovoytenko was the first representative of the authorities who began to attend the synagogue during religious holidays.[7]

In the late Soviet era, the Sholom Aleichem Jewish Culture Society began to operate in Dnipropetrovsk and other Ukrainian cities with a significant Jewish population. They organised courses in Yiddish which had been banned by the Soviet authorities (unlike the Hebrew language and Jewish holy books), conducted popular lectures on Jewish history and culture, held concerts, and shared information on emigration to Israel. Moreover, humanitarian aid was given to the participants of these events, which popularised the Society.

---

[4] Nikolay Shulga, Nataliya Panina, Yevgieniy Golovaha and I. Zisels, 'Emigratsiya yevrieyev v kontiekstie obshchey migratsionnoy situatsii v Ukrainie,'Sotsiologiya: tieoriya, metody, marketing, 2, 2001, 82.
[5] On Arkady Shmist see 'Pamiati Arkadiya Shmista.' https://www-djc-com-ua.translate.goog/news/view/new/?id=655&_x_tr_sl=uk&_x_tr_tl=en&_x_tr_hl=en
[6] A. Bystriakov 'Khronika zhyzni yevreyev Yekatierinoslava – Dniepropietrovska.'
[7] Yevgeniy Evshteyn, 'Oni byli soviestyu nashey obshchiny: intervyu s A. Friedkis,' Shabat Shalom, 6, 2014, 9.

Two groups of Jewish activists formed in Dnipropetrovsk with different positions, differing perspectives on the revival of the Jewish community and significant age gap. The first group were mostly elderly people who had survived the Holocaust and, even during the worst period for Jews in the USSR, never severed ties with the synagogue and Jewish religious traditions. 'I well remember our old synagogue with a stove, a broken plumbing fixture and a basement which flooded when it rained,' Hryhoriy Korol recalled.[8] They saw the prospect of community development in the revival of Judaism. Among its leaders were Korol[9] and Alexander Fridkis.[10] In addition to the significant age gap between Jewish community leaders, community development was not a very popular concept among the older generation who had been traumatised by the Holocaust and Soviet anti-Semitism, and for whom there was the problem of perceiving their own religious and ethnic identity. However, the younger generation showed themselves to be more willing to identify themselves openly and actively as Jews.

Representatives of the younger group wanted to revive the life of the Jewish community based on a secular model. A group of activists adhered to this concept, which became the core idea of the Dnipropetrovsk branch of the All-Union Association of Hebrew Teachers. Activists of the group included Stanislav Hlavnovych (Chairman), Faina Bulavina, Alla Yeshchyna, Marina Lantsman, Alice Litinsca, Igor Pochtar, Emilia Pugach, Stella Rusova, brothers Jan and Felix Sidelkovski, Marat Sorkin, Alla Hlavnovych, Elena Shafir, Vladimir Cherkassky, and Irina Shwartzman[11] Classes were held in private flats and secondary schools. Jewish youth considered Yiddish as their 'home language,' thus, they started to learn Hebrew as the state language of Israel for the possibility of emigration.

The School of Jewish Traditions, founded in 1989, played a significant role in the revival of the Dnipropetrovsk and Dnipro Jewish community. The revival of the city's Jewish community was significantly influenced by the School of Jewish Traditions, which emerged through the efforts of mostly young people – Dina Fisher, Viktor Gutin, Yevhenia Karpova, Mykhailo Khalifa, Semen Lurie, Nathan Meller, Arkady Shmist, Olena Tartakovska, Borys Tseitkin, Borys Yerukhimovich, Oleksandr Zamanskyy and others. The founder of the school was a parishioner of the synagogue and activist of the Jewish religious community, Victor Rabkin. After his emigration to Israel, Shmist became the

---

[8] *Mikwa* is a ritual pool for purification. Women visit the *mikvah* once a month and men before the morning prayer. It is believed that ritual ablution is necessary for utensils. It is customary to build a *mikvah* before the synagogue.
[9] On Hryhoriy Korol, see E. Yevshteyn, 'Oni soli soviestyu nashey obshchiny.'
[10] On Aleksander Fridkis see Boris Feldman, 'Sovmiestimy li mieditsina i rieligiya? Intervyu s Alieksandrom Fridkisom,' Shabat Shalom, 3, 1993, 5.
[11] Ester Tahtierina, 'S yubilieyem doktor Fridkis! Shabat Shalom, 1, 2014, 5.

head of the school.[12] Activists of the school sought to assist the Jews of Dnipropetrovsk to return to their national culture and revive the traditions of Jewish family and community life. They gathered in the synagogue where lectures were given, studied Hebrew and gave practical advice on emigration and living in Israel.

The Jewish Centre for Culture and Charity was later established on this basis. The constituent assembly of the Jewish Centre for Culture and Charity was held in December 1989 in the premises of the Taras Shevchenko Ukrainian Drama Theatre. For many Jews, this event marked the beginning of the community's revival.[13] Shmist, who was present, mentioned that 'so many Jews came there that there was nowhere for a stone to fall if someone had dared to throw it' (Bystriakov 2002, 86). Since then, the Jewish Centre for Culture and Charity has become the region's main secular Jewish organisation. Despite its declared 'secularism,' the Centre popularised Jewish culture and traditions in the Dnipropetrovsk and Dnipro Jewish community.

In the early 1990s, the board of the Jewish Centre for Culture and Mercy approved a flag designed by Shmist which became the first flag in the history of Ukraine of the Jewish community. In the spring of 1990, the centre held an unprecedented event of the celebration of the Jewish holiday of Purim outside the synagogue. Schmist recalled,

> There was a rumour that a Jewish pogrom was being prepared. In response, I proposed to organise a mass celebration of Purim... The regional party committee received permission. Two thousand five hundred people came to the religious holiday, including Valeriy Pustovoytenko. This was the first time since the Russian Revolution that the mayor had congratulated Jews on this holiday (Bystriakov 2002, 86).

Twelve hundred Dnipropetrovsk Jews celebrated Passover[14] with Kosher products[15] provided by the American Distribution Committee 'Joint' (see Magocsi and Petrovsky-Shtern 2016).

In January 1990, during the first congress of Jewish organisations of the USSR, the leadership of the Jewish Centre (Shmist, Yuri Stupniker and Alexander Zamansky) met with guests from Boston (USA) and invited them to

---

[12] Vladimir Vinogradov, 'Shkola yevrieyskih traditsiy,' *Shabat Shalom*, 2, 1991, 3.
[13] E. Yevshteyn, 'Oni byli soviestyu nashey obshchiny.'
[14] The Passover *Seder* is a ritual family meal held at the beginning of the Passover for which a famous rabbi was invited from Israel. See E. Yevshteyn, 'Oni byli soviestyu nashey obshchiny.'
[15] Kosher products are those that comply with Jewish rules of cooking.

visit Dnipropetrovsk, marking the beginning of many years of fruitful cooperation between the Jewish communities of both cities (see Bystriakov 2002). With the assistance of the Boston community an extensive medical programme was successfully implemented. The best Dnipropetrovsk doctors were given the opportunity to train in Boston hospitals while Boston doctors regularly visited Dnipropetrovsk. These medical care programmes were used not only by the city's Jews, but also by a wide range of its residents.

Revival of the Jewish Community in Independent Ukraine

The further revival of the Jewish community is closely bounded with the arrival of representatives of the Chabad movement, which has Ukrainian roots (Magocsi and Petrovskyy-Shtern 2016, 134–136). An important role was played by the leader of Chabad, Menachem-Mendla Schneerson who was a resident of Dnipropetrovsk. Schneerson attached great importance to the revival of Hasidism in the post-Soviet space, particularly in his hometown of Dnipropetrovsk and Dnipro.[16]

There is a legend in the Jewish community about the death bed testament of the last Lubavitcher Rebbe (Schneerson passed away in 1994) to revive Jewish communities in the countries of the former USSR and especially in Ukraine (Androsova, 2008, 253–269). Therefore, he led one of his best adherents, Shmuel Kaminetskyy, to Dnipropetrovsk. At first, it was difficult for foreign Jewish religious leaders to adapt to conditions in 1990s Ukraine, which was devoid of food and experienced long queues, hyper-inflation and problems with electricity and water supplies. Kosher food could not be found in Dnipropetrovsk, where tens of thousands of Jews lived.

Traditionally, the Chabad missionary becomes a permanent resident of the city they move to and settle in. The community elected Kaminetskyy as its rabbi. The arrival of the Kaminetskyy family was a powerful impetus to the revival of the community. Kaminetskyy eventually became a recognised leader of Jews in Dnipropetrovsk oblast following the instructions of his

---

[16] The *Chabad* movement formally ceased to exist on Soviet territory after the Sixth Lubavitcher Rebbe Josef-Yitzhak Schneerson was expelled from the USSR. Along with him, his future son-in-law Menachem-Mendel Schneerson left the USSR. After the death of Josef-Yitzhak in 1950, Menachem-Mendel Schneerson became the leader of *Chabad*, the Seventh Lubavitcher Rebbe. The promotion of atheism among Soviet Jews and anti-Jewish repression depressed *Chabad* but did not destroy it completely. Contacts between the centre of *Chabad* in the United States and Ukrainian Jews were not systematic as they were carried out sporadically through envoys of the Seventh Lubavitcher Rebbe who travelled to the USSR disguised as tourists. See Siemion Charnyi, 'Iudaizm na prostorah SND. Yevraziyskiy yevrieyskiy yezhegodnik,' *5766*, 2005–2006, 71–93.

teacher Menachem-Mendla Schneerson, who had given his blessings to serve in Dnipropetrovsk.

The beginning of Kaminetskyy's activities coincided with the disintegration of the USSR, which the Jewish community welcomed, and the emergence of an independent Ukraine. The Ukrainian state, despite its institutional weaknesses, showed a desire to distance itself from Soviet traditions of anti-Semitism and anti-Zionism. Traditional tolerant attitudes in Ukrainian society to non-Orthodox religious communities and Jews became noticeable, which assisted the revival of Jewish communities in Ukraine and allowing them to be more active than in other post-Soviet countries (Androsova 2008, 261–262).

Certain priorities were established for the activities of Lubavitcher Hasidism, unlike organisations which focussed on emigration to Israel, which included restoring traditions in the Jewish community, building networks and ties to government bodies and developing relations with a wide range of non-Jewish Ukrainian citizens based on tolerant interfaith relations (Zisels 2004, 55–57).

The arrival of representatives of *Chabad* in Dnipropetrovsk began a process that corresponds to the concept of 'rabbinical revolution'[17] – the revival of Jewish religious life with the rabbi as the spiritual leader and core of the new community. The renewal of the extensive infrastructure of the community required knowledge, energy, as well as premises and funding. Concerning the premises, the aim was to lobby for restitution of property confiscated from the Jewish community by the Soviet regime.[18] International charitable Jewish organisations helped the Jewish community in the initial stages of the revival. Domestic charitable organisations began donating funds to Dnipropetrovsk and Dnipro Jewish community after the emergence by the late 1990s of oligarchs and businesspersons.

Dozens of Jewish organisations established representation in Ukraine to coordinate charitable funds. The American Distribution Committee 'Joint' and the Jewish Agency '*Sokhnut*' played important roles in the development of the Dnipropetrovsk and Dnipro Jewish community. However, their approaches differed. The American Distribution Committee 'Joint' aimed to establish favourable conditions for Jews in their communities, while '*Sokhnut*' focused on emigration to Israel. The activities of the American Distribution Committee 'Joint' were therefore more directly associated with the revival of the Jewish community in Dnipropetrovsk. Registered in 1992 in Ukraine, the American

---

[17] 'Mirnaya rievoliutsiya Khabada.' https : // lechaim . ru / ARCHIVE / 165 / VZR / 01.htm
[18] See 'Restytutsiya mizhnarodnoho mayna: mizhnarodnyy ta vitchyznianyy dosvid.' Kyiv: Collection of Documents, 2007, 14–147.

Distribution Committee 'Joint' has regional offices in Dnipropetrovsk, Kyiv, Odessa and Kharkiv.[19] '*Sokhnut*' undertook educational programmes for young Ukrainian Jews which were implemented in Israel (e.g., multilevel Hebrew schools) and by the Israeli Cultural Centre in Dnipropetrovsk, supported by the Israeli Embassy in Ukraine.

Initially, international Jewish organisations wanted to be sure their funds were used wisely and eventually they discovered the potential of assistance from wealthy Jewish members as part of a transition to financial self-sufficiency for the Jewish community. Initially, this only consisted of one-off charitable contributions, but this gradually changed.[20] As big business and oligarchs emerged during Leonid Kuchma's presidency, businesspersons in the Jewish community in Dnipropetrovsk began increasingly to provide financing. This process began happening at the same time as a large proportion of the city's Jewish community came to realise its importance as a unique space for the development of the individual as well as its positive impact on the family world.

A breakthrough came in 1998 when a Board of Trustees was established which began to determine the main directions of the development of the Jewish community in Dnipropetrovsk and Dnipro. The Board brought together industrialists, businesspersons and bankers who resolved to ensure permanent and stable activities of the Jewish community of Dnipropetrovsk. Hennadiy Bogolyubov became the Board's president,[21] and one of its members was Kolomoyskyy.[22]

Philanthropy was not evident everywhere among the new class of big businesspersons, as many of them were not religious Jews and therefore had not been educated in the spirit of providing charitable donations. Making philanthropy to the Jewish community a fashionable gesture took time. A decisive role in the transformation of attitudes was played by Rabbi Kaminetskyy, who is also called 'the mentor of Ukrainian oligarchs,'[23] and who developed the relationship from a one-sided dependency to a mutually beneficial partnership.[24]

---

[19] Lieonid Kagan, 'Nash 'Joynt i stroit, I zhyt pomogayet,' *Shabat Shalom*, 12, 2001, 4.
[20] Boris Feldman, 'Chto den griadushchiy nam gotovit: interviu s predsedatieliem pravlieniya Dniepropietrovskogo blagotvoritelnogo phonda 'Hesed Menahem' Viktorom Danovishem,' Shabat Shalom, 8, 2002, 5.
[21] See Bogoliubov's biography at: https://1-ua--rating-com.translate.goog/gennady-bogolyubov/?_x_tr_enc=1&_x_tr_sl=uk&_x_tr_tl=en&_x_tr_hl=en
[22] See Kolomoyskyy's biography at: https://thepage.ua/ua/dossier/kolomojskij-igor
[23] Yekatierina Shapoval, 'Rosiyskiyey evriei zombirovany tielievid ieniy em.'
[24] Daryna Pryvalko, 'Yevreyske zhyttia v Ukrayini,' 44–46.

Creation of Jewish Educational Institutions

The intensification of Judaism in Dnipropetrovsk and Dnipro was originally tied to Chabad Lubavitch and the development of educational knowledge and training. Education is a prerequisite and mandatory factor for the successful development and sustainable growth of the Jewish community. An important component of the revival of the Jewish community has been the creation of Jewish educational institutions ranging from pre-school to higher education The patron of the educational system of the Dnipro Jewish community is oligarch Viktor Pinchuk who is a member of the Board of Trustees.

Children from Jewish families can attend the Ilana nursery and Beit Zindlikht kindergarten (named in honour of Fanny and Joseph Zindlichtov, grandparents of Ukrainian oligarch and philanthropist Pinchuk).[25] Jewish education facilities include the Jewish secondary school of Dnipro which is the largest in the former USSR. According to the memoirs of one of its teachers, A. Kaplunska, in order to convince the local authorities of the need to open a Jewish school, a group of activists led by Shmist held a rally near the city of Dnipropetrovsk Executive Committee.[26] Beforehand, Korol organised the first street poll of Dnipropetrovsk residents in the history of the city.[27]

In 1991, due to public pressure during Gorbachev's liberalisation, permission was obtained to open Jewish classes in secondary school № 58 where children were taught in the second shift of teaching. At the end of 1992, the Jewish school received a dilapidated building which had been a former boarding school which the Jewish community had renovated. The school is located on one of the Central streets of Dnipropetrovsk which under decommunisation legislation was renamed in 2015 Menachem Mendla Schneerson Street. The popularity of the school steadily increased, primarily due to its curriculum, which combined government programmes, Jewish educational subjects (taught six to eight hours per week) and foreign languages, including Hebrew. Parents and children were also attracted by the intensive extra-curricular programme which included the celebration of Jewish holidays, and finally, the warm family atmosphere of the school.

---

[25] 'Doshkolnoye obrazovaniye i vospitaniye.' http://djc.com.ua/obchina/project/?id=7785&lang=ru; Doma yevrieyev na Dnieprie and https://lechaim-ru.translate.goog/ARHIV/165/VZR/d4.htm?_x_tr_sl=uk&_x_tr_tl=en&_x_tr_hl=en
[26] Alexandra Kaplunska, 'Shmist i nasha yevrieyskaya shkola.' http://99897.blogspot.com/p/blog-page_31.html and I. Manievich, 'Piervyi diriektor: intervyu s S. Kaplunskim,' *Shabat Shalom*, 6 and 7, 2014.
[27] E. Yevshteyn, 'Oni byli soviestyu nashey obshchiny.'

Maon and Yeshiva educational institutions were later opened for young women and young men, respectively, which accept students from different cities and regions of Ukraine. Initially, *yeshivas* operated in Dnipropetrovsk for adult unmarried (*Yeshiva gdola*) and married (*Yeshiva koylel*) men. In 1993, after it became clear that there was a demand for more intensive Jewish education from the Jewish youth of the city and region, it was decided to open a junior *yeshiva* (*ktana*) at Jewish school № 144. The age range of pupils ranges from 15 to 32 years of age.[28]

Yeshiva graduates receive internationally recognised diplomas required for the functioning of Jewish communities to be a teacher of Hebrew and Judaism, an educator, a *shoikhet*, a *soyfer*, a *mashgiah* (specialist in *kashrut*), and a *moel*.[29] Study schedules in *yeshiva* schools are extremely busy. The main disciplines studied are Hebrew, *Torah*,[30] *Talmud*, writing and repairing old copies of the *Torah*, preparation of Tefillin, *mezuzahs* and other items necessary for Jewish religious life. Upon completion of their studies, *yeshiva* graduates perform professional duties in Jewish communities around the world and the most successful become rabbis. Graduates from the *yeshiva* are the pride of the city of Dnipro and members of the National Sofruta Centre. No similar union of professionals exist elsewhere in Ukraine or anywhere else in the former USSR.

A special place in the Jewish education system in Dnipro is occupied by the Beit Khana International Humanitarian and Pedagogical Institute (MHPI) college for girls. MHPI was founded in September 1995. The aim was to prepare teachers for the Jewish community and kindergartens, as well as private teachers and educators for Jewish families. In addition, rabbis often chose MHPI graduates as their brides.

MHPI students are provided with scholarships and guaranteed employment after their graduation. Among its advantages are the teaching of linguistic, religious, and regional studies. MHPI is also popular among Jewish girls because it enables orphans and children from low-income families to attend. One of the pupils wrote that her grandmother ordered her not to lose her Jewish roots before she died, and she therefore tried to fulfil her wish.[31]

---

[28] Yevgieniy Yevtushenko, 'Dniepropietrovskiy Natsionalnyi Soyphierskiy tsentr Popadaniye v diesiatku,' Shabat Shalom, 2, 2014, 5.
[29] *Moel* was a specialist who performed the Jewish circumcision ritual.
[30] The *Torah* is the Law of Moses, the Pentateuch of Moses, the first part of what Christians call the Old Testament of the Bible.
[31] I. Karpienko, 'Beyt-Hana – kuznitsa zhenskih kadrov.' https://lechaim.ru/ARHIV/165/VZR/d6.htm)

Restitution of Religious Properties

Religious properties confiscated by the Soviet authorities were returned to the Jewish community, the most important of which was the choral synagogue. In 1992, shortly after the establishment of diplomatic relations between Ukraine and Israel, President Leonid Kravchuk issued the decree, 'on measures to return religious property to religious organisations', which decreed that confiscated religious buildings and property must be returned to religious communities,[32] leading to the gradual return of synagogues. In Dnipropetrovsk, four synagogues survived from the USSR and three of them were returned to the Jewish religious community: choral synagogue (built in 1868), small Synagogue on Kotsyubynskyy Street and a synagogue on Mironov (renamed European Street).[33]

Between 1987-1996, the Dnipropetrovsk Jewish community fought for the return of the choral synagogue and when it was returned it was in a terrible condition with no proper floor and holes in the walls and ceilings. The synagogue was reconstructed in four years with financing initially only coming from abroad, but eventually Ukrainian businesspersons (Hennadiy Bogoliubov, O. Kaganovsky, D. Mishalow, A. Hanis) donated some funds as well.[34] There was no tender for architects to produce different designs as this was awarded to Aleksander Dolnik, a well-known Jewish architect from Dnipropetrovsk.[35]

Dolnik's vision was of a sacral interior consisting of the ark with six steps representing the number of days of the creation of the world; above the ark are five arches which represent the five books of Moshe (Moses); twelve pillars under the arches represent the twelve tribes of Israel and twenty-six rays emanating from the ark flow from God.[36] The restored synagogue includes an amphitheatre. The names of the benefactors are perpetuated on the walls of the lobby of the reconstructed choral synagogue. Tens of thousands of people attended the opening of the reconstructed choral Golden

---

[32] The restitution of Jewish property was undertaken by the VAAD of Ukraine (Association of Jewish Organisations and Communities of Ukraine) and OIROU. In 1995, a programme began to catalogue Jewish property in Ukraine and out of 2,500 premises, approximately fifty were returned over the next fifteen years. See D. Pryvalko, 'Yevreyske zhyttia v Ukrayini.'

[33] See I. Karpienko, 'Dniepropietrovsk obietovannyi.'

[34] Eduard Akselrod, 'Interviu s glavnym rabinom Dniepropietrovska Shmuelie Kaminietskim,' *Shabat Shalom*, 9, 2000, 1.

[35] Liev Lieynov and Aleksandr Dolnik, 'Ya na puti k odnoznachnomu otvietu,' *Shabat Shalom*, 10, 2000, 2.

[36] Grigoriy Revzin, 'Dniepropietrovskiye chudiesa.' https://lechaim.ru/ARHIV/195/revzin.htm

Rose Synagogue with Zelikh Breza, head of the Jewish community in Dnipropetrovsk.[37] Beza had been visited by President Kuchma the evening before the opening.[38] The choral Golden Rose Synagogue became the religious and cultural centre of the Jewish community in Dnipropetrovsk and Dnipro.

With the financial support of 'Joint' and big Ukrainian businesspersons a large Menorah complex was built by 2012 as a multifunctional centre of the Jewish community. Hennadiy Akselrod, President of Dnipropetrovsk Jewish community Bogoliubov and President of the United Jewish Communities of Ukraine Kolomoysyy played a decisive role in its creation. The opening of the Menorah in October 2012 was attended by 10,000 people. The Menorah consists of seven towers that symbolise the traditional Jewish candlestick. The highest part of the Menorah is a central 22-storey tower which is 77 meters high which includes business offices, the Israeli Consulate, the Jewish Medical Centre, educational, cultural, and social foundations, conference and celebration halls, a hotel, kosher food restaurants, art studios, sports gyms and shops.

The construction of the Menorah had a much more sincere significance of cultural Westernisation, which represented a break with the pattern of self-awareness among the residents of Dnipropetrovsk of their city as a closed industrial zone that was highly important but monotonously uninteresting.[39] Therefore, the Menorah not only decorated the centre with an unusual architectural contour, but also added to the city's mental appeal of a complex polyethnic mosaic. Eventually, the theme of the Jewish revival became synonymous with the city's acquisition of new meanings of modernity and the creation of new cultural values and demands.

Museum and Research into the Holocaust

The Ukrainian Institute for Holocaust Studies 'Tkuma' and Museum of Jewish Memory and the Holocaust in Ukraine are to be found inside the Menorah alongside the choral Golden Rose Synagogue.[40] Work on the creation of the museum began in 1999 with the collection and systematisation of documents and materials of Jewish history, research and development of its exposition.

---
[37] Y.Yevtushenko, 'Ironiya sudby ili kolieso istorii Zeliga Breza,' 5.
[38] E. Akselrod, 'Nie byvaiet yevreyev religioznyh I nierieligioznyh. Yest yevriei,' *Shabat Shalom*, 1.
[39] T. Portnova, 'Tema 'zakrytoho mista' v istoriyi radianskoho Dnipropetrovska 1950–80 rokiv. http://www.historians.in.ua/index.php/en/doslidzhennya/2351-tetyana-portnova-tema-zakritogo-mista-v-istoriji-radyanskogo-dnipropetrovska-1950-80-kh-rokiv
[40] Pavel Giner, 'Ot staroi sinagogi k Mienorie,' *Shabat Shalom*, 10, 2013, 6.

In 2010, the concept of the museum was finally adopted after it was developed by artist Viktor Gukailo, Director of the Centre for the Study of Judaism in Eastern Europe at the National University of Kyiv-Mohyla Academy Leonid Finberg, and Director of the Ukrainian Institute for Holocaust Studies 'Tkuma' Ihor Shchupak.

The head of the project was a member of the Advisory Board of the Dnipropetrovsk Jewish community Mark Shlyak, and its chief architect was Alexander Sorin. The project was implemented by the Chief Rabbi of the Jewish community of Dnipropetrovsk Shmuel Kaminetskyy, leaders of the Jewish community Bogoliubov and Kolomoyskyy, 'Joint' and other Jewish organisations. The museum consists of four halls.

The first hall 'The World Destroyed by the Holocaust' reconstructs the main events of Jewish life in Ukraine during the seventeenth to twentieth centuries, the spiritual world of Judaism, family and community traditions, the life of *shtetls* and history of Hasidism and Zionism. Attention is drawn to the traditionally close ties between Russian chauvinism and anti-Semitism, largely inherited from the USSR (Zaslavsky 1982, 17). There are exhibitions dedicated to the Holodomor and Joseph Stalin's repressions, including Jewish victims of these tragedies. Eventually, the role of denationalized communists of Jewish origin is recognized, who, along with communists of Russian, Ukrainian, and Polish origin, were the organisers of the Great Terror. This is important to explain the commonly held anti-Semitic, negative feelings of Soviet citizens towards the communist system (Kuromiya 2002, 199).

In the second hall devoted to the Holocaust the exhibition is implemented in a semantic triad format which includes the mass murder of Jews, their resistance by organising uprisings in the ghetto and concentration camps, participation of Jews in the Soviet partisan movement and underground and in the ranks of the Soviet Army, and reaction of the local population which ranged from collaboration with the occupiers and assistance in conducting anti-Jewish actions to rescuing Jews. The very difficult question of the participation of Ukrainian nationalists in anti-Jewish pogroms at the beginning of the Nazi-Soviet war is exhibited as manifestations of anti-Semitism and xenophobic Ukrainian nationalist ideology that existed during the 1930s and early 1940s. At the same time, exhibitions demonstrate dynamic changes in nationalist ideology during the 1940s when Ukrainian nationalists rescued Jewish lives and Jews participated in the OUN and the Ukrainian Insurgent army (UPA). These exhibitions reflect a desire to harmonise Jewish and Ukrainian historical narratives while preventing confrontations and heightened emotions (Kasianov 2018, 134; Shlogel 2016, 223–225).

A separate section of the exhibition is dedicated to the 'Righteous Among the Nations,' the official title given on behalf of Israel by the Yad Vashem World Holocaust Remembrance Centre to people of different nationalities who selflessly and risking their lives rescued Jews during the Holocaust. Ukraine (2,634) ranks fourth in the world after Poland (6,992), Netherlands (5,778) and France (4,099) in the number of recognised righteous (Shchupak 2016, 224). Belarus (660) and Russia (209) are ranked ninth and thirteenth places respectively. The exhibition contains materials about distinctive people such as Ukrainian Greek-Catholic Church Metropolitan Andriy Sheptytskyy, Greek-Catholic Church priest Omelian Kovch, and the Hlaholev family who were Ukrainian Orthodox. The Dnipropetrovsk and Dnipro Jewish community has long advocated the official awarding of the status of Righteous Among the Nations to Metropolitan Sheptytskyy by the Yad Vashem Commission.

The third hall 'Jews after the Holocaust' is dedicated to the situation of Jews in the post-war Soviet Union, to anti-Semitic policies undertaken by Soviet leaders Joseph Stalin and Leonid Brezhnev, and to the common fight of Jewish and Ukrainian dissidents demanding their national and democratic rights.

Also included in this hall is the participation of Dnipropetrovsk Jews in the Euromaidan Revolution and in the Russian-Ukrainian war in Eastern Ukraine. This area of the museum hosts meetings of soldiers, volunteers and city residents with exhibits that are continuously updated by donations from the war zone. In May 2015, the Museum was visited by volunteer Michael Sahakyan who at his car garage repaired and sent to the war zone more than 30 vehicles. He donated to the exposition the doors of a van that transferred wounded soldiers from Donetsk airport which had been pierced by dozens of shells. Member of the Jewish community and head of the country's Defence Fund Pavlo Khazan donated to the Museum a family heirloom, the belt of his grandfather Boris Khazan used during World War II which had been a symbol of the unity of generations of his family (Shchupak 2016, 224). Khazan explained the motivation for his participation in Ukraine's defence:

> My family lives here, my ancestors lived here... My great-grandfather and grandfathers fought in World War II. I merely follow their path; I am a reserve officer and I have a duty to protect my family, people, and country. I recalled my military expertise when hostilities began and believed I could be useful.[41]

---

[41] Y. Yevtushenko, 'Pavel Khazan: Phamiliya obiazyvayet!' *Shabat Shalom*, 10, 2014, 5.

Honouring the Holocaust

Honouring Jewish victims of the Holocaust from Dnipropetrovsk oblast was and remains an important factor of national identity and development of the Jewish community. Of the 1.5 million Jews murdered by the Nazis in Ukraine during World War II, up to 21,000 were killed in Dnipropetrovsk.

The Soviet regime deliberately ignored the Holocaust and repression of Jewish dissidents, while others who honoured Jews murdered by the Nazis had considerable civic courage. Since 1985, after Gorbachev came to power, Jews began to hold informal meetings near the monument in Dnipropetrovsk's Gagarin Park which was close to the site of the mass shooting of Jews in 1941 (Borodin, Ivanenko and Niedosiekina 2008, 32). A small monument established in the 1970s had the Russian inscription 'civilians – victims of fascism' without the nationality of the victims specified because of Soviet ethnic nihilism. In addition, the monument was not in the exact place where the mass murder of Jews had taken place (Shchupak 2017, 256). Despite the vagueness and uniformity of the memorial, it nevertheless became a place of memory and reflection. According to O. Fridkis, in the Soviet era some people advised the Jewish community not to gather by the memorial in order not to expose themselves to the wrath of the authorities, but gradually the number of people who gathered near the monument increased.[42]

On 2 May 1989, the first officially sanctioned rally in memory of the Day of Catastrophe and Heroism took place in the Botanical Garden of Dnipropetrovsk State University, and in the fall of that year a delegation of the newly formed People's Movement of Ukraine (*Rukh*) joined the commemoration. Eventually, the Jewish community actively discussed the need to install another monument devoted to the Holocaust in Dnipropetrovsk. The Jewish community collected $10,000 in April 2001 and installed a larger memorial in Gagarin Park in the form of a *matzevot*[43] with an inscription in Hebrew and Ukrainian. Designed by A. Shmist, the monument has twelve faces and twelve candles which symbolize the twelve tribes of Israel, with a broken *Magen David* (The Star of David) in barbed wire as the symbol of the Holocaust of Eastern European Jewish civilisation.[44]

---

[42] 'A. Fridkis rasskazyvayet o tom, kak yevriei Dniepra sokhraniali pamiat o Holokoste.' http://djc.com.ua/news/view/new/?id=22168
[43] *Matseva* is a traditional Jewish tombstone.
[44] A. Medvedovska, 'Pamyat pro Holokost u symvolichnomu prostori Dnipra.'

The Jewish Community, Euromaidan Revolution and Russian-Ukrainian War

The Euromaidan Revolution was a litmus test both of Ukraine's support for European values as well as whether these would be supported in Eastern Ukrainian regions such as Dnipropetrovsk. There was no unanimity in Dnipropetrovsk's Jewish community towards the Euromaidan Revolution. Most of the older generation agreed with the position of the Chairman of the Council of Jewish Veterans of World War II, retired Colonel Solomon Flax who said,

> Why are you ready to destroy the country? Why do you risk the health of future children left out in the cold? Why did they support bloodshed? Are there enemies who want to kill you? In 1941 there were and then I fought against the enemy's army, not against my compatriots. And now there are no enemies in our country...all of this is manipulation in return for money, power, a sense of self-importance, and over geopolitical games.[45]

However, Flax later mentioned Russian 'aggressors who invaded and occupied Ukraine want to destroy it.'[46]

The middle and younger generations were less equivocal in their support for the Euromaidan Revolution as they had no nostalgia for the USSR. They had adjusted to the new realities of post-Soviet life, had travelled abroad, and were not attracted by authoritarianism – a repressive system of government, powerlessness, economic and cultural stagnation, and Russian imperial ambitions.

As the spiritual leader of Dnipropetrovsk Jews, Kaminetskyy had significant influence in the Jewish community. Already at the beginning of the Russian occupation of Crimea, Rabbi Kaminetskyy talked about Ukraine with its centuries-old Jewish history: 'Here are to be found the origins of Hasidism, here are the graves of our righteous, here the Jewish community has been revived after the fall of communism, and here there is hope for the future.'[47] Dnipropetrovsk's Jewish community tried in any possible way to spread information about its support for the Euromaidan Revolution and the core ideas behind the Revolution of Dignity, its unity with the Ukrainian people, and

---

[45] Siemion Flaks, 'Ya obrashchayus ko vsiem,' *Shabat Shalom*, 2, 2014, 3.
[46] 'Obrashcheniye priedsiedatielia Sovieta yevreyev veteranov Dniepropietrovska Solomona Flaksa k vietieranam Vielikoy Otiechestviennoy voiny i vietieranskim organisatsiyam, Shabat Shalom, 5, 2014, 9, and Nataliya Bulgarina, 'Samyi glavnyi prazdnik,' Shabat Shalom, 6, 2014, 3.
[47] 'Biesiedy s ravinom,' *Shabat Shalom*, 3, 2014, 2.

readiness to defend their joint Motherland as citizens of different nationalities.[48] In 2014, the Menorah became a symbol of the unity of all ethnic groups in Ukraine and their readiness to defend the country's sovereignty and European integration.

The Dnipropetrovsk Jewish community helped Jewish refugees from Russian-occupied Crimea and IDPs from the Donbas region of Eastern Ukraine forced to flee their homes in the face of Russian-backed hybrid warfare.[49] Dnipropetrovsk's Jewish community assisted in restoring documents, providing medical care, providing shelter for IDPs in the Beit Baruch[50] boarding houses of the *Yeshiva* and *Beit Khana* schools, finding permanent housing and finding places for children in kindergartens and school. 'Everyone who came from there was pleasantly surprised, and sometimes even shocked by the consistently peaceful and good-natured situation in the city. They were only instinctively frightened when the explosions of fireworks and the roar of thunder were heard somewhere up close,' said director of the Jewish community Zelig Brez, one of the main organisers of volunteer activities.[51] According to Borys Treyherman, it would be extremely difficult to cope with the big influx of IDPs on their own, and therefore community leaders attempted to involve international resources in embassies and international organisations, with the most helpful being the United Nations High Commissioner for Refugees.[52]

The community also coordinated the activities of synagogue parishioners to donate food and humanitarian aid which was sent to Ukrainian soldiers, national guard, and military hospitals 'What is important was that we did not set any tasks or give orders but nevertheless people offered assistance,' Oleh Rostovtsev said.[53] Rostovtsev emphasised the uniqueness of Ukraine as a tolerant country and Dnipropetrovsk, where people of different nationalities but with common values live peacefully. The lobby of synagogue's had *tsdokas* (boxes for donations). Donations of food and water were transported

---

[48] Vitaliy Portnikov, 'Vsi my ukrayintsy,' *Shabat Shalom*, 2, 2015, 11; O. Rostovtsev, 'Demokratiya-eto liudi. Intervyu s zamiestitieliem gossiekrietaria SS HA Vendi Sherman,' *Shabat Shalom*, 4, 2014, 2.
[49] N. Bulgarina, 'Protianut ruku pomoshchi,' *Shabat Shalom*, 9, 2014, 3, and O. Liebiedinskaya, 'V voynie niet ni pravyh, ni vinovatyh,' *Shabat Shalom*, 8, 2014, 7.
[50] 'Beyt Baruh – dvoriets dlia pozhylyh.' https://lechaim.ru/ARHIV/165/VZR/d5.htm
[51] See 'Iudiei Dniepropietrovska aktivno pomogayut biezhentsam i ukrainskoy armii,' 31 July 2014. https://www.religion.in.ua/news/ukrainian_news/26503-iudei-dnipropetrovska-aktivno-pomogayut-bezhencam-i-ukrainskoj-armii.html
[52] Olga Miedviedieva, 'Vriemia niestandartnyh riesheniy ili povezlo roditsia jevreyem: intervyu s sovietnikom glavy Dniepropietrovskoi gosadministratsii Boris Traigermanom,' Shabat Shalom, 10, 2014, 7.
[53] Rostovtsev is the head of the 'Menora' Information Centre, member of the Civic Council of the Dnipro city council and an adviser to Mayor Filatov.

to the 93rd Mechanised Brigade base in Cherkaske in Dnipropetrovsk oblast and personal hygiene products and food and medicines were taken to the hospital on Komsomolskaya Street and the Dnipropetrovsk oblast Mechnikov hospital.[54]

As a front-line city the Dnipropetrovsk and Dnipro Jewish community had received substantial foreign assistance from abroad to deal with trauma as well as individual medical kits for soldiers. Dnipropetrovsk oblast Mechnikov hospital was visited by American specialists in field surgery who conducted operations to save wounded soldiers and helped to improve the rehabilitation process.[55] Each morning a prayer was said during morning service at synagogues for the recovery of wounded Ukrainian soldiers.[56]

In the first months of the Russian-Ukrainian war, a practice began of Jewish students visiting wounded soldiers. Sarah, the daughter of Rabbi Kaminetskyy, while an eleventh-grade student, wrote a newspaper article after visiting a hospital with wounded soldiers. She said she had been afraid to go to the hospital because of the fear of looking into the eyes of seriously injured soldiers. She overcame these fears because she knew how important it was to help those who had given their lives and become wounded in the defence of their country.[57] Another Jewish school pupil Sonia Zaydner after visiting a hospital wrote in a newspaper that she was most impressed by the fact wounded soldiers dreamt of returning to the war zone to be re-united with their friends.[58]

Kolomoyskyy's Strategic Role

In discussing the rise of Ukrainian patriotism between 2014–2015 and the part in this played by the Jewish community, one cannot ignore the role played by Kolomoyskyy. At that time, Kolomoyskyy vividly represented the Jewish component of the struggle for Ukrainian sovereignty and a guarantor of stability at a time of a weakened central government. Researchers emphasise the crucial role of local business and political elites, which, given the weakness of the central government, helped prevent the war spreading to Dnipropetrovsk

---

[54] 'Kak yevreyskiye struktury pomogayut biezhentsam i poddierzhivayut Vooruzhennyie sily Ukrainy i Natsionalnuyu gvardiyu.'
[55] Elena Torban, '911- Skoraya pomoshch iz Bostona,' Shabat Shalom, 12, 2014, 6, 'Yevrieyskiye obshchiny Boston i Dniepropietrovska cotrudnichayut , pomogaya spasat ranienyh.' http : // www . jewseurasia . org / page 16 / news 51990. html
[56] E.Yevshteyn, 'The arrival of the synagogue –to wounded soldiers,' Shabat Shalom, 8, 2014, 2.
[57] Sara Kaminietskaya, 'Viernities domoy zhivymy i zdorovymi,' Shabat Shalom, 10, 2014, 2.
[58] Sonya Zaider, 'Den, koly ya zustrilasia z viynoyu,' Shabat Sholom, 10, 2014, 2.

and Kharkiv (see Portnov 2015; Kononczuk 2015; Buckholz 2019).[59] However, in Dnipropetrovsk the business elite acted in a concentrated and personalised form. At that time, Kolomoyskyy was the guarantor of the city's stability during a period of weak central government and was the leader of the region that maintained Ukrainian sovereignty. The warm support given to Kolomoyskyy by Ukrainian patriots assisted in the process of overcoming historical legacies of anti-Semitism. It is noteworthy that in the Russian-occupied territories of Donetsk and Luhansk regions, anti-Semitic tendencies became increasingly apparent in the official ideology of the so-called DNR and LNR (Likhachov and Bezruk 2015, 41–42). The DNR and LNR had revived Soviet era anti-Zionism which had always been a camouflaged form of anti-Semitism (Kuzio 2019, 197–213).

On 22 February 2014, Kolomoyskyy issued a statement where he said that Russian-backed separatism would not spread to Dnipropetrovsk oblast. On 2 March 2014, Acting Head of State Oleksandr Turchynov appointed Kolomoyskyy governor of Dnipropetrovsk oblast. At his own financial expense, Kolomoyskyy bought petrol for the Ukrainian army. In April 2014, Kolomoyskyy funded volunteer battalions, paying each soldier a personal allowance in addition to his salary.[60] In April 2014, on the initiative and financing of Kolomoyskyy, the formation of battalions of volunteers began.

On 17 April 2014, Deputy Governor Boris Filatov announced that Kolomoyskyy would pay $10,000 for each Russian saboteur handed over. Five days later, the National Defence Headquarters of Dnipropetrovsk oblast reported that Kolomoyskyy had paid $10,000 for eight captured Russian saboteurs. On 3 June 2014, the National Defence Headquarters announced a reward of half a million dollars for the capture of Oleh Tsaryov, a former Party of Regions deputy from Dnipropetrovsk oblast who was working with the pro-Russian separatists.[61] Kolomoyskyy had telephoned Tsaryov and warned him that because of the murder in Mariupol of Shlemkevich, 'a member of the Jewish community,' a large ransom was imposed on Tsaryov's head.[62] On 8 June 2014, he offered to confiscate the property of separatist supporters, which was undertaken in the case of Tsaryov's assets. On 1 June 2014,

---

[59] A. Portnov, 'Chomu Kharkiv i Dnipropetrovsk ne staly Donetskom i Luhanskom?' *Ukrayinska Pravda*, 4 February 2016. https://www.istpravda.com.ua/articles/2016/02/4/148912/

[60] 'Oligarkh Kolomoiskiy sozdayot sobstviennuyu armiyu dlia voiny s Donbasom.' https://www-ntv-ru.translate.goog/novosti/975396/?_x_tr_sl=uk&_x_tr_tl=en&_x_tr_hl=en

[61] 'Kolomoyskyi oholosyv vynahorodu za Tsariova u pivmiliona dolariv.' https://www-5-ua.translate.goog/polityka/kolomoiskyi-oholosyv-vynahorodu-za-tsarova-u-pivmiliona-dolariv-32869.html?_x_tr_sl=uk&_x_tr_tl=en&_x_tr_hl=en

[62] 'Kolomoiskiy Tsarevu: Za tvoyu golovu dayut million dolarov.' https://bitva-wiki.translate.goog/ru/news/text/360-kolomoiskii-caryovu-za-tvoyu-golovu-dayut-million-dollarov?_x_tr_sl=uk&_x_tr_tl=en&_x_tr_hl=en

Kolomoyskyy was placed on the wanted list of the Investigative Committee of the Russian Federation.

Kolomoyskyy supported government proposals to build a fortified wall of barbed wire along the border with Russia which would run through Donetsk, Luhansk and Kharkiv oblasts. On August 28, Deputy Governor Hennadiy Korban made a statement that Kolomoyskyy could expand his governorship to neighbouring Zaporizhzhya oblast and adjacent areas of Ukrainian-controlled Donetsk oblast. The Kremlin's financial channels throughout Southern-Eastern Ukraine were shut down, which assisted in preventing pro-Russian separatists from expanding beyond the Donbas (see Kulick, 2019). In 2014–2015, Kolomoyskyy's team successfully transformed Dnipropetrovsk into a *Forepost* (Outpost) of Ukraine's defence against Russian military aggression.[63] In this endeavour the Jewish community played an important supporting role, as did the civic patriotism of Jewish citizens of Ukraine.

Certainly, the pragmatic aspect in the motivation of Kolomoyskyy and his team cannot be denied. 'Kolomoyskyy-businessman' acted in agreement with 'Kolomoyskyy-politician'. Among the Ukrainian oligarchs, Kolomoyskyy distinguished himself by the fact that long before the events of the Euromaidan Revolution, he far-sightedly reoriented his own business to the West (Olearchyk 2007; Paxton 2007). Thanks to his pro-Ukrainian position, he successfully defended his assets in Dnipropetrovsk and the region and sought to take advantage of his growing influence. Apparently, it was their determination to defend their own business interests that worried the central government, which was also headed by former President Petro Poroshenko, who was well versed in ways to convert growing business assets into political influence (Carroll 2015).

Kolomoyskyy was removed from the post of governor on 24 March 2015 while he was still a popular and influential political figure. A large crowd of Dnipro residents gathered at the farewell rally with the governor to thank Kolomoyskyy's team for saving their city from a Russian military scenario. They compared his patriotic position with that of Donetsk oligarch Rinat Akhmetov, whose uncertainty during the so-called 'Russian Spring' contributed to the occupation of part of Donbass. Dnipro residents held blue-yellow and red and black OUN flags with the Star of David attached to them. However, the removal of Kolomoyskyy did not significantly change the civic pathos of the city. Dnipro continued to assert itself as a city of much greater ambition than a centre of regional significance: it became a *Forepost* for the defence of all of Ukraine from Russian military aggression, an invincible patriotic polis in the Ukrainian East. And the Jewish community of

---

[63] A. Portnov, 'Chomu Kharkiv i Dniepropietrovsk ne stali Donetskom i Luganskom.'

Dnipropetrovsk and the Ukrainian patriotism shown by Jewish citizens played a central role in this.

The symbol of a Jewish warrior for Ukrainian independence was Asher Cherkaskyy,[64] who had been a senior sergeant of the Dnipro-1 special-purpose police battalion of the Ministry of Internal Affairs. He fought three kilometres from Donetsk airport against the pro-Russian separatist *Vostok* (East) battalion.[65] Cherkaskyy ensured the withdrawal of Ukrainian wounded soldiers from Ilovaisk, where hundreds of Ukrainian servicemen were killed after Russian President Vladimir Putin gave his 'guarantee' to a corridor for the withdrawal of Ukrainian troops. He was wounded in September 2014 and the following month was transferred to a military hospital.

Cherkaskyy experienced no problems with his ethnic or religious affiliations; on the contrary, he emphasised that other fighters in his unit respected his way of life and recalled the tolerant attitude of his fellow comrades in arms towards Jewish values:

> No one was bothered by my long beard…Everyone in the battalion knew that my Jewish friends Andrew Savchuk and Dmitry Pylypenko were killed in the Ilovaisk massacre. Contrary to stereotypes about nationalist *Pravyy Sektor* (Right Sector) battalion, he never experienced anti-Semitism. In order not to violate *kashrut* (Jewish rules for eating food), Cherkaskyy ate cereals and canned fish. 'While I was there, out of respect for me, they did not eat *salo* (bacon lard) or cook pork. This was not my request but their decision.[66]

In April 2016, on the initiative of Dmytro Yarosh, the former head of *Pravyy Sektor* (Right Sector), a Jewish company was created commanded by Maxim Khorev, a veteran of volunteer battalions Dnipro-1 and *Pravyy Sektor*. The company included representatives of Jewish citizens of Ukraine who had military experience in other volunteer and military units which had fought against Russian military aggression in Eastern Ukraine. Between 2016–2017, the Jewish company was based in sector 'M' and fought for the villages of Shyrokyne and Marinka, with many members being awarded medals for valour in combat. In September 2016, an improvised synagogue was opened

---

[64] On Cherkasskyy, see Y. Yevtushenko, 'Intervyu s Asherom Cherkaskim: 'Iz religioznykh yevrieyev Ukrainy na Donbase voyuyu ya odin,' *Shabat Shalom*, 1, 2015, 6.
[65] Y.Yevtushenko, 'Interviu s Asherom Cherkaskim.'
[66] Liba Liberman, 'Asher Cherkaskyi: menia ubierieg Vsievyshniy,' *Khadashot*, 1, 2015.
https://hadashot-kiev-ua.translate.goog/content/asher-cherkasskiy-menya-ubereg-vsevyshniy?_x_tr_sch=http&_x_tr_sl=uk&_x_tr_tl=en&_x_tr_hl=en

at the base of operations of the Jewish company.[67] Cherkaskyy wrote that 'there are no atheists in the trenches.' At the initiative of veterans and Jewish military instructors, G. Mashinzon, M. Mykulych, T. Zlatkin and Cherkaskyy, on the eve of Passover, Jewish volunteers visit military units on the front line and break matzo with soldiers.[68]

The contribution of Jewish intellectuals from Dnipro to the development of technological equipment for the Ukrainian army is unprecedented. Volunteer specialists Pavlo Hazan and Hennadiy Mashynzon developed a unique system of digital communication which allowed the Ukrainian military to control checkpoints in Dnipropetrovsk and Zaporizhzhya oblasts adjacent to Russian-occupied territories in Donetsk oblasts and in Dnipropetrovsk and Mariupol airports, which were important military bases and staging posts for combat operations. This represented a major step towards the modernisation of the Ukrainian army; before this initiative there was limited communication between units and mobile phones were being used which, in addition to being tapped by Russian intelligence, were also used by the enemy to detect and attack targets. With this invention by Jewish designers, military operators received the opportunity to maintain continuous flows of communication through video and radio signals with units located in sectors 'B' and 'M' and Dnipropetrovsk and Mariupol airports.

The phenomenon of so-called *Zhydo-Banderivtsi* (Jewish Banderites) was Kolomoyskyy's mocking and humorous response to Russia's information warfare of a 'Nazi-backed putsch' in Ukraine and fascists running the country. In fact, Kolomoskyy's team in 2014–2015 included two Jews (himself and Korban) and a Russian (Filatov). *Zhydo Banderivtsi*, a slogan which became common on t-shirts, reflected the active assistance of Russian-speaking Jews in Dnipropetrovsk oblast in defending Ukrainian statehood. Further, the slogan undermined Russian propaganda and disinformation about anti-Semitism in Ukraine. Russia's information warfare claimed that Jewish volunteers were 'particularly brutal and bloodthirsty, they do not take prisoners and shoot everything that moves. They do not neglect the ritual eating of raw liver of separatists to inflame themselves before going into battle'.[69] Such statements show to what degree Russian information warfare is out of touch with realities in Ukraine.

---

[67] Yelena Belozierskaya, 'Yevreyskaya rota Ukrainskoy dobrovolcheskoy armii Dmitriya Yarosha.' https://mayak-org-ua.translate.goog/news/in-a-jewish-company-in-the-area-of-the-ato-opened-the-synagogue-looking-for-the-rabbi-video/?_x_tr_sl=uk&_x_tr_tl=en&_x_tr_hl=en

[68] 'Pesach in ATO. Matca dlya karateley.' https://hurtmann.livejournal.com/1407916.html

[69] Mikhail Gold, 'A vy ikh antisiemitizmom nie probovali?' *Khadashot*, 8, 2014. https://hadashot-kiev-ua.translate.goog/content/vy-ih-antisemitizmom-ne-probovali?_x_tr_sch=http&_x_tr_sl=uk&_x_tr_tl=en&_x_tr_hl=en

Conclusion

Dnipropetrovsk Jews, who are a highly influential community in the oblast centre of Dnipro, hold no nostalgia for the USSR for several reasons. The Soviet system promoted anti-Semitism and anti-Zionism and hid the Holocaust inside the myths of the Great Patriotic War, with Jewish victims of Nazi war crimes included in the 'twenty million Soviet dead.' The lack of Soviet nostalgia undoubtedly explains why Dnipropetrovsk evolved so effortlessly from a closed and important Soviet city associated with nuclear weapons, the military industrial complex, and Soviet leaders, into a centre upholding Ukrainian statehood.

The revival of the Dnipropetrovsk and Dnipro Jewish community is unparalleled in the former USSR. From the late 1980s to 2013, Ukrainian patriotism deepened among Ukrainian Jews. The Jewish community was only able to revive and rebuild and honour the memory of the Holocaust in an independent Ukrainian state where anti-Semitism, particularly in Dnipropetrovsk oblast was practically non-existent. All of what had been achieved could have been lost in 2014 if Russian-backed hybrid warfare and Putin's *Novorossiya* (New Russia) project had spread to Dnipropetrovsk oblast. In 2014–2015, during the midst of the Russian-Ukrainian war, the Dnipropetrovsk and Dnipro Jewish community, which is predominantly Russian-speaking, exhibited a high level of patriotism which helped to strengthen the emergence of a Ukrainian civic nation.

In the last three decades the Dnipropetrovsk Jewish community has become united and part of the oblast centre's urban community. Jews no longer must hide their nationality or religious preferences as they did in the USSR and have the tools, institutions, and resources to continue to preserve and develop their Jewish identity.

References

Androsova, Valeriya. (2008). 'Habad v konteksti religiynoho vidrodzhennia ukrayinskoho yevreistva,' *Ukrayinske religiyeznavstvo*, 48, 253–269.

Borodin, Yevgen, Ivanenko, Valentyn, and Niedosiekina, Tetiana. (2008). *Istoriya ridnoho kraiu. Dnipropetrovshchyna. Pidruchnyk dlia 11 klasu zahalnoosvitnioyi*. Dnipropetrovsk: Vydavnytsvo.

Buckholz, Quentin. (2019). 'The Dogs That Didn't Bark. Elite Preferences and the Failure of Separatism in Kharkiv and Dnipropetrovsk,' *Problems of Post-Communism*, 66, 3: 151–160.

Bystriakov, Alexander. (2002). *Yevriei Yekatierinoslava – Dniepropietrovska (XX century)* Dnipropetrovsk: ART.

Carroll, Oliver. (2015). 'Star Wars in Ukraine: Poroshenko vs. Kolomoisky,' *Politico*, 21 December. https://www.politico.eu/article/star-wars-in-ukraine-poroshenko-vs-kolomoisky/

Kasianov, Heorhiy. ed., (2018). *Polityka i Pamyat. Dnipro-Zaporizhzhya-Odesa–Kharkiv* Lviv: FOP Shumylovych.

Kononczuk, Wojciech. (2015). 'Oligarchs After the Maidan: the old system in a 'new' Ukraine,' *Commentary* no. 162, Warsaw: Centre for Eastern Studies. https://www.osw.waw.pl/en/publikacje/osw-commentary/2015-02-16/oligarchs-after-maidan-old-system-a-new-ukraine

Kulick, Orysia. (2019). 'Dnipropetrovsk oligarchs: Lynchpins of Soverignty or Sources of Instability?' *The Soviet and Post-Soviet Review*, 46, 3: 352–386.

Kuromiya, Hiroaki. (2002). *Svoboda i terror u Donbasi: Ukrayinsko-rosiyske prykordonnia,1870–1990*. Kyiv: Osnovy.

Kuzio, Taras. (2019). *Viyna Putina Proty Ukrayiny. Revolutsiya, Natsionalism, i Kriminalitet*. Kyiv: Dukh i litera.

Likhachov, Vyacheslav. and Bezruk, Tetyana. *Xenophobiya v Ukraine v 1914 na fone revolutsii i interventsii: Informatsiono-analiticheskiy doklad po rezultatam monitoring*. Kyiv: Kongres natsionalnyh obshchin Ukrainy. https://bit.ly/2SsfIDH (PDF) 41–42.

Loshak, Aleksandra. and V. Starostin, Valentyn. (2019). *Sinagogi Yekatierinoslava*. Dnipro: Gerda.

Magocsi, Paul. R. and Petrovsky-Shtern, Yohanan. (2016). Yevreyi ta ukrayintsi: tysiacholittia spivisnuvannia. Uzhhorod: Vydavnytstvo Valeriya Padiaka.

Olearchyk, Roman. (2007). 'Evraz Buys Steel Assets in Ukraine,' *The Financial Times*, 12 December.

Paxton, Roger. (2007). 'Russia's Evraz to Pay $2 Billion for Ukraine Assets,' *Reuters*, 13 December. https://www.reuters.com/article/evraz-ukraine-idUSL1352492320071213

Portnov, Andriy. (2015). 'Post-Maidan Europe and the New Ukrainian Studies,' *Slavic Review*, 74, 4: 723–31.

Shlogel, K. (2016). *Ukrayinskyi vyklyk. Vidkryttia yevropeyskoyi krayiny*. Kyiv: Dukh i Litera.

Shchupak, Ihor. ed., (2016). *Pravednyky narodiv svitu. Directory*. Dnipro: Ukraiinskyy instytut vyvchennya Holokostu 'Tkuma.'

Shchupak, I. ed., (2017). *Holokost u Dnipropetrovsku*. Dnipro: Ukrayinskyy instytut vyvchennya Holokostu 'Tkuma' and LIRA.

Zaslavsky, Vladimir. (1982). *The Neo-Stalinist State: Class, Ethnicity, and Consensus in Soviet Society*. Armonk, NY: M. E. Sharpe.

Zisels, Iosyf. (2004). 'Fatal konflic tsivilizatsiy niet,' *Yevroaziatskiy yevrieyskiy yezhegodnik*, 55–57.

Zhuk, Sergei. (2009). "Bytva za kulturu' v zakrytomu misti Sovietskoiy Ukraiyny v period piznioho sotsializmu, 1959–1984,' *Skhid-Zakhid*, nos. 13–14.

4

Memory Politics in Dnipropetrovsk, 1991–2015

OLEH REPAN

This chapter is the first scholarly study of memory politics in Dnipropetrovsk between 1991 and the 2013–2014 Euromaidan Revolution. The Russian-speaking city of Dnipropetrovsk has been traditionally viewed as pro-Russian while at the same time, results from elections over this period show a gradual but steady increase in the share of votes won by pro-European parties. Memory politics and de-Sovietisation played an important role in the decline of pro-Russian political forces in Dnipropetrovsk.

In this chapter, historical memory is defined as the interaction of family and public memory. Family memory is transmitted mainly in the form of traditional stories and folklore from the older generation to youth, not necessarily within one family. This type of memory can be learnt from the experience of the older generation who are recognised as an authority by the recipient.

Pro-Ukrainian and pro-Russian actors fashioned memory politics in Dnipropetrovsk. Each of them has its own vision of what constitutes memory. Those considered pro-Ukrainian were liberal and conservative while pro-Russian actors were nostalgic for the Tsarist Russian Empire and Soviet era. Scholarly research has analysed how each of the two groups interpreted three key historical periods: the Cossack era, Tsarist Russian Empire and Soviet Union. In analysing pro-Ukrainian and pro-Russian memory politics it is important to bring in policies by state and local authorities.

Scholarly Research on Memory Politics in Dnipropetrovsk

Since 1991, memory politics in Dnipropetrovsk has been a neglected field of academic research. Despite the importance of Dnipropetrovsk to Soviet and

Ukrainian politics, scholars have largely ignored the city and region, preferring instead to focus on the Lviv-Kyiv-Donetsk axis. Among the few exceptions is the collective monograph *Historical memory of the Dnipropetrovsk region* which includes a chapter devoted to memory politics undertaken by the regional authorities during the celebrations of the 75th and 80th anniversaries of the region, as well as the activities of institutions such as the Dmytro Yavornytskyy Dnipropetrovsk National Museum. Another chapter analysed the transformation of historical memory in the region through the development of historical and local lore (Svitlenko 2012, 344–427).

An interesting analysis of different approaches to the problem of the emergence of the city was provided by Andrii and Tetiana Portnova (2015, 223–250). They outlined the main approaches to the founding of the city of Dnipropetrovsk within the 'imperial' paradigm, noting that typologically, celebration of the city's 100th anniversary in 1878 and the city's 200th anniversary in 1976 were very similar. Their theory is based on the idea of Russia's civilising role for the region. After the disintegration of the Soviet Union, some historians in Dnipropetrovsk began to substantiate the idea of the emergence of the city from settlements in the Cossack era, an approach aimed at searching for a Ukrainian identity for the city.

Memory politics in Dnipropetrovsk was analysed in *Politics and Memory. Dnipro-Zaporizhzhya-Odesa-Kharkiv: From the 1990s to the Present* by several authors, including myself (Kasianov 2018, 20–21, 39, 54–56, 67–68, 78–79, 84–85, 87, 94–95, 100–101, 108–110, 133–135, 138–140, 202–219). This detailed study identified the main contours of memory policies undertaken by the authorities and public figures during historical events. The material on each of the cities is divided into sections, with authors analysing the 'myths of the foundation,' the Tsarist Russian Empire in memory politics and memory politics in the twentieth century. The study (Kasianov 2018) analyses competition between Cossack and imperial myths of Dnipropetrovsk's emergence, uncertain perceptions in the nineteenth century and controversial approaches to events in Soviet history. The authors emphasise that controversy is inherent in all areas of Ukrainian memory politics, with a specific focus on the period after World War II when the city was closed to foreigners and became the centre of Soviet nuclear missile production. Textbooks on the history of the region describe the post-Soviet era as a period of prosperity.

The second part of the study is devoted to analysis of public opinion polls conducted in 2013 and 2015 in several Ukrainian cities, including Dnipropetrovsk, which showed attitudes to Ukrainian history and memorialisation of history in public spaces. The study included several interviews with Dnipropetrovsk residents from different generations who outlined their perception of the city and memory politics. Researchers have found that the most dramatic historical event in the city is World War II.

Perceptions of Historical Memory in Dnipropetrovsk

To understand the mechanisms of memory politics in Dnipropetrovsk one must first analyse the perceptions of its residents about the history of their region. In general, there are two images of the past, Cossack and Tsarist Russian imperial with Soviet memory divided into several components.

If we discuss oral traditions, the Cossack past continues to be developed through two types of legends, family through ancestors of Cossacks, and toponymic, through the origin of names associated with events or figures from the Cossack era. The Tsarist Russian imperial era is represented somewhat more broadly. There is also a living tradition; for example, legends about landlords and their influence (both negative and positive) on the life of a particular village.

Memory politics of the Soviet era is very different in terms of how it is evaluated and very much dependent upon a family's experience of the communist system. The key historical moments are in 1917–1921; the Holodomor, collectivisation, and political repression; and the Second World War. Memory politics of the post-Stalin era is divided into when the USSR was led by Nikita Khrushchev (1953–1964), Leonid Brezhnev (1964–1982) or Mikhail Gorbachev (1985–1991). Here, to a certain extent, we find a public perception that during the second half of the twentieth century there was a gradual improvement of standards of living, a myth of a 'golden age' in the 1970s and deterioration of living standards in the second half of the 1980s.

Another approach to the interpretation of historical memory in Dnipropetrovsk is by dividing public opinion into on the one hand pro-Ukrainian (both conservative and liberal) and on the other, pro-Russian Imperial and Soviet. Despite the existence of certain differences within these two large groups (pro-Ukrainian and pro-Russian Imperial and Soviet), they are quite clear in how they identify themselves when discussing with the competing 'Other.'

Now let us attempt to instrumentalise the history of these two groups. There is a certain consensus between them in recognising the Cossack era. At the same time, those with a pro-Ukrainian identity emphasise the place of Cossacks in their historical memory while those holding a more Imperial and Soviet identity typically display, with certain exceptions, an ignorance about them (which is discussed below).

Interest in Cossacks had always existed in the region; Ukrainian Communist leader Petro Shelest had praised them in his 1970 book *Ukrayina nasha radyanska* (Ukraine. Our Soviet Land) for which he was accused of 'national deviationism' and removed two years later (Tillett 1975). It was not surprising that interest in Cossack history was revived in the late Mikhail Gorbachev era during the uncovering of 'blank spots' in Ukrainian history. This came to the fore in 1990 during the 500th anniversary of the formation of Ukrainian Cossacks when Dnipropetrovsk and Zaporizhhya hosted events which gathered upwards of 20,000 people from the region and visitors, mainly from Western Ukraine and Kyiv. Rallies were held and a monument to a young Taras Shevchenko was unveiled.

A striking event was the march by thousands of people along the central avenue of Dnipropetrovsk to the D. Yavornytskyy Museum and a rally at the end of the commemoration in the Taras Shevchenko Park. There were minor skirmishes in the city with Soviet veterans from the Afghanistan war who opposed the Ukrainian national revival. This commemoration not only revived and reclaimed the Cossack past, but also other national liberation struggles in 1917–1921 by the Ukrainian People's Republic (UNR) and in the 1940s by the Organisation of Ukrainian Nationalists (OUN) and Ukrainian Insurgent Army (UPA).[1]

Since the early 1990's the Dnipropetrovsk region has registered 49 so-called pro-Ukrainian and pro-Russian Cossack organisations. Most of them were interest clubs who occasionally gather a small number of their members and undertake respectable activities. *Kodak Palanka* of the Zaporizhzhyan Cossack Army, which stands out among the pro-Ukrainian organisations, and regularly participates in the 'Sokil-Yura' regional competition, has defended a school playground from illegal construction, created a 400-strong Maidan self-defence group, and defended state buildings in Dnipropetrovsk in spring of 2014 from their take-over by Party of Regions and pro-Russian vigilantes.[2]

The most successful pro-Russian Cossack organisation is the Ekaterinoslav Cossack District, ideologically based on the not so historically important Ekaterinoslav Cossack army which fought for the Tsarist Russian Empire.

---

[1] Mykhaylo Tverdokhlib, 'Ukrayina vidznachaye 500-richchya ukrayinskoho kozastva.' http://www.spas.net.ua/index.php/news/full/755, and 'Yak nad Dnipropetrovskom vpershe derzhavnyy prapor pidiymaly,' http://gorod.dp.ua/news/94123#

[2] 'Kodaska palanka viyska Zaporozkoho nyzovoho.' http://vk.com/club66159938; 'Kozaski orhanizacii Dnipropetrovshhyny.' http://otkozachestvod.jimdo.com; Hlib Pryhunov, 'Kozastvo Ukrayiny – slava Ukrayiny,' *Vidomosti*, 11 October 2006; 'Samarska pokrova,' http://foundationsirko.blogspot.com/p/blog-page_17.html; 'U Dnipropetrovsku vyrishyly pidtrymaty kozastvo.' http://24tv.ua/ukrayina/u_dnipropetrovsku_virishili_pidtrimati_kozatstvo/n290979

They strongly support the concept of the Russian World and have organised processions with the Russian Orthodox Church in Ukraine in honour of military victories by the Tsarist Russian Empire. They established a Cadet Corps for young Cossacks and organised visits by Cossacks from Russia. Since 2014, they have been not surprisingly inactive.[3]

Cossack organisations in Dnipropetrovsk traditionally celebrate the Intercession, the Day of Remembrance of Hetman Ivan Sirko on 14 October. In 2000–2010, the *Samarska Pokrova* festival took place on the territory of the Old Samara fortress (located in the modern village of Shevchenko in Dnipropetrovsk). On 1–2 August, commemorations of Hetman Sirko are traditionally held at his gravesite in the village of Kapulivka. During celebrations prior to 2014, there were often conflicts between pro-Ukrainian and pro-Russian Cossack organisations, with the latter supported by the authorities during Viktor Yanukovych's presidency (2010–2014).[4]

Competition Over Who Founded Dnipropetrovsk

One of the important areas of conflict between pro-Ukrainian and pro-Russian Imperial and Soviet memory politics is the founding of the city of Dnipropetrovsk. The year 1776 was celebrated by the Soviet regime in the 1970s as a way of deliberately coinciding with the 70th anniversary of Brezhnev's birth. This replaced the previously dominant date of the founding of Dnipropetrovsk during the visit of Tsarist Empress Catherine II in 1787 which was traditionally used by historiography as the city's foundation year. Since the 1990s, attempts have been made to revise these Tsarist and Soviet

---

[3] 'V Dnepropetrovskoj eparkhii proshly torzhestva, posvyashennye pobede nad Napoleonom,' 21 July 2007. http://www.patriarchia.ru/db/text/272220.html; Iryna Ehorova, 'Pochemu vozrozhdenye kazachestva – myf?' http://gorod.dp.ua/news/18161?page=3; 'Katerynoslavskoe kazachestvo otkryvaet novye stranyci ystoryy goroda.' https://sites.google.com/site/nashdnepropetrovsk/novosti/ekaterinoslavskoekazacestvo; 'Kozaski orhanizasii Dnipropetrovshhyny.' http://otkozachestvod.jimdo.com; 'Po blahoslovenyyu pravyashheho arkhyereya v eparkhii proshly prazdnovaniya 222-letyya sozdaniya Ekaterynoslavskoho kazachestva.' http://www.eparhia.dp.ua/news.php?id_news=176; 'Pryhunov H. Kozastvo Ukrayiny – slava Ukrayiny,' *Vidomosti*, 11 October 2006; 'Sostoyalos otkrytye pervogo na Ukraine kazaskoho kadetskoho korpusa,' 6 September 2007, http://www.patriarchia.ru/db/text/291086.html

[4] 'V seli Kapulivka vidbulosya shchorichne vshanuvannya pamyati I. Sirka.' http://dp.ridna.ua/2015/08/04/v-seli-kapulivka-vidbulos-schorichne-vshanuvannya-pamyati-ivana-sirka; Yuliya Zabyelina, 'Kozaske svyato: hulyay, narode!' *Visti Prydniprovya*, 9 August 2011; Alena Makarenko, 'Den kazaskoj slavye u kurgana Syrko,' 4 August 2009; Anatoliy Ovcharenko, 'Chto ne mogut podelyt kazachi atamanye?' *Reporter*, 10 August 2006.

dates and, more importantly the context by expanding discussion into the media. In the 1990s, the most prominent scholar who regularly addressed this topic was Yuriy Mitsik who argued that the history of the city should be dated earlier from the construction of the Cossack Kodak Fortress in 1635.[5]

Discussion about the origins of the city of Dnipropetrovsk intensified following the 2004 Orange Revolution when several civic organisations and academic centres (e.g., Institute of Ukrainian Studies, Institute of Social Research), appealed to scholars and local historians to begin research into the Cossack era foundation of Dnipropetrovsk. Based on the monograph *Palimpsest: settlements of the sixteenth to eighteenth centuries in the history of Dnipropetrovsk*, they launched a public campaign to redefine the origins of Dnipropetrovsk by proposing 1645 as its founding year. Press conferences in Dnipropetrovsk and Kyiv, round tables, petitions to the city's mayor, billboards on streets, and the unveiling of a memorial on the territory of Novyy Kodak were used to popularise the Ukrainian claim to having established the settlement of Dnipropetrovsk.

The city authorities moved towards the Ukrainian claim to having founded Dnipropetrovsk through symbolically recognising the Cossack component of the history of Dnipropetrovsk by naming one of the streets in the centre of the city of Polovytska in honour of the settlement of Polovytsya established around 1743. Interestingly, the names of districts within Dnipropetrovsk, such as Mandrykivka, Diyivka, Kamyanka, and others are linked to Ukraine's Cossack past. The biggest revival of Cossack historical names took place during the process of decommunisation in 2015–2018 which is analysed in Chapter 6 by Ihor Kocherhin (see Repan 2007).[6]

Pro-Russian Imperial and Soviet memory politics on the founding of Dnipropetrovsk is weakly endowed with scholarly support; nevertheless, it was dominant among the city's political elites prior to the 2014 crisis. The *History of the City of Dnepropetrovsk*, which was commissioned by the City's Council, uses 1776 as the date of the founding of Dnipropetrovsk which influences the city's annual Day of the City holiday and the celebration of other anniversaries. Even between 2014–2015, during the Russian-Ukrainian war, social advertising was embellished in the city centre with the foundation

---

[5] Ihor Kocherhin, 'Pohlyad na deyaki aspekty rannoyi istoriyii mista.'
[6] 'Istoryky namahayutsya utochnyty daty zasnuvannya ukrayinskykh mist.' http://photo.ukrinform.ua/ukr/current/photo.php?id=243472; 'Katerynoslav? – Ni! Novyy Kodak!' http://www.radiosvoboda.org/content/chapter/1112256.html; 'Vidkryty lyst shchodo zasnuvannya m. Dnipropetrovska.' http://maidan.org.ua/arch/petit/1207140563.html; 'Mizh Polovytseyu ta Katerynoslavom.' http://visnyk.dmr.org.ua/statti/istoriya-v-osobistostyakh/12-mizh-polovitseyu-ta-katerinoslavom.html; Polyn Iryna 'Goroda kornevyshche,' *Dnepr vechernyj*, 17 August 2003.

year of 1776 – supposedly to promote local unity in the face of the threat from foreign invasion (Bolebrukh 2006).

At the heart of the pro-Russian Imperial approach is a thesis of the civilising influence of the Tsarist Russian Empire on the development of the Dnipropetrovsk region. Tsarina Catherine II and Prince Potemkin allegedly aimed to fashion Katerynoslav into the third capital of the Tsarist Russian Empire. In the 1990s, this thesis was used to justify the uniqueness of Dnipropetrovsk. The costumed characters of Tsarina Catherine II and her favourite courtiers participated in the Day of the City celebrations and were aired in television commercials. Local businessman Hennadiy Balashov named his chain of 'Moskva' shops after figures from the Tsarist Empire, such as Katerininsky, Potemkin, Orlovsky and others. These shops were part of the city landscape for a long period of time.[7]

In 2005–2006, following the Orange Revolution, a heated debate broke out in the local media over the erection of new monuments. Attempts to erect monuments to Tsarina Catherine II were successful in several Ukrainian cities and in Dnipropetrovsk there was an initiative to install a monument to her next to the building of the Central Cathedral of the Russian Orthodox Church in Ukraine. The head of the Dnipropetrovsk state administration Yuriy Yekhanurov, appointed by President Viktor Yushchenko, was opposed to this proposal, arguing it represented homage to the Tsarist Empire and demanded an end to its construction. Supporters of the pro-Russian Imperial approach to memory politics actively promoted 'St. Catherine' by attempting to provide the Empress with a saintly image.

The importance of the mythology about Tsarina Catherine II was demonstrated during the 2012 visit of Russian President Vladimir Putin's political technologist Konstantyn Zatulin, who was accompanied by a team of historians and a film crew from the Russian *Kultura* television channel to Dnipropetrovsk and other cities in Southern-Eastern Ukraine. The visit was to mark the 225th anniversary of the so-called 'Great Journey' of Tsarina Catherine II and to promote her memory as that of a 'civilising mission' into so-called 'wild lands.' The Party of Regions organised several supporting events in Dnipropetrovsk oblast library, promotions in the media, and presentations by Party of Regions deputy Oleh Tsarev (who in the 2014 crisis became a separatist leader). Subsequently published Russian media reports and pseudo-academic work by Russian historians were of low scholarly quality, primarily consisting of disinformation about the life of 'Russians' living

---

[7]   Hennadyy Balashov, http://510.ukr/_party/leader.php; Borys Petrov, 'Dnepropetrovsk – tretyj Rym?' *Dnepropetrovsk*, 30 November 1995; 'Pyyte Dnipropetrovske!' *Nashe misto*, 18 October 2002.

in Dnipropetrovsk.[8] This view of 'Russians' inhabiting Southern-Eastern Ukraine had already been propagated by Putin in 2008 to a NATO audience.[9]

Not all historic figures were unacceptable in the competition over the origins and identity of Dnipropetrovsk. Two historical figures, Dmytro Yavornytskyy and Olexandr Pol, were acceptable to pro-Ukrainian and pro-Russian Imperial and Soviet memory politics of Dnipropetrovsk. They were both represented in the public space with monuments. During the decommunisation process the central avenue of Dnipropetrovsk was renamed after Yavornytskyy while a large avenue on the right bank of the city was named after Pol. Besides a monument to him as a historian on Dnipropetrovsk's central avenue the city's Historical Museum also bears his name.[10]

Yavornytskyy satisfied supporters of the pro-Ukrainian interpretation of Dnipropetrovsk history because he was a populariser of Cossacks, an archaeologist, and activist of the Ukrainian cultural organisation *Prosvita*. His work made him a legendary figure during his lifetime and following his death, positive memories were published of Yavornytskyy which were incorporated into the city's folklore. Consequently, his legacy did not provoke opposition from civic groups.

Pol's memory was revived after it had been banned in the Soviet era. In the late nineteenth and early twentieth centuries, Pol was influential as a historian who imbued a self-confident identity to Dnipropetrovsk. Pol was traditionally supported by those holding a pro-Russian Imperial identity of Dnipropetrovsk because he was an aristocrat, had taken part in the *Zemstvo* movement, and actively lobbied for the construction of a railway through Ekaterinoslav which had assisted the development of the region's metallurgical industry. At the same time, he was favourably received by those upholding a pro-Ukrainian identity of Dnipropetrovsk because he identified himself as a 'Little Russian' with Cossack ancestry and because he was interested in Ukrainian ethnography. Pol's memory was revived through many newspaper articles, publication of a monograph and a popular scholarly book, opening of a monument to him near the City Council's building, and the re-naming of a street after him. In 2020 on the initiative of Dnipro Mayor Boris Filatov his anniversary was honoured in official ceremonies (Kocherhin 2002; Platonov 2002).

---

[8] 'Navyazlyva uvaha 'russkoho myra'.' http://www.day.kiev.ua/uk/chapter/cuspilstvo/navyazliva-uvaga-russkogo-mira

[9] https://www.unian.info/world/111033-text-of-putin-s-speech-at-nato-summit-bucharest-april-2-2008.html

[10] 'Dnepropetrovsk. Prospekt Karla Marksa.' http://iloveua.org/chapter/77; 'Memorialnyj budynok-muzej D. I. Yavornyskoho,' https://www.facebook.com/budynok?fref

Ukrainian National Liberation Struggle in Dnipropetrovsk Memory Politics

The 1917–1921 national liberation struggle was not actively debated in Dnipropetrovsk during the first two decades of Ukrainian independence. Dnipropetrovsk inherited street names which commemorated the Soviet interpretation of the 'Russian civil war,' such as the plaque on the *Holovposhti* (Main Post Office) which commemorated the Bolshevik victory against 'counter-revolutionaries.'

Prior to, and especially since 2014, there have been attempts to rethink the 1917–1921 period of Ukrainian history. A crucifix was installed at the burial place of UNR soldiers on Zhovtnevyy (re-named Sobornyy) Square in the upper part of the city of Dnipro. Initially, the city authorities did not allow the installation of the crucifix memorial and dismantled it, but it was replaced by a stone cross unveiled by Mayor Filatov.[11] Other memorials to UNR officers installed by civic activists were unveiled in the villages of Dniprovokamyanka (Spyrydon Tropko) and Verkhnodniprovsk (Nykyfor Avramenko).[12]

Reviving the memory of anarchist leader Nestor Makhno was less problematical. In the Dnipropetrovsk and Zaporizhhya regions many legends about Makhno continued to persist with one of the most common being his mistress had lived 'in our village.' A memorial plaque was erected at the *Ukrayina* Hotel where Makhno established his headquarters during his occupation of Katerynoslav. A Makhno Public Bar also operates on a street in the centre of Dnipro. A monument to Makhno was erected in Nikopol.[13]

Other ways in which historical memory has been revived is through the romanticisation of the 1917–1921 Ukrainian national revolution through the songs of the Dnipro *Vertep* (travelling drama theatre). The 'ultras' (football club extremists) of the Kryvyy Rih football club *Kryvbas* are fond of the UNR Hetman Kost Pestushko who was one of the most ardent anti-Bolshevik leaders in the Dnipropetrovsk region.[14]

---

[11] 'U Dnipropetrovsku vkotre vidnovyly khrest na mohyli biytsiv UNR.' http://m.tyzhden.ua/News/27932

[12] 'Na Sicheslavshchyni vidkryly pamyatni znaky biytsyam armii UNR.' http://geroika.org.ua/sicheslavshyna-21-07-13/

[13] Anna Demyna, 'Makhno v kamne,' *Nashe misto*, 5 August 2009; 'Dnepropetrovsk. Prospekt Karla Marksa.' http://iloveua.org/chapter/77; 'Makhno-pab,' http://makhnopub.dp.ua/; Mykola Chaban 'Yak «bratchyky» doshky vidkryvaly...' *Zorya*, 25 January 2007; 'Yak Makhno batkom stav.' http://www.umoloda.kiev.ua/regions/56/286/0/61695/

[14] 'Prezentasiya novoho muzychno-heroyichnoho albomu hurtu Vertep.' http://artvertep.com/news/25102_Prezentaciya+novogo+muzichno-geroichnogo+albomu+gurtu+VERTEP+%22Mamaj.+Gajdamacki+pisni%22.html; 'A chy znayete vy, shcho na

The Holodomor was denied by the Soviet regime until 1990. Knowledge about the Holodomor was revived during the Gorbachev era's unveiling of blank spots in history and of course from 1991 in independent Ukraine. President Viktor Yushchenko devoted a good deal of attention to reviving memory of the Holodomor and mobilised an international campaign to persuade governments it constituted a genocide against Ukrainians. A memorial to the victims of the Holodomor in Dnipropetrovsk was unveiled in 2008.[15] Yanukovych's presidency adopted a Russophile stance on the 1933 famine as an all-Soviet tragedy (not a Ukrainian genocide) leading to a decline in interest in the Holodomor by state institutions. In the public arena the Holodomor continued to be of interest to civic groups and scholars.

Great Patriotic War and World War II

In 2000–2010, the most heated discussions in memory politics dealt with the myth of the Great Patriotic War and OUN and UPA. Dnipropetrovsk had many Soviet memorial plaques and monuments upholding the Soviet myth of the Great Patriotic War. Ukraine inherited celebrations of the Liberation Day of the city and Victory Day (9 May). The Party of Regions exported to Dnipropetrovsk the transformation in Putin's Russia of the Great Patriotic War into a quasi-religious cult and promotion of the St. George ribbon. This was especially evident in the 'Immortal Regiment' of people marching on 9 May with portraits of Soviet heroes from their families; in reality, they were often teachers and state officials ordered to attend.

In 2013, the cult of Victory Day was promoted by a huge injection of resources into the re-staging of the crossing of the Dnipro River in 1943 during the Great Patriotic War during which hundreds of thousands of Soviet soldiers died.[16] In May 2013, a march by pro-Ukrainian civic groups and activists was attacked by young vigilantes from a sports club funded by the Party of Regions.[17]

Memory politics aimed at honouring the memory of OUN and UPA was systematic but slow. The Dnipropetrovsk branch of the Brotherhood

---

prapori ultras Kryvbasvu?' http://vinteresah.com/

[15] Iryna Reva, '1932: molotom – po serpu!' *Dnepr vechernyj*, 27 February 2007; 'Yushchenko vidkryv Memoryal zhertvam Holodomoru.' http://tsn.ua/ukrayina/yushchenko-vidkriv-memorial-zhertvam-golodomoru.html

[16] Alexandr Belyj, 'Ne dadym perepysat istoriyu,' *Dnepr vechernyj*, 5 October 2012; 'V Dnepropetrovske proshla mashtabnaya rekonstruktsiya forsyrovaniya Dnepra.' http://dnepr.comments.ua/news/2013/10/29/180049.html; 'Kovtochok pravdy u mutnij void.' http://www.dniprograd.info/ua/videoreportone/119

[17] 'Prymyrennya ne vsim do vpodoby.' http://www.dniprograd.org/ua/news/events/15402

of Soldiers of UPA had operated since the 1990s and public commemorations of UPA on 14 October were regularly held. Publications in the mass media and scholarly conferences devoted to the Ukrainian nationalist movement led to bitter debates in the city. Supporters of pro-Ukrainian memory politics and nationalist groups publicised OUN and UPA through torchlight processions in Dnipropetrovsk. After 2014, 'ultras,' civic activists and patriots held portraits of OUN leader Stepan Bandera in marches to demonstrate their hostile attitudes to Putin and Russian military aggression against Ukraine.[18]

Negative attitudes towards Ukrainian nationalism in response to Russian military aggression waned and since 2014 more Ukrainians have had a positive view of OUN and UPA (Oliinyk and Kuzio 2021, 831–832). An ethnic Russian fighting in Ukraine's armed forces compared volunteers like himself with the volunteers who had joined OUN and UPA. Bandera had, Anatoliy Lebidyev believed, in the same manner as they were, defended their own land, seeing nationalism as 'vaccine' against genocide by Ukraine's neighbours and believing that if there had been no nationalism in Western Ukraine there would have been 'genocide' against the local Ukrainian population (Reva 2020, 250).

Jewish Life in Dnipropetrovsk Memory Politics

The Ukrainian Institute for Holocaust Studies 'Tkuma' and the Museum of the History of the Jewish People and the Holocaust in Ukraine, both located in the city of Dnipro, were created, and headed by historian and author of school textbooks Ihor Shchupak (see Chapter three). They became a public platform which provided an opportunity for dialogue and presentation for supporters of both the liberal and conservative wings of pro-Ukrainian memory politics. Their premises were used by the Dnipro Historical Club[19] which regularly invited Ukrainian historians, such as Vladyslav Hrynevych, Volodymyr Vyatrovych, Ivan Patrylyak, Yaroslav Hrytsak, Paul R. Magocsi, Sergei Zhuk

---

[18] 'Banderivtsi na Dnipri.' http://politiko.ua/blogpost83480; Serhiy Dovhal, 'Dnepropetrovsk – «stolyca» banderovtsev na vostoke Ukraynj?' *Kryvorozhskye vedomosty*, 9 June 1995; Hryhoriy Ilchenko Hryhorij (head of the regional branch of the Brotherhood of OUN-UPA), 'Nevyznani, ale neskoreni (Do 65-richchya stvorennya viyka UPA),' *Pershotravenskye novosty*, 19 October 2007; Serhiy Kopanyev, 'Nam Ukrayina vyshcha nad use,' *Sicheslavskyy kray*, January 23, 1995; Iryna Reva, 'Pochemu moj dedushka – vrag?' *Dnepr vechernyj*, 29 March 2003; 'U Dnipropetrovsku proyshly zi smoloskypamy na chest S. Bandery.' http://www.radiosvoboda.org/content/chapter/25218304.html; 'Ultras Dnipra zaspivaly pisnyu pro «papu» Banderu y «katsapa» Putina.' http://prosport.tsn.ua/sport/ultras-dnipra-zaspivali-pisnyu-pro-banderu-ta-putina-348836.html

[19] 'Dniprovskyy istorychnyy klub.' http://www.tkuma.dp.ua/index.php/ua/prosvescheniye/istoricheskiy-klub

and Timothy Snyder. The contents of their lectures expanded discussions of Ukrainian history in the local media.[20]

The museum's exposition presented materials which demonstrated a moderate stance towards Ukrainian nationalism while seeking to advance understanding between Jews, who had no love for the USSR, and Ukrainian patriots. The exhibition included examples of cooperation between the OUN and Jewish community during World War II, participation of Ukrainian nationalists in the Holocaust, rescuing of Jews by Ukrainian nationalists and participation of Jews in the UPA.

The museum exhibition presents far more than the Holocaust with visitors experiencing the Jewish world of Ukraine which preceded the Shoah. The museum does not attempt to show the history of the Jews in an unblemished manner, and they are represented as both victims and perpetrators. Ukrainians are similarly presented not as one homogenous group of murderers or patriots, but as both indifferent to what is taking place around them, and rescuers in the Holocaust. It is noteworthy the museum's exposition presents the tragedies of a broader number of peoples that include Armenians, Chechens, and Crimean Tatars who have also suffered genocides.[21]

Euromaidan Revolution and Russian-Ukrainian War

Historical debates over memory politics subsided during the Euromaidan Revolution. The exception was how the greeting 'Glory to Ukraine! Glory to its heroes!' became popular at that time. Dnipropetrovsk experienced its own Maidan which was savagely attacked by Party of Regions vigilantes in January 2014.

After Yanukovych fled from office in February 2014, the situation in the city became precarious. At a time when there were demoralised and paralysed

---

[20] 'Nevidomyi holod v Ukraini 1928–1929 rr.' http://tkuma.dp.ua/ua/prosvescheniye/ istoricheskiy-klub/123-nevidomij-golod-v-ukrajini-1928-1929-rr., 'Dniprovskyi istorychnyi klub provodyt zasidannia na temu Velykoho teroru u SRSR.' https://gurt.org.ua/news/events/29564/; Ihor Shchupak, 'Ukrayinski yevrei: velyke yednannya.' https://zbruc.eu/node/33921; 'Vidbulos cherhove zasidannia Dniprovskoho istorychnoho klubu.' http://tkuma.dp.ua/ua/prosvescheniye/istoricheskiy-klub/645-vidbulos-chergove-zasidannya-dniprovskogo-istorichnogo-klubu

[21] Yuliya Ratsybarska, 'Muzey Holokostu v Dnipropetrovsku ne unykaye skladnykh pytan ukrayinskoi istorii.' https://www.radiosvoboda.org/a/24758348.html; Yuliia Ratsybarska, 'Muzey Holokostu u Dnipropetrovsku vidviduyut lyudy riznykh natsionalnostey.' https://www.radiosvoboda.org/a/24894797.html; 'Kontseptsiya ta istoriya stvorennya Muzeyu.' https://www.jmhum.org/uk/about/history

state structures, following the disintegration of the Party of Regions, the vacuum was filled by Euromaidan Revolution supporters and Ukrainian patriots. On a symbolic level, the removal of the large Vladimir Lenin monument in the central square of Dnipropetrovsk was an early important victory. Its removal over eight hours was broadcast live by several local television channels.[22]

St. George's ribbons were worn by supporters of the anti-Maidan and Party of Regions vigilantes. Annual 9 May Victory Day celebrations often experienced fierce confrontations between those holding a pro-Russian Imperial and Soviet identity who insisted on the right to wear the St. George's ribbon and those holding a pro-Ukrainian identity who interpreted the ribbon as a symbol of the Russian World and Russian military aggression against Ukraine. In 2015, after the adoption of four decommunisation laws, poppies dominated the public space in Dnipropetrovsk and a far smaller number of supporters of the Opposition Bloc (one of two successor parties to the Party of Regions) continued to wear the St. George ribbon. In 2017, and therefore beyond the scope of this chapter, Ukraine's only exposition dedicated to the Russian-Ukrainian war, the Museum of the ATO[23], was opened in Dnipro.[24]

Conclusions

In 1991–2015, memory politics in Dnipropetrovsk resembled that found on the national level, but with some local differences as memory politics in Dnipropetrovsk were often inconsistent and schizophrenic prior to the Orange Revolution. Yushchenko's presidency officially promoted the Holodomor and a pantheon of heroes of Ukrainian nationalism. Yanukovych's presidency attempted to undertake a counter-revolution against pro-Ukrainian memory politics and imported Russian approaches to the 1933 famine and quasi-religious cult of the Great Patriotic War propagated in Putin's Russia.

---

[22] 'U tsentri Dnipropetrovska skynuly pamyatnyk Leninu.' https://www.radiosvoboda.org/a/25272954.html; 'Lenina znesly u Dnipropetrovsku, Poltavi ta Chernihovi.' https://www.bbc.com/ukrainian/news/2014/02/140221_lenin_monuments_ak
[23] http://www.museum.dp.ua/ato-book.html
[24] '9 travnia u Dnipropetrovsku zustrichaiut z «heorhiivskymy» i syno-zhovtymy strichkamy y chervonymy makamy.' https://www.radiosvoboda.org/a/25379019.html; Vadym Ryzkov, '9 travnia v Dnipropetrovsku - pid riznymy partiynymy praporamy ta symvolikoyu.' https://m.day.kyiv.ua/uk/news/090515-9-travnya-v-dnipropetrovsku-pid-riznymy-partiynymy-praporamy-ta-symvolikoyu; 'U Dnipri vidkryly muzey ATO z frahmentamy Donetskoho aeroportu.' https://dnipro.depo.ua/ukr/dnipro/u-dnipri-vidkrili-muzey-ato-z-fragmentami-donetskogo-aeroportu-25052016124200

Yanukovych and the Party of Regions built on pre-existing Soviet memory politics. Post-Soviet local elites in Dnipropetrovsk had tolerated the Cossack past of the region but strongly objected to memory politics of the UNR and especially OUN, which had operated a sizeable underground in the city during World War II. The only significant event which was firmly entrenched in the public space was the Holodomor because of support given by the central government coupled with a strong memory of the tragedy which had survived in local family history.

Fundamental changes occurred in response to the victory of the Euromaidan Revolution, 2014 crisis and Russian military aggression. Prior to then there had been a gradual growth in pro-European and Ukrainian patriotism and those holding this identity came to power in 2014. This was ironically personified in Deputy Governor and (from 2015) Mayor Filatov, Governor Ihor Kolomoyskyy and Deputy Governor Hennadiy Korban, an ethnic Russian and two Jewish-Ukrainians respectively, leading the counter-offensive against pro-Russian forces and Russian military aggression. Their support made Dnipropetrovsk and Dnipro the most radical implementor of decommunisation in Southern-Eastern Ukraine.

The roots of the gradual change in electoral sentiment and coming to power of pro-Ukrainian forces is to be found in the revision and desovietising of identity and promotion of pro-Ukrainian memory politics which had taken place since 1991. Other important factors were a pluralistic approach to the Ukrainian past (unlike in neighbouring Donbas), diversity of activists and scholars working in the field of memory politics and official support given to a pro-Ukrainian identity by government institutions.

Supporters of Soviet memory politics were clearly at a disadvantage during the bulk of the period from 1991–2013, except during Yanukovych's presidency, and were completely defeated in 2014–2015. The smaller influence of pro-Russian memory politics is explained by two factors. Firstly, their activities were to a great extent inspired by external support through funding from the Russian World Foundation or the Donetsk-based Party of Regions, rather than from local support. Secondly, their activities most often relied on the support of state institutions (such as during Yanukovych's presidency) or the Russian Orthodox Church in Ukraine – rather than from local civil society.

Figures

4.1 – 500 Years of Ukrainian Cossacks, Zaporizhzhya, Taras Kuzio, 1990.

4.2 – 500 Years of Ukrainian Cossacks, Zaporizhzhya, Taras Kuzio, 1990.

4.3 'Away with Kremlin Occupiers of Ukraine! KPRS (Communist Party of the Soviet Union) to Nuremberg! (DS-UNDP [Democratic Union-Ukrainian Peoples Democratic Party], Kryvyy Rih, 500 Years of Ukrainian Cossacks, Zaporizhzhya, 1990, Taras Kuzio, 1990.

References

Bolebrukh, Anatoliy. ed., (2006). *Istoriya mista Dnipropetrovska*, Dnipropetrovsk: Grani.

Kasianov, Heorhiy ed., (2018). *Polityka i Pammyat. Dnipro-Zaporizhzhya-Odesa-Kharkiv. Vid 1990-x do syohodni,* Lviv: FOP Shumylovych.

Kocherhin, Ihor. (2002). *Oleksandr Pol: mrii, spravy, spadshchyna*, Dnipropetrovsk: NHA.

Platonov, Vladimir. (2002). *Chelovek-legenda: Aleksandr Pol*, Dnipropetrovsk: Prospekt.

Portnov, Andriy and Portnova, Tetiana. (2015). 'The 'Imperial' and the 'Cossack' in the Semiotics of Ekaterinoslav-Dnipropetrovsk: The Controversies of the Foundation Myth,' In: Igor Pilshchikov, ed., *Urban Semiotics: The City as a Cultural- Historical Phenomenon*, Tallinn: TLU Press, 223–250.

Repan, Oleh. (2007). Valentyn Starostin and Olexandr Xarlan, *Palimpsest poselennya XVI–XVIII st. v istoriyi Dnipropetrovska*, Kyiv: Ukrayinski propiley.

Svitlenko, Serhiy. eds., (2012). *Istorychna pamyat Dnipropetrovshchyny*, Dnipropetrovsk: Monolyt.

Tillett, Lowell. (1975). 'Ukrainian Nationalism and the Fall of Shelest,' *Slavic Review*, 34, 4: 752–768.

5

The Outpost of Ukraine: The Role of Dnipro in the War in the Donbas

NICHOLAS KYLE KUPENSKY AND OLENA ANDRIUSHCHENKO

On 3 May 2014, fans of two competing football clubs – FC Dnipro and Lviv's FC Karpaty – gathered in the centre of Dnipropetrovsk to promote a march *Za yedynu Ukrayinu* ('For a United Ukraine'). Less than a month after the seizure of government buildings in Donetsk and Luhansk by pro-Russian separatists and just weeks after the government's launch of the Anti-Terrorist Operation (ATO), the march was organised at a crucial juncture for the city. Many worried that the escalating violence in the east could spill over into the Dnipropetrovsk region at a moment's notice. Indeed, Dnipropetrovsk was typically included in discussions of a 'New Russia' (*Novorossiya*) buffer state, even though polling suggested that support for unification with Russia was extremely low (Plokhy 2015, 341–342; O'Loughlin, Toal, and Kolosov 2017, 125).

The fans marched down the main thoroughfare of the city, Karl Marx Prospect, along the city's famous embankment, and ultimately arrived at the *Parus* Hotel, a half-completed and long-abandoned eyesore on the banks of the river. With hundreds of litres of blue and yellow paint, a few dozen marchers scaled the 17-story building, and, by evening, they turned one of *Parus* drab concrete faces into a massive Ukrainian coat of arms, the largest *tryzub* in the world ('Fanaty 'Dnepra' preobrazili' 2014). A month later, a flash mob commemorated those who were killed during the Euromaidan Revolution protests by illuminating the *tryzub* (trident) with torches (Dnepropetrovtsy 2014; Dnepropetrovsk 28 iunia 2014). And then in July, fifty volunteers organised by the Dnipro Ultras scaled the hotel to paint the other face of the building in the colours of the Ukrainian flag (Gostinitsu 'Parus' 2014; see figures 5.1 and 5.2).

The choice of the *Parus* (the 'sail') as a site to signal the changes in Ukraine's political winds was not coincidental. The longest-running construction site in Ukraine, *Parus* was originally a pet project of Leonid Brezhnev, the adoptive son of the city whose ascendance to power gave rise to the 'Dnipropetrovsk clan' of Soviet politicians (Zhuk 2010). According to the original plans, the building was designed to be a luxury hotel for party conferences and foreign delegations to the city, the 'symbol of the golden age of prosperity under Brezhnev.' Construction began in the mid-1970s; however, problems in financing caused the construction to drag into the 1980s. In 1987, the project completely stalled when the building was 80 per cent complete. After the collapse of the Soviet Union, the *Parus* was looted and stripped of its useful materials, and residents of the city long began to view the hotel as a 'symbol of the unrealised dreams of the Soviet era' (Iasko 2019).

Thus, the transformation of the *Parus* Hotel from a perpetual reminder of Dnipropetrovsk's lost Soviet glory into a brightly coloured billboard signifying the city's optimism, patriotism, and strength is one of many of examples how the threat of war in the east provoked a radical change in the city's spirit and urban spaces. Indeed, as Sophie Pinkham aptly observed, 'now the hotel would have to be finished: demolishing the building would look like the destruction of Ukraine itself' (Pinkham 2016, 262). No longer clinging to its past laurels as the 'Rocket City,' Dnipropetrovsk not only received a new name: since 2016 the city changed its name to Dnipro to remove the legacy of one of the organisers of the Holodomor, Hryhorii Petrovskyi, in the wake of the 2015 Decommunisation Laws (Oliinyk and Kuzio 2021, 7). It also embraced a new identity since the start of the war – *forpost Ukrayiny* (outpost of Ukraine) – a metaphor which reflects its strategic role in both defending and protecting the Ukrainian state.

Originally a German military term, *forpost* carries both offensive and defensive connotations. On the one hand, a *forpost* can refer to a unit of soldiers situated in an advanced position, which places them on the front line in the event of an attack or allows them to warn their comrades about an enemy advance. At the same time, a *forpost* also signifies a fortification or fortress in an advanced position, which provides protection from the dangers outside its walls. And these dual meanings of Dnipro's new identity – both as the city best suited to support the Anti-Terrorist Operation (ATO) and the city most capable of offering refuge from it – were broadly embraced as the conflict escalated.

While the change in Dnipro's civic identity was swift, its origins remain a source of scholarly debate. Yuri M. Zhukov has focused on the 'opportunity cost' of rebellion, which he argues was highest in the Dnipropetrovsk region and lowest in the economically vulnerable Donetsk and Luhansk regions, which were 'heavily dependent upon trade with Russia' (Zhukov 2016, 2). However, Quentin Buckholz (2019, 152) has argued how 'elite preferences' proved to be more determinative than economic factors or 'mass popular attitudes,' especially in Kharkiv and Dnipro. Indeed, many have shown how the city's powerful oligarchs and a vocal minority of Euromaidan Revolution activists were the primary actors fuelling Dnipro's transformation into a 'bastion of civic Ukrainian nationalism' (Zhurzhenko 2014, 11; Portnov 2015b, 729). Andrii Portnov has been the most forthright in crediting Ihor Kolomoyskyy and his associates in the Privat Group Borys Filatov and Hennadiy Korban with 'creating Dnipropetrovsk's "pro-Ukrainianness"' (Portnov 2016). Silviya Nitsova also has shown how Kolomoyskyy's support of the state inspired small- and medium-sized businesses to provide materials and funds for the war effort (Nitsova 2021, 20). While Orysia Kulick has emphasised that it is best to understand how a 'perfect storm' of circumstances – including the collapse of central authority, the delegitimisation of the Party of Regions, and the annexation of Crimea – convinced the city's businessmen to prevent 'a cascade of destabilizing acts' (Kulick 2019, 354), she too acknowledges Kolomoyskyy's central role. In fact, for Ilya Gerasimov, that Dnipro's elite was made up of Russian-speaking but pro-Ukrainian Soviet Jews, or 'Russo-Jewish-Banderites,' is a testament to the 'new Ukrainian hybridity' of the 'Dnipropetrovsk phenomenon,' the emergence of a coalition of Ukrainians of hyphenated or hybridised identities who were inspired by the Privat Group's model of civic nationalism (Gerasimov 2014, 34–35).

Our study does not speculate on the origins of Dnipro's surge in 'local patriotism' (Portnov 2015a, 66). Instead, it chronicles and analyses the public discourses of civic nationalism that emerged in the immediate aftermath of the war and crystalised in the years since. What we are interested in is how Dnipro's residents came to understand their decisive role in the defence of the country and how they came to spontaneously articulate these experiences in verbal and visual forms. Drawing upon representations of Dnipro's role in the war in the local and national media, memory institutions, and urban spaces, we argue that the city's new political identity cannot merely be reduced to 'the result of successful crisis management' on the part of the Privat Group (Portnov 2015a, 70), even if Kolomoyskyy's actions were definitive in the earliest days of the war. In the months and years that followed, the metaphor that Dnipro was the 'outpost of Ukraine' proved to be a particularly effective new myth, one with the power to signify both strength and compassion and synthesize a wide array of civic activity: volunteering to fight, caring for IDPs, healing the wounded, and facilitating new social relations.

The Evolution of a Metaphor

Many have observed that the individual most responsible for deciding the fate of the city was the oligarch Kolomoyskyy (Gerasimov 2014; Wilson 2014; Zhurzhenko 2014; Portnov 2015a; Portnov 2015b; Portnov 2016; Sakwa 2015; Buckholtz 2017; Kulick 2019; Nitsova 2021). Early on, Kolomoyskyy and his associates in the Privat Group in January 2014 demonstrated public support for the Euromaidan Revolution by projecting coverage of the protests in Kyiv on the side of the shopping mall Passage (Kulick 2019, 366). After becoming governor of Dnipropetrovsk region in March 2014, Kolomoyskyy launched an all-out campaign to ensure that separatist sentiment did not spread beyond the Donbas. He personally subsidised the Ukrainian Air Force, offered a $10,000 reward for the capture of a pro-Russian separatist, and backed the creation of the highly effective Dnipro battalions (Sakwa 2015, 128; Portnov 2015a, 67; Kulick 2019, 382–385). For these reasons, many have argued that the Maidan itself represented a 'major victory of Dnepropetrovsk over the Donbas' in the triumph of Kolomoyskyy's clan over the one controlled by ousted President Viktor Yanukovych (Sawka 2015; Portnov 2015a, 66). Indeed, as one member of a Kolomoyskyy-funded militia commented, Dnipropetrovsk was 'just lucky to get a better oligarch' (Baczynska 2014).

It was in the wake of these interventions that Dnipropetrovsk began to be known as the *forpost Ukrayiny* (outpost of Ukraine) because of its strategic role in stemming the tide of pro-Russian activity. 'Sergei Taruta in Donetsk can't manage to control the situation,' one Dnipropetrovsk resident commented in April 2014, 'but Kolomoyskyy in a short amount of time turned the neighbouring Dnipropetrovsk into a *forpost* of Ukrainian statehood' (Boris Filatov 2014). In May, fans of the Dnipro Football Club mobilised the phrase to channel the team's civic pride into a victory on the football pitch. 'We are living through the very peak of historical time. Dnipropetrovsk has become the *forpost* of the Ukrainian state,' the letter reads: 'Leave everything on the field [...] for Dnipropetrovsk.' (Fanaty 'Dnepra' obratilis' 2014).

Local media outlets picked up references to the 'outpost' image in the national and international press. After former United States Secretary of State Henry Kissinger argued that Ukraine must be a bridge between Russia and the West — 'not either side's outpost against the other' — the journalist Iurii Romanenko responded by rebuking Kissinger and making the case that the 'outpost' identity was a positive one: '[Ukraine must] only be an outpost,' he writes. 'Only a wall. Only a moat with crocodiles and crucified boys for intimidation. Only a complete cure for schizophrenia' (Kissinger 2014; Romanenko 2014). At the same time, local organisations used the term in their names and branding, such as the Dnipro-based NGO Forpost, and rehabilitation centre Forpost HELP, which provide legal and psychological assistance to soldiers and IDPs (Forpost-Centre 2021).

By 2015, the term began to appear in scholarship about the war when the historian Andrii Portnov suggested that Dnipropetrovsk had become the *forpost* of Ukraine (Portnov 2015a, 65). It also made its way to the highest levels of national politics. Former President Leonid Kuchma began to use the term (To, chto Aleksandr Vilkul vydvinul sebia 2015). And President Petro Poroshenko used it frequently in his speeches about the city. 'The Dnipropetrovsk region was and will remain the outpost of Ukrainianness,' he said during one visit in 2015 (Bilovyts'ka 2015; Rybal'chenko 2015; Babenko 2017). Thus, while other cities such as Kharkiv and Mariupol also have been called outposts in the conflict (Petrak 2015, Poroshenko 2018), even Poroshenko has suggested that Dnipro's early 'decisive position' to resist the 'Russian spring' earned it the right to be the 'main outpost of Ukraine' (Babenko 2017).

Thus, beginning in the spring of 2014, the *forpost* metaphor was used and reused in the press and came to be picked up by a diverse group of individuals and organisations who mobilised it to describe four interrelated but distinct aspects of the city's new identity: Dnipro's role as a city-defender, city of refuge, city-hospital, and city of love.

City-Defender

The first meaning of Dnipro's identity as the 'outpost of Ukraine' came from its identity as the 'city-defender' (*gorod-zashchitnik / misto zakhysnyk*), a formulation that was often used for the roughly 20,000 soldiers from the region who were mobilised to fight in the ATO and the 559 who lost their lives between 2014 and 2018 (Vpervye traditsionnoe 2018; Voytsekhovska and Yakushenko 2018). One of them was Petr Sirota, an engineer from Dnipropetrovsk's National Mining University (now, the Dnipro Polytechnic National Technical University) who in the spring of 2014 felt that his technical expertise might be of some benefit on the front. After serving as a volunteer for a few uneventful months at a checkpoint away from the front, Sirota came back home; however, he ultimately had a change of heart after attending a speech in Dnipropetrovsk delivered by Mikhail Saakashvili. After Saakashvili reminded the residents of the city that 'if Ukraine holds back this aggression, it will defend both itself and Europe,' Sirota remembers experiencing the overwhelming feeling of responsibility to take up arms and return to the conflict. 'I'll go myself,' he said: 'You won't stop me from defending my country' (Andriushchenko 2014e, 16). What is significant about Sirota's narrative is the spontaneity in which he came to feel that he was in a unique position to change the course of history. As part of Dnipropetrovsk's cadre of engineers – the legacy of the city's 'Rocket City' days – he indicates that he was sure his skills could help defend his city and country. Furthermore, during a moment of doubt, his desire to take up arms was rekindled at the thought that living in Dnipropetrovsk gave him the unique opportunity to make a difference and play a meaningful role in the affairs of the nation, if not the continent.

Many of the volunteers who came to the front in the early days of the war remembered that the ranks had a clear contingent from Dnipropetrovsk, such as Taras Litkovets from Lutsk. The assistant dean of the history department at the Lesya Ukrayinka East European National University, Litkovets fought in the Donbas in 2015. 'Around 70 per cent of the battalion were Russian speakers. Most of the guys were from Dnipropetrovsk region and from Dnipro itself,' he said. This observation is backed up by statistics about the number of fallen soldiers, for the Dnipropetrovsk region has suffered the highest number of casualties (Zahybli hromadyany Ukrayiny za mistsem narodzhennya v mezhakh Ukrayiny 2021). Litkovets also added: 'Dnipro had a special, good standing among the soldiers. Everyone knew that the city has fantastic doctors and a wonderful attitude towards servicemen' unlike some cities, such as Kharkiv, where he often preferred to walk around in civilian clothes to not be identified as a soldier (Andriushchenko 2017, 13). Indeed, even before the Euromaidan Revolution, Dnipropetrovsk was a city with strong patriotic sentiments, which only grew in intensity after the war. From 2013 to 2015, the per centage of residents of the Dnipropetrovsk region who answered the questions 'I love Ukraine' and 'I feel Ukrainian' grew from between 88.8 to 92.8 per cent and 85 to 90.1 per cent [BK1] (Bureiko and Moga 2019, 151).

City of Refuge

Meanwhile, residents in the Donbas caught in the crossfire began to escape the violence by coming to Dnipropetrovsk, which led to its reputation as a city of refuge. While this specific formulation was not frequently used, it can be identified in the many accounts of individuals who fled the war. Initially, these individuals were referred to as 'refugees' (*bezhenets / bizhenets'*) and are commonly called 'resettlers' or 'relocatees' (*pereselenets / pereselenets'*); however, Ukraine eventually adopted the term 'internally displaced person' (IDP, or *vnutrishn'o peremishchena osoba*) (Kabanets 2019, 5). One of the first IDPs was Iryna Stepanova, an engineer from Slovyansk, who fled to the city in May 2014 after her religious community was targeted by pro-Russian separatists. 'The route to Dnipropetrovsk (about 231 kilometres) took us twenty hours,' she remembers: 'When I finally saw Ukrainian flags, we started crying' (van Metre, Steiner, and Haring 2017, 17). And Stepanova was not alone. Many recalled that they felt free, safe, or protected only after arriving in Dnipropetrovsk.

From the earliest days of the conflict *Dopomoha Dnipra* (Dnipro Aid) became the primary coordinating centre helping the IDPs, the first wave of which were mainly women, children, and the elderly (Kabanets 2019, 17). Elena Nesterenko, a Chinese-language teacher from Luhansk, came to Dnipropetrovsk in July 2014 after her neighbourhood came under fire. She took cover in her basement, where she managed to calm herself by studying Chinese language and philosophy. Having given up on the dream of teaching Chinese in Luhansk, Nesterenko hoped to share her love of Chinese culture with the residents of her host city (Andriushchenko 2014c).

Another IDP, the 85-year-old Anna Baulova, came to Dnipropetrovsk Aid from the village of Zuhres in the Donetsk region. 'I remember the Great Patriotic War well,' said Baulova: 'We also hid in the same way then. Only for some reason we were less afraid then. I guess it's because we were young' (Andriushchenko 2014b, p.4). When her area was bombed, she took cover in a basement, where there were a few other pensioners who remembered World War II. Initially, they intended to wait out the conflict and 'softly sang war songs' to distract themselves from the bombings; however, Baulova concluded that 'one war a lifetime is enough' and left for Dnipropetrovsk.

By the fall of 2014, the number and nature of the IDPs began to change as more Donbas residents came to realise that the conflict would drag on (Kabanets 2019, 17). Lyudmila Khapatko, one of the coordinators at Dnipro Aid, said that the organisation was taking in as many as 60 IDPs a day in the wake of the attacks on the cities of Mariupol and Avdiyivka (Andriushchenko 2015b). By spring, the need for assistance was so high that the United Nations High Commissioner for Refugees (UNHCR) opened a second Ukrainian headquarters in Dnipropetrovsk that would cover all Eastern Ukraine (Andriushchenko 2015a).

Amidst the chaos and upheaval, some of the IDPs from the first wave began to find a sense of purpose in helping those from the second, like Tatiana Gladkova, who had arrived from Novoazovsk in August 2014. Even though much of her time was occupied with finding a stable source of work, Gladkova nonetheless volunteered in her free time at Dnipro Aid, where she was proud to 'help those like me, other resettlers' (Andriushchenko 2015b). At the centre, Gladkova helped invigorate an arts and crafts workshop where IDPs could learn how to produce handcrafts and, most importantly, 'get rid of stress' (Andriushchenko 2015c, 15). One of the IDPs who especially valued the workshop was Irina Terekhova, who came from Luhansk. Initially, Terekhova thought she would be able to quickly return to her home and business, but she found herself in a 'heavy emotional state' when she struggled to find 'something to distract herself' from the realities of resettlement. At the workshop, she took great pleasure from making children's toys and stuffed animals, often painted in patriotic colours, and the collective began selling their wares at a local market to support wounded soldiers.

Yevheniya Shevchenko, another coordinator at Dnipro Aid, was particularly impressed with the generosity of many of the IDPs: 'Some want to donate blood for the soldiers wounded in the ATO. [...] Others get involved with the work of the coordinating centre. Yet others organise charitable fairs to help the soldiers. It's like balm for the soul. You see that all your efforts aren't in vain, that the world around you, even if slowly, is getting better. And then your belief in the bright future gets stronger, the strength to go on and do good appears' (Andriushchenko 2015d, 25). In this respect, she began to feel that her work as a volunteer was complementary to those fighting on the front lines. 'The soldiers in the ATO are giving their lives for my safety. I won't go to fight, but I have the power to take care of the resettlers,' she said: 'This is my small fight for peace' (Andriushchenko 2015d, 25).

While many IDPs expressed their gratitude at the hospitality of Dnipropetrovsk's residents, others were blamed for the economic problems of the city. 'When I moved to Dnipropetrovsk, I only met positive people on my journey,' said Lyudmila Yermak: 'But many encountered people with negative attitudes towards them. Like, because of you there's no jobs and the rent is too high' (Andriushchenko 2016, 2). As a result, Yermak was moved to ease the tensions between the city's residents and the new arrivals and, as such, organised a series of roundtables so that the community could frankly discuss the cultural and economic issues standing in the way of a smooth integration. The difficulty of finding sustainable work and adequate housing were the most pressing struggles, but the events also sought to break down negative stereotypes many held about IDPs. One of the claims that was often made was that the IDPs have helped strengthened the economic stability of Dnipropetrovsk, though a group of scholars at the University of Birmingham found that there was not convincing evidence to suggest that IDPs had a positive effect on 'increased consumer demand' or 'faster economic growth' in their host communities (Kuznetsova, et. al. 2018, 4).

Sophie Pinkham has reported that some Dnipropetrovsk residents felt that those from the Donbas had a 'strong sense of entitlement,' were 'aggressive,' and could not be trusted because they were 'simply another kind of people' (Pinkham 2016, 259). Similarly, the volunteers at Dnipro Aid also cited examples of conflicts when IDPs arrived and expected more provisions than the centre could provide. Oftentimes, skirmishes took place because the IDPs had recently survived heavy shelling and showed up in a state of shock. Others, the coordinators reported, are 'professional provocateurs, who instilled in the displaced people unpleasant feelings. They said that Ukraine needs to be wiped off the face of the earth, that Ukrainians should be exterminated, [that] Obama bombed us, and we're being pacified with buckwheat' (Andriushchenko 2015d, 25). Yet, Shevchenko insisted that the vast majority were good, sympathetic, and positive.

Another Dnipro-based organisation that actively helped the IDPs is the Human Rights Group *Sich*. Founded by Dmytro Reva, Andrii Denysenko, and Oksana Tomchuk in the summer of 2014, *Sich* aims to provide comprehensive legal assistance to victims of the war: soldiers and their families, IDPs, the families of missing persons, former hostages, victims of torture, volunteers, and civilians in the conflict areas (Pravozakhystna hrupa Sich 2019). Nina Panfilova, one of their clients, turned to the group for help after her house in the Donetsk region was destroyed in a bombing and all her possessions were engulfed in a subsequent fire. 'That night we were warned about the danger. We hid in one of the basements. By morning I discovered that my apartment was destroyed,' Panfilova said: 'Nothing is left, except to live in a basement.' After she appealed to *Sich*, however, her case seeking monetary compensation for her losses is one of a few awaiting judgments in the Supreme Court of Ukraine (Andriushchenko 2018b). Another client of *Sich* is Valentina Buchok, a former electrician at Donetsk Regional Energy who was abducted during one of her shifts, humiliated and tortured, and then held as a prisoner of war for nearly a year. '[A member of the Donetsk People's Republic] decided that I was a spy,' Buchok remembers: 'They threw a cellophane bag over my head and handcuffed my hands behind my back. And they tortured me for twenty hours, trying to get me to confess to murder' (Andriushchenko 2018a). After she was released during a prisoner exchange, Buchok began to seek monetary compensation for her period of captivity, including back pay from her employer since she was captured performing her duties at work. In 2018, *Sich* took her case before the European Court of Human Rights, which ruled in her favour (Ekspolonena boyovykiv 'DNR' 2019). *Sich* also works closely with their partner, the NGO *Forpost* and rehabilitation centre *Forpost* HELP, which was founded in early 2015 and provides psychological support to approximately 70 individuals affected by the war each month (V Dnepre otkryli Tsentr 2016).

The City-Hospital

As IDPs and POWs turned to Dnipropetrovsk as a refuge from the violence in the east, those wounded in the combat zone also frequently ended up in the city's Dnipropetrovsk Military Hospital or I. I. Mechnikov Hospital, one of

Ukraine's leading trauma centres. From the earliest days of the conflict, many recognized that the city's doctors were helping soldiers return to the battlefield and saving the lives of the most gravely wounded, which transformed Dnipro into a 'city-hospital' (*gorod-gospital'*/*misto-shpital'*), a term typically used during World War II to describe cities where injured soldiers were sent for treatment and rehabilitation.

It was largely at the Mechnikov Hospital where the city's doctors gained local and national fame for their life-saving procedures. Founded in 1798, the hospital has over 2,000 employees, including 400 physicians, who see over 40,000 admitted patients and about 300,000 outpatients a year (Likarnya Mechnykova 2019). At the start of the war, many of Mechnikov's physicians were drawn to the metaphor of Dnipropetrovsk as the 'outpost' of Ukraine and began to frame their work in support of the soldiers arriving from the front in these terms (Stolyarova 2014). 'The Mechnikov doctors remain a trusted *forpost*,' remarked the head of medicine Serhiy Ryzhenko: 'Every day we are defeating death' ('Peremirye' 2015). 'The Mechnikov Hospital has become a real medical *forpost* of Ukraine and Dnipro,' a journalist remarked: 'Nearly every day the wounded are brought to the hospital, and the doctors carry out great deeds in saving the life and health of these people' (Tatyana Rychkova 2016). Indeed, the Mechnikov doctors have saved the lives of over 2,000 soldiers since the start of the war. 'Dnipropetrovsk has become the *forpost* of the country,' the deputy head of medicine at the hospital Oleksandr Tolubaev said during a blood drive for wounded soldiers: 'Two thousand defenders of Ukraine, real heroes have survived. Doctors, volunteers, donors – only together are we a force! The force of Dnipropetrovshchina!' (Bilan 2016).

Furthermore, Dnipropetrovsk also was one of the cities where soldiers on the front had access to mental health care. On 1 August 2015, the Dnipropetrovsk oblast State Administration opened a hotline for participants in the ATO. At its height, the centre was receiving as many as fifteen calls a day, many directly from the front. One of the psychologists at the hotline, Olha Korinchuk-Shtykova, remembered a typical scenario when one young soldier contemplating suicide called in. 'You understand, I'm tired. I can't do it anymore,' he said: 'There's no exit.' She described how 'a long conversation started. The young man talked about the hell that he has lived in for many months, about how he lost one friend after another... He finally started to cry and wasn't afraid to be weak. And then relief set in. The fighter recognised that he should value life and fight for peace for the sake of the bright future of his children in Ukraine. His role is invaluable' (Andryushchenko 2016a, 25). Again, for many ATO fighters, if the Donbas was associated with violence and danger, Dnipropetrovsk was associated with safety and care, both physical and mental.

The City of Love

Not everyone who came to Dnipropetrovsk from the front was in search of refuge or physical or mental care: many soldiers came to the city on leave to relax and, more often than not, go on dates. For this reason, Dnipropetrovsk often was represented as a city of love by local media outlets in human interest stories about soldiers.

One the individuals who came to Dnipropetrovsk for romantic reasons was Serhiy Ponomarenko, a retired lieutenant in the Ukrainian army who volunteered for combat and ended up in the ATO. His wife of twenty-two years, Svetlana, remained behind in Dnipropetrovsk. 'It was really hard for me to leave my family behind,' Ponomarenko said: 'I saw that my wife's eyes were tearing up. But I couldn't do anything else, to defend my native land is my debt. Who would if not me?' (Andriushchenko 2014d, 4). But as the fighting continued into the summer of 2014, the couple decided that they wanted a religious ceremony in the Ukrainian Orthodox Church-Kyiv Patriarchate, which required Serhiy to leave his post. Much to his surprise, his commander not only approved his leave but also granted leave to his comrades, all of whom escaped the combat zone for a day to attend the wedding.

Meanwhile, other soldiers serving on the front met their future wives in the city thanks to the Facebook group ATO Acquaintances (*ATOshni znayomstva*), a project launched by the Dnipropetrovsk resident Natalia Koval. An active participant in the Women's Volunteer Battalion, an organisation that delivered supplies to the front, Koval noticed that many soldiers were asking her to include the phone numbers of the women who prepared the packages or personally introduce them to women from the city. 'At first I took it all as a joke, but then, when I had more free time one day, I sat down and created the 'ATO Acquaintances' group on Facebook,' Koval said. Although Koval primarily envisioned the group to be a pleasant distraction for soldiers to pass the time when they were deployed, many began to use the site as a dating platform to find partners who shared their commitment to self-sacrifice (Andriushchenko 2016c, 4). 'Because of everything that has recently taken place in Ukraine, many of us have lost our familiar circle of friends or our families,' reads the description of the Facebook group: 'Every day we meet wonderful people — enchanting volunteers and fearless courageous fighters, who, unfortunately, are alone. Precisely for this reason we decided to create this group of acquaintances, both romantic and friendly. Everyone deserves happiness!' (ATOshni znayomstva 2019). In fact, after a year, five couples had been married, and today the group has over 82,000 members.

In short, from the beginning of the war in Donbas, Dnipro's role in the conflict has been deep and wide. It has sent troops to the front and served as a base for military operations. It has taken in IDPs and provided them with housing and elementary necessities. Its lawyers and advocates have helped veterans and victims receive legal status and monetary compensation. Its hospitals have saved the lives of the injured, and its psychologists have comforted the distressed. Finally, it has been a place of leisure — and even love — for demobilised soldiers, some of whom even met their future spouses in the city. And all these elements coalesced into the frequently used metaphor that Dnipro is the 'outpost of Ukraine,' both the defender of the state and the protector of the most vulnerable victims of the conflict in the east.

ATO Museum: Shock

Meanwhile, Dnipro's artists, curators, and filmmakers also have begun to integrate the region's post-Maidan identity into its public spaces, and the visual narratives that engage the 'outpost' metaphor similarly register a wide range of responses to the war, including shock (the ATO Museum), solemnity (Heroes' Square), and satire (the street art of Zdes Roy).

In February 2016, a group of activists and veterans began to collect artefacts from the front with the hopes of curating an exhibition about Dnipro's role in the war. After storing them in various garages around the city for months, they were allowed to put many of the objects on display in May in a park adjacent to the Dnipro National History Museum, which became the open-air museum *Shyakhami Donbasu* (Following the Roads of Donbas). 'In the exposition we showed everything that you really could see in the zone of military activity,' said Vladislav Sologub, a veteran and volunteer who helped create the 1,000-square-meter space: 'We tried to cram in as much as possible – from the ruins of the airport and the half-destroyed bus stop to elements of a fortification' (Muzei ATO v Dnepre 2016).

As a result, 'Following the Roads of Donbas' is a shocking space, one that brings the chaos, destruction, and violence from the front to the centre of Dnipro (see figure 5.3).

Street signs are snapped off at right angles. City signs are peppered with bullet holes. Rusted out sheets of metal are penetrated by shrapnel. The decapitated turret of a T-64 tank used in the defence of the Donetsk airport languishes on the ground. A damaged medical evacuation vehicle used to transport the wounded from the battlefield is missing doors. A hastily assembled army checkpoint is the only structure that offers refuge from the chaos on the streets of Donbas. Inside the checkpoint, a message scrawled by a soldier on one of the walls tells us that *boyatsya bessmyslenno* ('it's pointless to be afraid'). On the ground, an overturned table lays on its side, an improvised extra layer of protection against errant bullets (see figure 5.4).

In Catherine Wanner's study of how the Euromaidan Revolution protests and war in Donbas are 'made material in urban public space,' she observes that Kyiv's commemorative practices primarily 'foster moods that accentuate tragedy, loss, and sacrifice,' which are designed to stoke feelings of outrage to encourage ongoing support for the war (Wanner 2019, 328). 'People might have died, and the protests might have ended,' Wanner writes, 'but the outrage that fueled them can endure when their deaths are understood in terms of sacrifice in the defence of the nation' (Wanner 2019, 331). We find something similar in the performative disorder of 'Following the Roads of Donbas.' On the one hand, the space transports you to the hellish streets of a Donbas at war, which provokes emotions of fear, disgust, horror, anger, and terror. On the other hand, it forces visitors to image what the streets of Dnipro might look like if the fighting would spill over the border. In doing so, the exhibition transforms Dnipro into Donetsk, if only for a half a block. In this respect, the space consciously constructs the impression of a perpetual – and imminent – threat, one that calls upon its viewers to prevent such a possibility. It also demands the feeling of gratitude towards the soldiers and volunteers who defended the city in the most chaotic days of the war. In fact, the only element within the exhibition that does not bear the signs of violence or trauma is a sculpture, entitled *Vdyachnist* (Gratitude), which represents a young girl from the Donbas offering an apple to an ATO soldier. Nearby, a mailbox installation, *List Soldatu* (A Letter to a Soldier), encourages visitors to mimic the gesture and send a card or a drawing to the front (Muzei ATO Dnipro 2019, 11).

'Following Donbas Roads,' however, was just the first in a series of installations that now has grown into the *Hromadianskyy podvikh Dnipropetrovshchyny v podyakh ATO* (Museum of the Civil Feat of Dnipropetrovshchyna in the Events of the ATO). The museum, in fact, goes by four different names, each of which offers a different interpretive frame for its collection. The first name one encounters when approaching from Yavornytskyy Prospekt (formerly Karl Marx Prospect) is the Museum of the Civil Feat of Dnipropetrovshchyna in the Events of the ATO, which suggests that the museum's purpose is to chronicle and curate, for a local audience, the variety of ways that Dnipro's residents have changed and been changed by the war. The given English name of the museum, however, tells a different story: the Museum of Russian Aggression in the East of Ukraine. This title indicates that what a (likely foreign) visitor will encounter is not necessarily a positive story about the heroic contributions of the Dnipropetrovsk region, but a negative one about Russia's active military campaigns against Ukraine.

Here, the English title implies that the broader region has been victimised by a single external actor. Yet, in much of its own promotional material, the museum often uses yet another name – Ukraine's First ATO Museum – which emphasises that the organisers of the museum were the first to recognise that the material culture of the conflict must be catalogued and preserved for posterity (Ukraine's First ATO Museum 2019). At the same time, it purports to tell the story of the whole Anti-Terrorist Operation, not just the contributions of the Dnipropetrovsk region. Finally, most residents of Dnipro avoid the mouthful that is its official name and are not even aware of its English name; instead, they opt for a shorter, more convenient version of the third title and simply refer to it as the *Muzey ATO* (Museum of the ATO). Again, visitors who arrive expecting to see the story of the entire war in Donbas might come away with the impression that the single most decisive factor in the war was Dnipro.

The ATO Museum opened to the public in January 2017 within a different museum – the Battle for the Dnipro Diorama – which allowed ATO activists to house indoor galleries in its entrance hall. Its central installation is the documentary film *Dnipro – Forpost Ukrayiny* (Dnipro – The Outpost of Ukraine 2017), which weaves together the ways the city has supported the war effort: sending troops, caring for the wounded, and accepting IDPs. Like the open-air museum, the film is a powerful, sensorially overwhelming experience, in part, because it is screened in a 360-degree panoramic theatre that immerses viewers in the traumatic realities of the war. Furthermore, the film makes ample use of point of view shots, which force the viewer into a restricted sensorial environment that creates a specific set of heavy-handed emotional and moral outcomes. Its opening sequence sets the scene for what is to come. On the centre screen, a Ukrainian soldier on the outskirts of Donetsk hums a Cossack folksong as he solemnly prepares his weapon before battle (see figure 5.5).

To the left, mothers and children cheerfully play on a playground in Dnipro. However, the peace and tranquillity are suddenly disrupted when loud bombs begin to fall on the right side of the screen. The viewer spins 180 degrees and sees a series of images of the destroyed Donetsk airport, which is located, we are told, just 240 kilometres from Dnipro. The logic of the sequence is clear: the only thing preventing death and destruction from raining down on Dnipro as well is the age-old resolve of the battletested Cossack spirit now embodied in a new generation of Ukrainian warriors.

Subsequent episodes build upon this narrative by using point of view shots to shock and then calm the audience. When the film deals with the annexation of Crimea, the theatre goes completely black. Bullets begin to penetrate the darkness on all sides, which creates the feeling that we, the viewers, are taking cover. Not knowing where the shooting is coming from can be disorientating, and the gun shots only grow louder and faster. Suddenly, we are rescued when images of volunteer soldiers running through trenches take us back into the light, and a graphic to the left tells us that over 25,000 citizens of the Dnipropetrovsk region participated in the war. In other words, this sequence dramatises the motif of Dnipro as the 'city-defender' by first simulating the feelings of vulnerability and helplessness and then portraying the individual volunteers from Dnipro, who restore peace and order.

Another point of view shot puts viewers in the back of a medical evacuation vehicle. As we frantically race down a rural road, bombs nearly miss the van to the left and right, and the driver swerves and breaks to avoid the onslaught. The van eventually reaches a stabilisation point, where we are shown the graphic injuries of the soldier we were transporting: his ankle is so severely broken that we can see the bones penetrating through his skin, and his body is 80 per cent covered in burns (see figure 5.6).

In the foreground, we receive a text message telling us that the most severely wounded are being taken to the Mechnikov Hospital, and we see a helicopter with the soldier arriving in Dnipro, where a massive line of Dnipro residents have signed up to donate blood, some of which goes to the wounded soldier undergoing an operation to repair a badly mangled arm. Here, Dnipro's identity as the 'city-hospital' is fully on display, for the montage of the film shows, literally, how the blood of the city flows through the veins of the soldiers defending the nation.

Another sequence places the viewers in the back seat of a car that is slowly approaching a checkpoint out of Donbas. The car ahead of us is stopped, and its driver is being violently dragged out at gun point (see figure 5.7). The young couple in the front seat is anxious but composed, and if you turn 180 degrees, you notice that you are sitting next to a young girl, who nervously awaits the moment when we must face the guards. Our driver steps out of the car to show the contents of the trunk, and we wait, in silence, fixated on the anguished face of his young wife. Suddenly, he returns to the car, we drive away from the checkpoint, and the anxiety transforms into ecstasy as the car crosses into the Dnipropetrovsk region, where it is welcomed by the volunteers of Dnipro Aid. Again, the emotional resolution of a tense, sensorially immersive scene occurs when you are rescued by the people of Dnipro.

However, the metanarrative of the ATO Museum comes not from its content but its context. Its outdoor exhibition is located across from the tomb of the historian of the Zaporizhzhyan Cossacks Dmytro Yavornytskyy. Its indoor galleries share space with the Soviet-era Battle of the Dnipro Diorama, a massive immersive work that tells the story of the Red Army's liberation of Ukraine from Fascist control. Thus, the spatial juxtaposition of the ATO Museum and these other symbolic spaces analogises Ukraine's fight against Russian aggression to the continuation of the Zaporizhzhyan Cossacks' fight for freedom against the Russian Empire or the Soviet Union's victory over Nazi Germany. 'The whole museum is one big symbol of Ukraine,' one museum worker commented: 'And like there once was a battle for the Dnipro, there is also a battle for the Dnipro today – it is our deed. And if Dnipro is standing – Ukraine is standing' (Desyateryk 2018).

In this sense, *Dnipro – Forpost Ukrayiny* fully dramatises the central narratives of the 'outpost' metaphor, and like 'Following the Roads of Donbas,' it is designed to provoke feelings of shock, fear, and horror at the atrocities committed in the Donbas and gratitude, indebtedness, and awe at the sacrifices of Dnipro and the Dnipropetrovsk region. However, in doing so, it risks alienating viewers with connections on the wrong side of the simplified binary between the heroism of the 'good' citizens of Dnipro and the barbarism of the 'bad' residents of Donbas. Its reliance upon an 'emotional narrative' to deliver 'affective engagement,' argues Elżbieta Olzacka (2019), 'hinders an objective assessment of the events.'

Heroes' Square: The Solemn

While the ATO Museum primarily relies on shock, *Skver heroyiv* (Heroes' Square) offers a more solemn approach to the constellation of associations contained in the 'outpost' metaphor. Formerly Lenin Square, this bright, well-maintained park surrounds the Dnipropetrovsk regional State Administration (OGA). This space played an important role in the decisive days of the winter of 2014, when the square was briefly weaponised by the Yanukovych-appointed governor, who ordered the park to be flooded by fire hoses out of the fear that protestors would storm the building (Mitingi 2014; Dnepropetrovskuiu OGA 2014). In the frigid January 2014 winter, the water ended up freezing, which transformed the square into a massive, frozen lake that some compared to 'a moat around a medieval castle' (Andriushchenko 2014a). But today, the same space that once protected the Yanukovych administration now celebrates the heroism of those who fought to protect the city from his regime.

Heroes' Square features a series of distinct commemorative spaces whose narratives spill into one another during a stroll. The most prominent of them is easily Rocket Park (*Park raket*), a monumental installation that opened in October 2013. Rocket Park is an overt celebration of Dnipropetrovsk's Soviet industrial past. It features three rockets: the 8K11, the 8K99, and the Cyclone-3, which rises nearly 130 feet into the sky. They represent the city's role in ushering the Soviet Union from the military threats of the Cold War to the peaceful exploration of space (Park raket 2013; see figure 5.8).

While admiring the rockets, you immediately notice a long series of stands that contain the names, photographs, and memories of the hundred protestors shot on the Maidan and to those who lost their lives fighting in the Donbas (see figure 5.9). This is the *Aleya pamyiati heroyiv Nebesnoyi Sotni i ATO* (Alley to the Memory of the Heavenly Hundred and ATO Heroes). This public memorial is a series of interconnected cork boards, which allow residents to staple or tack their own tributes to the fallen. When many of the pictures and poems began to disintegrate over time, volunteers systematically replaced these sections with weather-resistant placards (Alleia geroev 2017).

The Alley of Heroes is a visually fluid space without a single aesthetic centre. But precisely because this is a more democratic memorial, it has become a type of sacred space passionately protected by the residents of the city. In her study of Kyivan memorials, Wanner observed that 'ritualized mourning converts mundane things initially placed around the shrines to protestors (such as paving stones, gas masks, tires, helmets, and make-shift shields) into sacred objects to evoke a righteous, yet violent, David and Goliath-like struggle' (Wanner 2019, 332). Similarly, when vandals tore down pictures from some of the stands in the Alley of Heroes, Yuriy Golik, an adviser to the Dnipropetrovsk governor, turned to Facebook to furiously rebuke the *negodiai* (wretches), calling them *nelyudey* (nonhumans) who should be 'immediately sent to the front' (Vandaly 2017).

Among the most poignant memorials are those dedicated to the Ilyushin Il-76 plane that was shot down outside of Luhansk on 14 June 2014; 40 of the crew were paratroopers who belonged to the 25th Separate Dnipropetrovsk Airborne Brigade (see figure 5.10). Framing their portraits is a text that reads, 'paratroopers do not die, they go to heaven.' Below the placards stands an anonymous handwritten poem, a lyric written in the voice of one of the paratroopers to his wife. Its final stanza reads:

> Know that our company has not disappeared.
> We all ascended to heaven.
> For after all we're not simple foot soldiers,
> We can handle any height.
> Знай, не исчезла наша рота.
> Мы все на небо вознеслись,
> Ведь не простая мы пехота,
> Нам по плечу любая высь (see figure 5.11).

Here, the poem inverts the tragedy of a plane crash and replaces it with an image of a triumphant flight into heaven, a sentiment that echoes the motif of flight across the alley in Rocket Park. In other words, the symbolic logic of Rocket Park creates a spatial and political hierarchy that draws in the Alley of Heroes: at the bottom are the smaller Cold War ICBMs representative of violence and destruction, the taller, Brezhnev-era Cyclone-3 symbolizing peaceful space exploration reaches higher in the sky, but the self-sacrifice, courage, and heroism of the post-Maidan paratroopers far supersedes the reach of the now-useless rockets of the past and ascend all the way to heaven.

In May 2017, the city opened a second section of the alley — the Heroes' Memorial — which is specifically designed to remind foreign visitors about Dnipro's contributions to the defense of Ukraine (Lyakh 2017; see figure 5.12).

Set off from the main sidewalks of the park, the Memorial evokes the feeling of a graveyard, for the names and portraits of those who lost their lives are printed on illuminated black glass panels in the dimensions of a standard tombstone. The panels remind passers-by that 'Heroes Never Die' in English, French, German, Hebrew, and Ukrainian (see figure 5.13).

In the centre of the Memorial is cobblestone preserved from Kyiv's Hrushevskyy Street, which materially transfers the spirit of the revolution from the streets of the capital to the outpost of the country. Likewise, its central panel draws attention to the fact that Sergei Nigoyan, a resident of Dnipro, was one of the Heavenly Hundred and among the first to give his life.

Furthermore, the Heroes' Memorial is in dialogue with yet another commemorative space, the Monument to the Victims of the Chornobyl Catastrophe (see figure 5.14).

The monument consists of an imposing arch, which represents the billowing nuclear explosion, and a bird that has fallen from the sky because of its wing scorched by the radiation. The Chornobyl memorial registers the irreparable damage done to the nation through an image of a grounded, disfigured bird; however, through the juxtaposition and intermingling of spaces, the eternal flight of the Heavenly Hundred and Dnipro's paratroopers symbolizes the resurrection of a national spirit brought down by tragedies of the past. In this respect, Dnipro's Heroes' Square manages to appropriate and re-signify the other memorials to the city's past. Without the war in Donbas, the park would end up mourning the city's lost Soviet glory and the national tragedy of the Chornobyl nuclear disaster. Instead, the Alley of Heroes memorialises the sacrifices of the city in a way that makes them inheritors and redeemers of the country's past triumphs and tragedies. Recently, the state oblast administration added one more symbolic space to Heroes' Square: an inclusive playground for children with disabilities.

'Many people associate Dnipro with the space industry or with the ATO Museum,' said Yuriy Holik: 'We really want the city to become a certain type of space where people can socialise and interact. We're building an inclusive park for this.' (Dnepr stanovitsia inkliuzivnym 2018). Here, Holik's comment reveals the essential tension within the 'outpost' metaphor: whether the civic pride of Dnipro comes from its offensive role in fighting off Russian aggression or its humanitarian role in protecting the vulnerable.

Zdes Roy: The Satirical

Holik isn't alone in his desire to play up Dnipro's welcoming side. If you walk to the corner of Heroes' Square, you will see one of the most prominent murals of the Dnipro-based graffiti artist Zdes Roy, whose work may exert the single biggest influence on the urban landscape of the city. While Roy's early work was an open challenge to the city's authority, he began to take up civic themes when the war in Donbas broke out, including what is perhaps his best-known mural *A Girl Alone* (see figure 5.15).

The mural depicts a young girl sitting atop an abandoned brick house, now overrun by weeds. In the foreground, a quote by Christian Morgenstern in Ukrainian translation reads: *Dim — tse ne tam, de ty zhyvesh, a tam, de tebe rozumiyut* (Home is not where you live, but where you're understood). *A Girl Alone* was sponsored by the United Nations High Commissioner for Refugees and is a tribute to Dnipro's willingness to open its arms to the IDPs (Roy 2018). The mural succeeds in acknowledging the longing for home, sadness, and trauma of the city's residents who had not planned to move to Dnipro, a narrative often lacking in other representations of the city's heroism.

In his other work, Roy's Dnipro murals represent high-minded civic subjects using visual language taken from lowbrow or popular culture, often with an aesthetic that echoes another Roy — the pop artist Roy Lichtenstein. In August 2016, with a commission from the MEDINUA clinic he completed a 23-foot mural on Dmytro Yavornytskyy Prospect *Supermural* (see figure 5.16) dedicated to Dnipro's superhero doctors;

> The idea was to represent the superpowers of doctors, who sometimes accomplish impossible things for humanity,' he said. 'This art is dedicated to all the doctors, who, daily, or at

least one time in their lives, have saved somebody's life (Roy 2019b).

While the theme of *Supermural* undoubtedly resonates with Dnipro's post-Maidan spirit, Roy is hesitant to verge into chest-thumping patriotism, and he rarely frames his own work within the context of the war. In fact, much of his street art consists of covering up Dnipro's post-Soviet blight with brightly coloured images inspired by Western pop culture. He transformed an unsightly dumpster on the city's famous embankment into a minion from the film *Despicable Me* (Bondarenko 2016). He painted over the old gates of a children's club using images from the *Simpsons* (see figure 5.17). And he enlivened the unadorned side of an outbuilding with Walter White and Jesse Pinkman from the TV series *Breaking Bad* (see figure 5.18). While none of these murals explicitly engage with the political realities of contemporary Dnipro, a closer look reveals that they share a common colour palate: the yellow and blue that emerged overnight on seemingly every surface of the city, like the *Parus* Hotel. In fact, the Simpsons mural was commissioned by the children's club, whose only demand was that the art object should have 'a yellow colour scheme' (Roy 2019a). Here, we can see the slippage between the patriotic desires of the client, who ordered a mural in one of the national colours, and the aesthetic choices of the artist, who opts for an image from Western, not Ukrainian, popular culture. Roy's Facebook and Instagram accounts include several examples of his use of yellow and blue for political purposes, including his graffiti of a *tryzub* in neon colours on a Dnipro underpass and his mural behind the entrance sign to Mariupol painted in patriotic colours (Roy 2014; Roy 2016a).

If Dnipro signalled its new identity by transforming its drab Soviet-era urban spaces into Ukrainian flags, street art by Roy plays with and parodies this phenomenon. And we can understand the meanings of this parody in several internally contradictory ways. On the one hand, since the Ukrainian national colours represent fields of grain and a clear blue sky, the paradigmatic landscape from the Ukrainian steppe, his murals may imply that Ukraine has always been an integral part of the Western visual landscape (see figure 5.19); it just took the threat of war and the surge in local patriotism to create the conditions to see it.

Similarly, we might also view this gesture as Roy inserting Ukraine into Western mass culture, perhaps just as the Euromaidan Revolution has compelled the country to turn to Europe and the United States. Yet, that his favourite archetypes tend to be drawn from American consumer culture suggests a critical attitude towards the commodification of Dnipro's awakening of civic nationalism, even as he has fundamentally altered the visual language of Dnipro's urban landscape. 'My work used to be patriotic. I tried to support this theme as much as I could so that people wouldn't forget what is happening in the east,' he said: 'But with time my opinions changed. I heard a lot from friends and acquaintances that were in the hot spots in the Donbas. And things there are not like they represent it in the media. A lot of what is happening in the war is business, and local people are suffering because of it' (Roy 2019c). Thus, read from this perspective, Roy's thesis is the following. The yellow and blue that has covered the city and has inspired patriotic fervour is no different than the chemically pure meth served up by Walter White and Jesse Pinkman: once you take a hit, you're hooked, but the high is ephemeral, and behind all of it is a dangerous gang of self-interested criminals making money off everyone.

Conclusion

In short, there were many factors that influenced Dnipro's sudden surge of patriotism and embrace of its new identity as the 'outpost of Ukraine.' Much has been made of Kolomoyskyy's role in financing the Anti-Terrorist Operation, in part as a way of protecting his business holdings and expanding his political influence; however, the spontaneous and creative ways that residents of the city picked up and developed this identity should not be seen as an epiphenomenon of the Privat Group's business strategy. The 'outpost' metaphor became an organisational principle for a wide range of civic activity: serving in the army, providing shelter to the homeless, caring for the wounded, creating spaces to remember the dead, and producing images to inspire the city to turn towards a better European future and away from its Soviet past.

Figures

5.1. Parus Hotel, 14 July 2014. Courtesy of editor, Oleksandr Pugach, freednipro.tv: https://www.youtube.com/watch?v=kcfh0OCVrB8

5.2. Parus Hotel, Courtesy of editor, Oleksandr Pugach, freednipro.tv: https://www.youtube.com/watch?v=kcfh0OCVrB8

5.3. 'Construction Pierced with Artillery Fire, 'Following the Roads of Donbas,' ATO Museum,' Nicholas Kyle Kupensky, 25 June 2019.

5.4. 'Checkpoint, 'Following the Roads of Donbas,' ATO Museum,' Nicholas Kyle Kupensky, 25 June 2019.

5.5. Yevhen Titarenko, 'Singing Soldier,' Dnipro — The Outpost of Ukraine, 2017 (2019). ATO Museum.

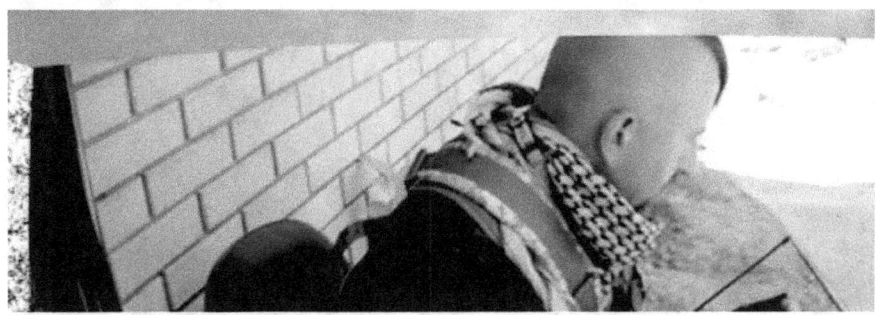

5.6. Yevhen Titarenko, 'Medical Evacuation' (Dnipro – Forpost Ukrayiny 2019). ATO Museum.

5.7. Yevhen Titarenko, 'Leaving Donbas,' Dnipro — The Outpost of Ukraine, 2017 (2019). ATO Museum.

5.8. 'Rocket Park,' Nicholas Kyle Kupensky, 22 July 2019.

5.9. 'The Heavenly Hundred, Heroes' Square,' Nicholas Kyle Kupensky, 22 July 2019.

5.10. 'Paratroopers Do Not Die, They Go to Heaven,' Heroes' Square,' Nicholas Kyle Kupensky, 22 July 2019.

5.11 "*Ushel, rodnaia, ne prostilsia…* (You have left us, my dearest, without saying goodbye),' Heroes' Square,' Nicholas Kyle Kupensky, 22 July 2019.

5.12 'Heroes' Memorial, Heroes' Square,' Nicholas Kyle Kupensky, 22 July 2019.

5.13 "Heroes Never Die,' Heroes' Square,' Nicholas Kyle Kupensky, 22 July 2019.

5.14 'Monument to the Victims of the Chornobyl Catastrophe, Heroes' Square,' Nicholas Kyle Kupensky, 22 July 2019.

5.15 Zdes Roy, 'Girl Alone,' Facebook, 25 September 2016.

5.16 Zdes Roy, 'Supermural,' Zdesroy.com, September 2016.

5.17. Zdes Roy, 'The Simpsons,' Zdesroy.com, 2018.

5.18. Zdes Roy, 'Heisenberg Coffee Lab,' Zdesroy.com, 2017.

5.19. Zdes Roy, 'Red Neck Style,' Instagram, 16 May 2017.

References

Alleia Geroev Nebesnoi Sotni v Dnepre teper' budet novyi vid. (2017). www.Gorod.dp.ua, 20 February. http://bit.ly/2PbMLNO

Andriushchenko, Elena. (2014a). 'Skver vozle Dnepropetrovskoi oblgosadministratsii kommunal'shchiki prevratili v ozero.' *Facebook*, 20 February. http://bit.ly/33UJAhS

Andriushchenko, E. (2014b). 'Ia snova begu ot voiny.' *Dnepr vechernii*, 9 July.

Andriushchenko, E. (2014c). 'Mir – eto –世界.' *Dnepr vechernij*, 24 July.

Andriushchenko, E. (2014d). 'Voin Svety.' *Dnepr vechernij*, 1 August.

Andriushchenko, E. (2014e). '45 dnei v ATO.' *Dnepr vechernij*, 22 August.

Andriushchenko, E. (2015a). 'Na chuzhoi storone zakona.' *Dnepr vechernij*, 15 January. https://bit.ly/2My4nlh

Andriushchenko, E. (2015b). 'V poiskakh mira.' *Dnepr vechernij*, 29 January.

Andriushchenko, E. (2015c). 'Masterskaia schast'ia.' *Dnepr vechernij*, 30 January.

Andriushchenko, E. (2015d). 'Liubit', kogda tebia nenavidiat.' *Dnepr vechernij*, 13 February.

Andriushchenko, E. (2016a). 'Lekary po telefonu.' *Dnepr vechernij*, 11 February.

Andriushchenko, E. (2016b). 'Net pereselentsev, est' – my.' *Dnepr vechernij*, 16 February.

Andriushchenko, E. (2016c). 'Koval' – kuznets schast'ia.' *Dnepr vechernij*, 24 March.

Andriushchenko, E. (2017). 'Cherez Dnepr — na voinu.' *Dnepr vechernij*, 2 March.

Andriushchenko, E. (2018a). 'Donetskaia plennitsa.' *Dnepr vechernij*, 28 February. http://bit.ly/2Bxq4vO

Andriushchenko, E. (2018b). 'Bez doma — vne zakona.' *Dnepr vechernij*, 5 July. http://bit.ly/2o7LjkH

ATOshni znayomstva. (2019). *Facebook*, 9 October. http://bit.ly/33MS9v1

Babenko, Iuliya. (2017). 'Petro Poroshenko: 'Vklonyayus dnipryanam za te, shcho misto zalyshayetsya holovnym forpostom Ukrayiny.' *Nashe misto,* 2 March.

Baczynska, Gabriela. (2014). 'Kiev pins hopes on oligarch in battle against eastern separatists.' *Reuters,* 23 May. https://reut.rs/33okJCO

Bilan, Olga. (2016). 'Bolnitsa Mechnikova snova zhdet donorov krovi.' *Dnepr vechernij,* 18 February. https://bit.ly/2OMKBUV

Bilovytska, Nataliya. (2015). 'Dnipropetrovshchyna – tse forpost Ukrayiny.' *Uryadovyi kuryer*, 28 March. https://ukurier.gov.ua/uk/articles/dnipropetrovshina-ce-forpost-ukrayini/

Bondarenko, Anna. (2016). 'Strit-art po-dnepropetrovski.' www.Gorod.dp.ua, 18 April. http://bit.ly/2Jo3NEN

Buckholz, Quentin. (2019). 'The Dogs That Didn't Bark: Elite Preferences and the Failure of Separatism in Kharkiv and Dnipropetrovsk.' *Problems of Post-Communism*, 66, 3: 151–160.

Bureiko, Nadiia and Teodor Lucian Moga. (2019). 'The Ukrainian-Russian Linguistic Dyad and its Impact on National Identity in Ukraine.' *Europe-Asia Studies*, 71, 1: 137–155.

Desyateryk, Dmytro. (2018). "Poky stoyit' Dnipro – stoyit' Ukrayina': Rozmova pro pershyy u krayini Muzeo ATO.' *Den*, 21 June. http://bit.ly/2P9Jw9E

Dnepr stanovitsia inkliuzivnym: v skvere Geroev stroiat park dlia detei s osobymi potrebnostiami. (2018). *Dnipropetrovska oblastna derzhavna rada*, 29 March. http://bit.ly/35VyZ81

Dnepropetrovsk 28 iunia fleshmob gostinitsa 'Parus.' (2014). *Novyny Dnipropetrovska,* 4 July. https://bit.ly/2VIcuPt

Dnepropetrovskuiu OGA opiat obnesli koliuchei provolokoi. (2014). *Unian,* 20 February. https://bit.ly/2IPWXHP

Dnepropetrovtsy 'zazhgut' gerb na nedostroennom otele 'Parus.' (2014). www.Gorod.dp.ua, 23 June. https://bit.ly/2qc4VVj

Dnipro – Forpost Ukrayiny. (2019). Directed by Yevhen Titarenko and produced by Natalia Khazan. http://bit.ly/2pIx7yJ

Dnipropetrovskyy Parus rozmalyuvaly yak derzhavnyy prapor. (2014). www.freeDnipro.tv, 14 July. http://bit.ly/2JlZxpq

Ekspolonena boyovykiv 'DNR' zayvlyaye pro vyyavlennia poztiazhky na podvirya svoho budynku na Donechchyni. (2019). *Radio Svoboda*, 23 October. http://bit.ly/33T4uxN

Fanaty 'Dnepra' obratilisk komande. (2014). *Dnepr vechernij,* 9 May. https://bit.ly/2pouXnU

Fanaty 'Dnepra' preobrazili gostinitsu 'Parus.' (2014). www.Gorod.dp.ua, 5 May. https://bit.ly/2oKdTsq

Filatov, Boris. (2014). 'Liudi razdeleny neponimniem, a tseli u vsekh pokhozhi'. *Dnepr vechernij*, 28 April. http://bit.ly/32BFZoz

Forpost-Centre. (2021). www.forpost-centre.org

Gerasimov, Ilya. (2014). 'Ukraine 2014: The First Postcolonial Revolution. Introduction to the Forum.' *Ab Imperio,* 3: 22–44.

Gostinitsu 'Parus' razrisovali v tsveta gosudarstvennogo flaga. (2014). www.Gorod.dp.ua, 14 July. https://bit.ly/2Mdv4f5

Iasko, Vlada. (2019). 'Simvol ushedshei epokhi: istoriia zabroshennoi gostinitsy 'Parus' v Dnepre.' www.opentvmedia, 20 September. https://bit.ly/31h9zy2

Ivanov, Ivan. (2017). 'Master graffiti Zdes Roy: Goni k svoei mechte, kak poezd.' www.49000.com.ua, 28 April. http://bit.ly/2N4xVGa

Kabanets, Yuliya. (2019). *Internally Displaced Persons (IDPs) in Kyiv: Lost in the City or Agents of Change? A Case Study of Refugees in Towns*. Medford, MA: Feinstein International Centre, Friedman School of Nutrition Science and Policy at Tufts University. https://fic.tufts.edu/wp-content/uploads/RITReportKyivUkraine.pdf

Kissinger, Henry A. (2014). 'To Settle the Ukraine Crisis, Start at the End.' *Washington Post*, 5 March. https://wapo.st/2P5C3sj

Kulick, Orysia. (2019). 'Dnipropetrovsk Oligarchs: Lynchpins of Sovereignty or Sources of Instability?' *The Soviet and Post-Soviet Review*, 46, 3: 352–386.

Kuznetsova, Irina, Mikheieva, Oksana, Gulyieva, Gulara, Dragneva, Rilka, and Mykhnenko. Vlad. (2018). *The Social Consequences of Population Displacement in Ukraine: The Risks of Marginalization and Social Exclusion*. Birmingham: The University of Birmingham.

Liakh, Kristina. (2017). 'V Dnepre otkryli unikal'nuiu Alleiu pamiati geroev ATO.' *Informator*, May 12. http://bit.ly/2JeCRaK

Likarnia Mechnykova. (2019). 'Pro nas.' www.Mechnikova.com. https://bit.ly/2p0RzuN

Mitingi v Dnepropetrovske 26 ianvaria: narodnoe veche i protesty vozle OGA. (2014). *Telekanal 34*, 26 January. https://bit.ly/33ysJku

Metre, Lauren Van, Steiner, Steven E., and Haring, Melinda. (2017). *Ukraine's Internally Displaced Persons Hold a Key to Peace*, Washington, DC: Atlantic Council. https://www.atlanticcouncil.org/in-depth-research-reports/issue-brief/ukraine-s-internally-displaced-persons-hold-a-key-to-peace/

Muzey ATO Dnipro. (2019). Dnipro: Muzey ATO.

Muzei ATO v Dnepre: ekskursiia po 'goriachim tochkam' Donbassa. (2016). www.vgorode.ua, 27 May. http://bit.ly/31IIrZh

Nitsova, Silviya. (2021). 'Why the Difference? Donbas, Kharkiv and Dnipropetrovsk After Ukraine's Euromaidan Revolution.' *Europe-Asia Studies*, 73, 10: 1832–1856.

O'Loughlin, John, Gerard Toal, and Vladimir Kolosov. (2017). 'The Rise and Fall of 'Novorossiya': Examining Support for a Separatist Geopolitical Imaginary in Southeastern Ukraine.' *Post-Soviet Affairs*, 33, 2: 124–144.

Oliinyk, Anna and Taras Kuzio. (2021). 'The Euromaidan Revolution, Reforms and Decommunisation in Ukraine.' *Europe-Asia Studies*, 73, 5: 807–836.

Olzacka, Elżbieta. (2019). 'The ATO Museum in Dnipro – Between Trauma and Propaganda.' *Transregional Academies*, 3 July. http://bit.ly/2JdwEfa

Park raket otkrylsia v Dnepropetrovske. (2013). *Novosti kosmonavtiki*, 30 October. http://bit.ly/35Zxbeo

Peremirie: za nedeliu – 17 ranenykh so strashneishimi travmami. (2015). *Dnepr vechernij*, 23 October. https://bit.ly/2BrgHhb

Petrak, Dmytro. 'Yak Mariupol' peretvoryvsya na 'forpost Ukrayiny.'' www.depo.ua, 25 May.http://bit.ly/33ObE6j

Pinkham, Sophie. (2016). *Black Square: Adventures in Post-Soviet Ukraine*. New York: W. W. Norton & Company.

Plokhy, Serhii. (2015). *The Gates of Europe: A History of Ukraine.* New York: Basic Books.

Poroshenko, Petro. 2018. 'Kharkivshchyna – spravzhniy forpost Ukrayiny.' *Facebook*, 30 September. http://bit.ly/35OGfml

Portnov, Andrii. (2014). 'Dnepropetrovsk. Tam, gde nachinaetsia Ukraina.' *Gefter*, 27 June. http://bit.ly/2P7AH0k

Portnov, Andrii. (2015a). ''The Heart of Ukraine'? Dnipropetrovsk and the Ukrainian Revolution.' In: Andrew Wilson ed., *What Does Ukraine Think?* London: European Council on Foreign Relations, 62–71. https://ecfr.eu/publication/what_does_ukraine_think3026/

Portnov, A. (2015b). 'Post-Maidan Europe and the New Ukrainian Studies,' *Slavic Review,* 74, 4: 723–731.

Portnov, A. (2016). 'Chomu Kharkiv i Dnipropetrovsk ne staly Donetskom i Luhanskom?' *Ukrayinska Pravda,* 4 February. https://www.istpravda.com.ua/%20chapters/2016/02/4/148912/

Pravozakhystna Hrupa Sich. (2019). 'Istoriya ta misiya.' www.sich-pravo.org. http://bit.ly/35V4NtO

Rybalchenko, Vladimir. (2015). 'Dnepropetrovshchina ostaetsia forpostom ukrainskosti.' *Golos Ukrainy*, 28 March. http://www.golos.com.ua/rus/article/253324

Romanenko, Yuriy. (2014). 'Ukraina – forpost ili most?' *Dnepr vechernij*, 12 November. https://bit.ly/2MiDMZp

Sakwa, Richard. (2015). *Frontline Ukraine: Crisis in the Borderlands*. New York: I. B. Tauris.

Stoliarova, Larisa. (2014). 'Pomoch ranenym.' *Dnepr vechernij*, 28 May. https://bit.ly/2W1mGCP

Roy, Zdes. (2014). 'Tryzub.' *Instagram*, 29 September.

Roy, Z. (2016a). 'Mariupol City.' *Facebook*, 30 July.

Roy, Z. (2016b). 'Segonia chetverg, operatsionnyi den'.' *Facebook*, 26 August.

Roy, Z. (2017). 'Red Neck Style.' *Instagram*, 16 May.

Roy, Z. 2018a). 'Mural dlia OON.' www.Zdesroy.com, 26 July.

Roy, Z. (2018b). 'Heisenberg Coffee Lab.' www.Zdesroy.com, 26 July.

Roy, Z. (2019a). 'Simpsons.' www.Zdesroy.com.

Roy, Z. (2019b). 'Supermural.' www.Zdesroy.com.

Roy, Z. (2019c). WhatsApp message to Nicholas Kyle Kupensky, 23 October.

Rychkova, Tatiana. (2016). 'My obespechim bolnitsu im. Mechnikova sovremennym oborudovaniem i sdelaem ee dostupnoi dlia gorozhan,' *Dnepr vechernij*, 11 July.

To, chto Aleksandr Vilkul vydvinul sebia kandidatom v mery, ia schitaiu eto khoroshei novost'iu, – Leonid Kuchma. (2015). www.Gorod.dp.ua, 11 September. https://gorod.dp.ua/news/108324

Ukraine's First ATO Museum. (2019). *Facebook*.

V Dnepre otkryli Tsentr psikhicheskogo zdorovia i travmaterapii Forpost HELP. (2016). www.Gorod.dp.ua, 15 December. www.gorod.dp.ua/news/126234

Vandaly oskvernili Alleiu geroev ATO v Dnepre. (2017). *Dnepr vechernij*, 28 July. http://bit.ly/2ob7w1h

Voytsekhovska, T. V. and V. V. Yakushenko, eds. (2018). *Memorial Book of Soldiers from Dnipropetrovsk Region Who Fell in ATO*. Dnipro: ART-PRESS.

Vpervye traditsionnoe podniatie flaga proshlo ne v Kieve, a v Dnepre — Petr Poroshenko. (2018). www.Gorod.dp.ua, 23 August. https://gorod.dp.ua/news/149476

Wanner, Catherine. (2019). 'Commemoration and the New Frontiers of War in Ukraine,' *Slavic Review,* 78, 2: 328–335.

Wilson, Andrew. (2014). *Ukraine Crisis: What it Means for the West*. New Haven: Yale University Press.

Zahybli hromadyany Ukrayiny za mistsem narodzhennya v mezhakh Ukrayiny. (2021). *Knyha pamyati polehlykh za Ukrayinu.* http://www.memorybook.org.ua/indexfile/statbirth.htm

Zhukov, Yuri M. (2016). 'Trading Hard Hats for Combat Helmets: The Economics of Rebellion in Eastern Ukraine,' *Journal of Comparative Economics*, 44, 1: 1–15.

Zhurzhenko, Tatiana. (2014). 'From Borderlands to Bloodlands.' *Eurozine*, 14 September. http://bit.ly/33OQdIK

6

Decommunisation in Dnipropetrovsk and Dnipro in 2014–2019

IHOR KOCHERHIN

Decommunisation and memory politics have been important to civil society activists, historians, and political scientists because of their influence on the social and political life of post-communist countries (see Motyl 2015; Portnov 2015; Oliinyk and Kuzio 2021). The launch of the process of decommunisation began on 9 April 2015, when the Ukrainian parliament approved four laws 'On access to Archives of Repressive Agencies of Totalitarian Communist Regime of 1917–1991'; 'On the condemnation of the communist and National Socialist (Nazi) totalitarian regimes, and prohibition of propaganda of their symbols'; 'On the Legal Status and Honouring the Memory of Fighters for Ukraine's Independence in the Twentieth Century'; and 'On Perpetuation of the Victory over Nazism in World War II of 1939–1945.'[1]

We first need to explain the terminology used in this chapter. *Decommunisation* is defined as the process of deprivation of the consequences of communist ideology on an internal level of human consciousness and on an external level by the removal of monuments and changes in street and city names. *Leninopad* (Lenin-fall), refers to the demolition of monuments of Soviet leader Vladimir Lenin in Ukrainian cities and towns, including Dnipropetrovsk, in 2014–2015. Despite declaring Independence in 1991, Ukraine inherited a considerable footprint of the Soviet past not only in the mindset of its citizens but also in the memorial space. Quite often, monuments to communist leaders, particularly those of

---

[1] Ukrainian Institute of National Remembrance (UINP). https://old.uinp.gov.ua/page/dekomunizatsiya-0

Lenin, were used by pro-Russian forces for destabilising the social and political situation before and after the launch of Russian military aggression against Ukraine in 2014.

During the Euromaidan Revolution, participants fought not only against usurpation of authority by President Viktor Yanukovych but also against symbols of authoritarianism in the form of monuments to Soviet figures and urban toponyms. In the wake of the Euromaidan Revolution, participants of the Dnipropetrovsk Maidan appealed to the authorities to remove the monument of 'the proletariat leader' from Lenin's square in Dnipropetrovsk. However, the central authorities were disorganised and reluctant to undertake any actions. Therefore, participants of the Dnipropetrovsk Maidan and civic activists did not wait for Kyiv's permission and on 22 February 2014 dismantled the monument, adding to *Leninopad* spreading throughout Central Ukrainian cities. Only a small number of people opposed the demolition of the Lenin monument. On the same day, deputies of the Dnipropetrovsk City Council renamed Lenin Square into Heroes of Maidan Square, because a tent camp had been based there during the Euromaidan Revolution.[2] For a long time, the remnants of Lenin's monument were used as an improvised memorial to the fallen heroes of the Dnipropetrovsk Maidan, and later those killed in the war in the Donbas region of Eastern Ukraine.

These events should be considered as the beginning of the changes which became known as decommunisation. The next steps in this direction took place in 2015.

Why in 2015 and Not Earlier?

In the context of the above three questions arise. Why did decommunisation not take place after Ukraine's Declaration of Independence in August 1991? Why did decommunisation not begin after the 2004 Orange Revolution? Why was decommunisation only possible in 2015?

Ukraine's 1991 Declaration of Independence took place without a radical change of former Communist Party elites or changes in public attitudes. Former communist party and '*nomenklatura* cadres' remained in power. Although the population no longer supported Marxist-Leninist ideological guidelines, it expected an improvement in social and economic conditions. Communist idols were only removed from the streets and squares of Western Ukrainian cities and Kyiv. There was no dismantling of monuments in

---

[2] 'U Dnipropetrovsku ploshchu Lenina pereymenuvali na ploshchu Heroyiv Maydanu,' 24 February 2014. http://www.istpravda.com.ua/short/530bb6fc91894/

Dnipropetrovsk oblast or other Russian speaking cities in Southern-Eastern Ukraine prior to the Euromaidan Revolution.

In May 2006, after the Orange Revolution the Ukrainian Institute of National Remembrance (UINP) was created. Its main task was to formulate and implement state policy in the revival and preservation of the national memory of the Ukrainian people.[3] A criminal case was opened in 2009 against the organisers of the 1932–1933 Holodomor which ended with their conviction. However, the lack of consensus of political forces in parliament, the unwillingness of local elites to dismantle the Soviet memorial legacy and the election in 2010 of Party of Regions leader Viktor Yanukovych were obstacles to decommunisation.

Ukrainian Patriotism versus the 'Russian Spring' in Dnipropetrovsk

In 2014, the population of Ukraine continued to live in the grip of historical myths and a distorted consciousness which could be described as a form of social schizophrenia. People knew or had free access to information about the crimes of the leaders of the Soviet state but continued to co-exist with streets named after them and walk alongside monuments erected in their honour.

The past never left the public consciousness; moreover, it distorted and disfigured the present and the future. The communist impasse of the past did not allow Ukrainian society to move forward. Memorial spaces and toponyms of towns and villages of Dnipropetrovsk oblast were the embodiment of the Soviet totalitarian past. Ukrainian citizens could not understand that the totalitarian past and democratic present could not coexist.

From this impasse there were only two exits. The first one was to remove the remnants of the Soviet totalitarian legacy in favour of a future based on human dignity, rule of law and Ukraine's integration of European values. The second would be resuscitation of the Soviet historical past through the Russian World with the prevalence of the state over human rights, no rule of law, absence of basic freedoms, and authoritarianism.

Patriotism grew exponentially in Ukrainian society after the Euromaidan Revolution and especially after the launch of Russian military aggression. This was reflected in the widespread hanging of national flags and other forms of Ukrainian symbolism, including artwork, on houses, balconies, and

---

[3] 'Pro stvorennya Ukrayinskoho institute natsionalnoyi pamyati,' 31 May 2006. https://zakon.rada.gov.ua/laws/show/764-2006-%D0%BF

cars. One of the most noticeable was the drawing of an image of the Ukrainian national emblem by FK Dnipro 'ultras' in May 2014 on the Parus Hotel, an uncompleted Soviet era building on the right bank of the Dnipro River, confirming the Ukrainian identity of the city of Dnipropetrovsk and Dnipro.

Pro-Russian forces in the spring and summer of 2014 were not very visible in Dnipropetrovsk, except for a few episodes when the Russian tricolour was raised near the City Council building. The balance of power in Dnipropetrovsk and the region had changed. In January 2014, you could have been beaten for flying the Ukrainian flag and four months later for flying the Russian flag. Participants of the Dnipropetrovsk Maidan did not represent a critical mass of the population but nevertheless it became the basis for civil society. They took an active pro-Ukrainian stance which intensified after the appointment of oligarch Ihor Kolomoyskyy in March 2014 as head of the Dnipropetrovsk state regional administration. Pro-Russian forces and those with nostalgia for the Soviet Union either hid themselves or left the territory of Dnipropetrovsk oblast.

One of the manifestations of an active stance was the dismantling of Soviet monuments by which the Soviet system had dominated the public space. Throughout February–December 2014 there was a spontaneous dismantling of Lenin monuments in the city of Dnipropetrovsk and the Dnipropetrovsk region by patriotic Ukrainians who saw this as a way to prove their resolve in the face of Russian military aggression. Sometimes, the authorities dismantled monuments themselves in order not to have political confrontation. The last Lenin monuments to be dismantled in the Dnipropetrovsk region were in Novomoskovsk and Synelnykove because of local opposition.

Ukrainian Institute of National Remembrance Takes Control of Decommunisation

From August 2014 the UINP resumed its activities as a government body and became the leader and generator of the decommunisation process. The staff of the UINP began to prepare a package of decommunisation laws. A public debate ensued on whether to dismantle Soviet monuments and rename toponyms. Opponents of this process presented three arguments.

Firstly, they appealed to the need to first deal with material and economic issues after which renaming could take place.[4] Those arguments had been

---

[4]   Yuliya Kokoshko, 'Yest li zhizn na Marksa?' Dniepr vechernij, 56, 7 July 2015.

heard for quite a long time since 1991 and if prolonged meant the renaming process would never take place. Secondly, Soviet monuments and the toponyms of the Soviet era were 'our past and we should not fight it, no matter what they are.' For some proponents of that argument, the Soviet past was indeed part of their identity which continued to impact their vision of the world and they perceived renaming as an insult to the historical memory of the city.[5] Despite the existence of an independent Ukraine, they continued to behave as if they were citizens of a country that no longer existed and were more impressed by Russia as the successor state to the USSR. Soviet toponymy and monuments resembled the visual image of the landscape of a territory which they used to inhabit. Thirdly, a very small group of Dnipropetrovsk inhabitants viewed Soviet works of art in the monuments as a cultural heritage. This was despite the fact most of those objects were created as shoddy fakes with little significant artistic value.

The three arguments did not stand up to scrutiny. Monuments and street names are not part of history but in fact events and people in whose honour they were created and named. Monuments and toponyms are part of the memorial space which have a significant impact on the formation of moral and ethical norms. Soviet leaders who committed crimes against millions of victims cannot serve as an example from a moral and ethical point of view.

Why then did some inhabitants of Dnipropetrovsk oppose toponymic changes and the removal of Soviet-era monuments? Firstly, change is not always acceptable to many people. Changes can be unpredictable, do not necessarily have positive consequences, and often do not achieve the desired effect. Changes are undertaken through the mobilisation of political will and resources. Secondly, fear of an unknown future paralyses political will and the desire for change. The Soviet totalitarian past was ingrained in the minds of some Ukrainian citizens who were born and raised in the USSR. They associated changes with famine, repression, war and other traumatic experiences. Thirdly, people were convinced that changes would not last for a long period of time. Toponyms in Ukraine have changed many times during the twentieth century by the Tsarist Russian Empire, Bolsheviks, Nazis, and nationalists after 1991. Why change anything if it will be changed again? Fourthly, Soviet monuments and toponyms testified to the longevity of communism and demonstrated that despite being an independent state since 1991, Ukraine continued to belong to the post-Soviet space. An inhabitant of the city of Dnipropetrovsk who lived on Lenin Street, near Lenin Square with its Lenin's monument when visiting Russian cities felt at home with the same street names and monuments.

---

[5] A. Beliy, 'Chto v imeni tvoem', Dniepr vechernij, no. 58, 10 July 2015.

Among the opponents of toponymic changes were moderates who believed that renaming should be to neutral names, such as Floral Street, Lilac Street, or Rainbow Street. They were characterised by an absence of any ideological beliefs, whether communist, pro-Russian, nationalist, or pro-Ukrainian. In their opinion, neutral names would help to avoid possible misunderstandings between different political camps and prevent another 'war of monuments and toponyms' in the future.

In the Mikhail Gorbachev era, the KGB hired veterans from the Soviet occupation of Afghanistan to attack *Rukh* (abbreviated for Ukrainian Popular Movement for Restructuring) activists and the national flags they carried (see figure 6.1). A quarter of a century of nation building in independent Ukraine, the Euromaidan Revolution and Russian-Ukrainian war, lay the ground for de-communisation.

In 2015 most inhabitants of Dnipropetrovsk opposed the dismantling of monuments and changing toponyms. This though, gradually changed over time. Importantly, few inhabitants of Dnipropetrovsk actively stood up to defend the monuments (as they may have done prior to 2014) and their opposition was therefore passive.

Toponym Changes in Dnipropetrovsk

The first renaming in the city of Dnipropetrovsk took place before the adoption of the decommunisation laws under public pressure and they were therefore not systemic. A more systemic process only appeared after the adoption of the decommunisation laws and the formation of the City Commission for naming (renaming) streets, alleys, avenues, squares, parks, squares, bridges, and other objects located in Dnipropetrovsk which began working in Summer 2015. The Commission was headed by the acting chairman of the City Council Halyna I. Bulavka with co-chairmen the executive committee manager of the City Council Vadym A. Shebanov and the Secretary Svitlana V. Gladka (Svitlenko 2016, 100).

The Commission included historians with a specialty in local history, architects, museum staff, public and political figures. The first organisational meeting of the Commission working group which took place on 10 June 2015, was headed by Dean of the History Department at Oles Honchar Dnipropetrovsk National University Serhiy I. Svitlenko. Between June and November 2015, members of the working group met and suggested proposals for renaming city toponyms which were submitted to the meeting of the City Commission. The concept of toponymic reforms at the national, regional, and local levels, was presented on 17 June 2015. The Commission working group proposed a wide range of names that reflected the entire Ukrainian historical narrative. Dnipropetrovsk and Dnipro's urban space now included historical figures tying it to other regions of Ukraine. Inhabitants of Dnipropetrovsk and Dnipro are no longer disconnected from national school textbooks and the names of streets and squares in other Ukrainian regions.

As a result of many months of work by the working group, the City Commission proposed changing 317 toponyms. Many of these names were fiercely discussed and debated. Most members of the Commission, who complied with the law, advocated renaming which considered the history and culture of the region, as well as the current political processes. A small number of Commission members attempted to use the decommunisation process for situational political interests and without a knowledge of local history proposed unreasonable and controversial names. On 24 November 2015, the city Council of Dnipropetrovsk agreed to change 57 toponyms.[6] On 26 November 2015, another 259 toponyms were added to the list, giving a total of 316.[7]

Members of the Commission disagreed on naming one of the streets after OUN leader Stepan Bandera after it had provoked heated discussions. Finally, the City Commission agreed on two alternative names for Lenin Street – its historical name *Voskresenska* or Stepan Bandera. The alternatives were handed over to the city council which chose the first.[8]

One of the oldest streets in the city had never changed its name but the Commission argued to rename it because Moscow is the capital of the state undertaking military aggression against Ukraine. *Moskovskaya* Street was renamed Kyiv Rus ruler Volodymyr Monomakh Street. Another street which was renamed without any provocations and conflicts was Dmytro Donskoy, who was one of the heroes of the Russian nationalist pantheon. Although it did not fall under the decommunisation law the City Commission proposed to change the ending of the name of the street and Dmytro Donskoy therefore became Dmytro Dontsov. Unlike the well-known Bandera, opponents of decommunisation had not heard of the nationalist ideologue Dontsov.

Some new toponyms re-affirmed the Pridniprovya region's close connections

---
[6] Resolution of the Mayor of Dnipro, 'Pro pereymenuvannya toponymy Dnipro,' 882, 24 November 2015. «https://dniprorada.gov.ua/upload/editor/882-%D1%80.pdf
[7] Resolution of the Mayor of Dnipro, 'Pro pereymenuvannya toponyms Dnipro city', 897-r, 26 November 2015. https://dniprorada.gov.ua/upload/editor/897-%D1%80.pdf
[8] Resolution of the Mayor of Dnipro, 'Pro pereymenuvannya toponyms Dnipro city,' 71, 19 February 2016. https://dniprorada.gov.ua/upload/editor/71-%D1%80.pdf

with neighbouring Cherkasy, Kirovohrad, and Poltava which re-orientated Dnipropetrovsk from being part of Ukraine's 'East' to its 'Centre' (at the very least, 'Central-East'). Additional new street names re-affirmed historical ties to Zaporizhzhya and Kharkiv. Lubenska Street was named after a district in the centre of Poltava oblast which had been an important trade route between Dnipropetrovsk and Poltava. Slobozhanskyy Avenue was renamed after an important trade route between Dnipropetrovsk and Kharkiv.

Re-Connecting to Ukrainian History

The new toponyms re-confirm connections of the Dnipropetrovsk region to different periods of Ukrainian history. The Prydniprovya region, the centre of which is the city of Dnipro, lies on both sides of the Dnipro River and the origins of the region's name is 'Land Beyond the Rapids.' Nomadic Iranian, Turkic-speaking, and agricultural Slavic communities settled in the region from ancient times and during the medieval era. The new names of Sarmatska, Derevlyanska and Tiverska streets appeared in memory of the history of these peoples in the Pridniprovya region. Sarmatians were an Iranian-speaking ethnic group who had occupied Southern Ukraine between the third century B.C. to the third century A.D. *Derevlyany* and *Tivertsy* were Slavic tribes who lived in the Pridniprovya region in Kyiv Rus. Other streets were named after the royal dynasty of Kyiv Rus during the tenth to thirteenth centuries: Princess Olha, Svyatoslav the Brave, Volodymyr the Great, Yaroslav the Wise, Volodymyr Monomakh, Roman Mstislavovych, and Danylo Halytskyy.

An important historical period for the Dnipropetrovsk region was the Cossack era. Streets were re-named after Prince Constantine of Ostroh, Prince and Cossack Hetman Dmytro Baida-Vyshnevetskyy, Hetmans Petro Doroshenko, Ivan Mazepa, Pavlo Polubotok, Danylo Apostle and many others. Historical ties to Zaporizhzhya are represented by Melitopolska Streets (Melitopol was a district in the centre of Zaporizhzhya oblast) and Khortytska. Khortytsya Island within the city of Zaporizhzhya was a major Cossack encampment destroyed by Russian Tsarina Catherine in the late eighteenth century. The Dnipropetrovsk and Zaporizhzhya regions were major centres of Ukrainian Cossacks from the fifteenth to eighteenth centuries. Five of the eight Zaporizhzhyan Cossack fortresses are to be found in what is now Dnipropetrovsk oblast.

The Cossack past of the Dnipropetrovsk region was reflected in a dozen new street names. *Starokozatska* (Old Cossack) Street is in honour of Ukrainian Cossacks as well as restoring historical justice; in the nineteenth century it was called *Kozatskaya* named after Cossack units in the Tsarist Russian imperial army. Haydamatska and Ivana Honta Streets refer to the uprising of

Ukrainian peasants and *Haydamaky* Cossacks and one of its important leaders Ivan Honta. The eighteenth century *Haydamaky* uprising against the Polish nobility took place in what are now Cherkasy and Kirovohrad oblasts.

The embankment on the right bank of the Dnipro River was named Sicheslav which pays tribute to the Zaporizhzhyan Sich Cossack state tradition. Ukrainian scholars and civil society activists have often used Sicheslav to describe the name of the city of Dnipropetrovsk and Dnipro. Sich lane is a new toponym referring to the historical existence of Zaporizhzhyan Cossacks in the Dnipropetrovsk region.

Kryshtof Kosynskyy, Ivan Sulyma, Pavlo But, and Yakov Ostryanyn Streets were re-named after Cossack Hetmans and leaders of anti-Polish uprisings during the sixteenth to seventeenth centuries. Other new street toponyms were named after Cossack Hetman Pylyp Orlyk (one of the authors of the first Ukrainian constitution of 1710, the second oldest in the world), Kostya Hordiyenko (the last Hetman of the *Chortomlyk Sich*), Dmytro Horlenko (Colonel of Pryluky and ally of Hetman Ivan Mazepa in the anti-Moscow uprising of 1708–1709), and Cossack chroniclers Hryhoriy Hrabyanka and Samiylo Velychko.

Re-naming fulfilled three purposes. Firstly, it replaced the Soviet name of Komsomolskaya (*Komsomol* [Communist Youth League]) Street. Secondly, the new name confirmed the existence of Ukrainian Cossacks in the Pridniprovya region during the fifteenth to eighteenth centuries long before the appearance of Tsarist Russian Empire Cossack units. The Cossack fortresses of old and new Kodaky was first built in 1635 on what is now the city of Dnipro over a hundred years before the founding of Yekaterinoslav in 1776. Two streets were re-named after Semen Bardadim, a Hetman of New Kodaky and Petro Kalnyshevskyy, the last Hetman of the *Pidpilna Sich*. Fortress Street referred to the Cossack fortress of Novyy Kodaky (the name of the city of Dnipro during the pre-Tsarist Cossack era).

Thirdly, pre-Tsarist Cossack toponyms undermined Russian President Vladimir Putin's so-called *Novorossiysk* (New Russia) project which made territorial claims against Southern-Eastern Ukraine. 'New Russia,' in the same manner as New France (Quebec), Nova Scotia (New Scotland) and New England, ignored native inhabitants in those four regions before the arrival of French, British and Russian colonists (Turchenko and Turchenko 2015, 18). The Tsarist Russian, French and British Empires all claimed there was no 'civilisation' before their arrival.

In fact, the Dnipropetrovsk and Zaporizhzhyan regions had been inhabited and developed by Ukrainian Cossacks for centuries before their annexation by the Tsarist Russian Empire. A street was re-named after Opanas Kovpak who belonged to the Mahdenko Cossack officer's family, a colonel of the *Pidpilna Sich* who participated in Ukrainian colonisation of the Prydniprovya. Another street was re-named after Cossack Maxim Diy who is one of the founders of Diyvka village, now within the confines of the city of Dnipro.

In addition to Kyiv Rus and the Cossack eras, the Tsarist Russian Empire is represented by Governor Andriy Fabr, founder of the Olena Blavatska Theosophical Society, religious intellectual Theodosius (Makarevskyy), philanthropist Nadiya Alekseenko, naturalist Ivan Akinfiev, engineer Volodymyr Khrinnykov, educator Kateryna Messarosh, Mayor Ivan Ezau, film director Danylo Sakhnenko, and historians Vasyl Bidnov and Antin Synyavskyy. Mykola Sadovskyy Street commemorates one of the luminaries of Ukrainian theatre whose life and activity were intimately connected with the city of Kropyvnytskyy in the centre of the Kirovohrad region.

Other new street names pay tribute to Ukraine's national and cultural revival in the nineteenth century, such as the writer Oleksandr Konyskyy, historian Volodymyr Antonovych, historian and philosopher Mykhaylo Drahomanov, and the *Tarasivtsi* Brotherhood youth organisation of Ukrainian patriots. Vasyl Karazin Street commemorates the founder of Kharkiv University in 1804 and Dmytro Bahaliy Street is named after a well-known historian who lived and worked in Kharkiv.

The next period of history with new toponyms relates to the Ukrainian national revolution of 1917–1921. Streets have been renamed in honour of historian and Chairman of the Ukrainian Central Council Mykhaylo Hrushevsky, Chairmen of the Directory Volodymyr Vynnychenko and Symon Petlyura, and founder of the Ukrainian Academy of Sciences Volodymyr Vernadskyy. Ukrainian cadets who died in 1919 fighting the Bolsheviks near Kyiv were immortalised with *Heroyv Krut* (Heroes of Kruty) Street. Other streets named after historical leaders from this era include partisan Hetman Tryphon Hladchenko, educator Fedir Storubel, engineer and educator Ivan Truba, and the anarchist leader of the Revolutionary Insurgent Army of Ukraine Nestor Makhno. Kholodnoyarska Street immortalises the anti-Bolshevik Ukrainian insurgents of the *Kholodnoyarsk* Republic in 1919–1922 in the Cherkasy region.

The Ukrainian nationalist movement of the 1930s and 1940s, which had fought Polish, Nazi, and Soviet occupations, never became a controversial issue in the decommunisation process in Dnipropetrovsk. Streets were re-named after the head of the Organisation of Ukrainian Nationalists (OUN) Yevhen Konovalets, commander of the Ukrainian Insurgent Army and head of OUN Roman Shukhevych and OUN leader Vasyl Kuk, who had run the OUN underground in Dnipropetrovsk in 1942–1943 during World War II. Streets were also named after Ukrainian nationalist ideologues Mykola Mikhnovskyy and Dontsov who were born respectively in the Poltava region and Melitopol, Zaporizhzhya oblast.

New street names of Soviet era intellectuals and scholars have appeared. These include former Dean of Dnipropetrovsk State University Volodymyr Samodryha Street, city architects Oleksandr Krasnoselskyy and Pavel Nirinberh Streets, writer Vasyl Chaplenko Street, composer Andriy Shtoharenko Street, artist Volodymyr Lyubarskyy, and Jewish religious figure and the last Lubavitcher Rabbi Menachem Schneerson. FC Dnipro player Petro Loiko is immortalised by the re-naming of the football stadium which is located on the left bank of the city.

A large group of new toponyms were named after important members of the dissident and cultural movement of the 1960s to 1980s, some of whom were from the Dnipropetrovsk region where they suffered from political repression by the KGB and from the KGB's use of Afghanistan veterans as vigilante's (see figure 6.2). These include dissident poets Vasyl Symonenko and Vasyl Stus, dissident Vasyl Makukh (who was buried in Dnipropetrovsk), Soviet General and leader of the Ukrainian Helsinki Group Petro Hryhorenko, poet and composer Volodymyr Ivasyuk (who was murdered by the KGB), sculptor Vadym Sidur (who was born in Katerynoslav), dissident Ivan Sokulskyy (see Zhuk 2010, 37–40, 48–52, 57–64) and historian and poet Borys M. Mozolevskyy.

The modern period of the history of the Dnipropetrovsk region honours the Heavenly Hundred who were murdered during the Euromaidan Revolution. Dnipropetrovsk City Council renamed Kalinin Avenue on 28 January 2015 in honour of Sergei Nigoyan, an Armenian refugee living in Dnipropetrovsk oblast, who was killed by a *Berkut* riot police or pro-Russian vigilante sniper in January 2014.[9] After the first attempt on 29 December 2014 was unsuccessful after infringing regulations, the renaming was adopted on the second attempt in Summer 2017. At a public hearing most of the participants and the city authorities led by Mayor Boris Filatov voted in favour of Sergei Nigoyan Avenue. Nigoyan is an iconic figure for the modern Ukrainian state because he is the personification of the desire for a free and democratic civic nation.

Dnipropetrovsk oblast has the largest number of security forces killed in the Russian-Ukrainian war.[10] Several patriots killed during this war are honoured by streets named after journalist Alexander Chernikov and railway man Oleksandr Serebryakov in the respectively Checheliv and Samara districts of

---

[9] Resolution of Dnipropetrovsk City Council, 22/80, 28 January 2015.
[10] http://memorybook.org.ua/index1.htm

the city of Dnipro. The Alley of Heroes, which immortalises the killed heroes of the Russian-Ukrainian war, was opened next to the Dnipro oblast state administration.

The Goals of the City Commission

Opponents of toponymic reform in Dnipropetrovsk claimed the City Commission intended to remove all Soviet names to erase this period of history from memory. This was also the mistaken claim made of decommunisation in general in the open letter by Western academics written by David Marples and James Sherr (see Oliinyk and Kuzio 2021, 819–821).[11] In reality, as this chapter shows, hundreds of Soviet-era names remain in the new toponyms alongside ones named after historical figures who had been previously ignored. In fact, most of the new toponyms are associated with individuals from the creative professions, not politicians, party, or military figures. The re-naming process was a means to revive spiritual and material values, rather than the goal of confrontation.

Special attention in the new city toponyms was given to avenues named after Oleksandr Pol and historian and archaeologist, and long-time Director of the Dnipropetrovsk National Historical Museum Dmytro Yavornytskyy who had decisive influences on the formation of the socio-economic and socio-cultural image of the city of Dnipropetrovsk. The commission faced a dilemma about what name to replace Karl Marx Avenue which runs through the centre of the city, and following discussions, it was named after Yavornytskyy who contributed to the development of historical scholarship in Ekaterynoslav. D. Yavornytskyy Dnipropetrovsk National Historical Museum has transformed into a leading centre of culture in a city where there had not been a university until 1918. During the Tsarist Empire the avenue had been called Ekaterynoslavskiy in honour of the Russian Empress Catherine II linking the city to Russian history. From 1923–2016 the avenue was named after Marx to demonstrate Dnipropetrovsk was part of the Soviet state.

Sergei Kirov Avenue, named after a communist functionary who had nothing to do with the city of Dnipro, was re-named Oleksandr Pol Avenue. In the nineteenth century, Pole helped to transform a provincial, small agricultural town into a powerful industrial and economic centre. The Dnipropetrovsk oblast state administration and Dnipropetrovsk *oblast* council are on Oleksandr Pol Avenue.

---

[11] https://krytyka.com/en/articles/open-letter-scholars-and-experts-ukraine-re-so-called-anti-communist-law

In his lifetime, Pole attracted European investments into the region's economy. Since 2014, Ukraine's European integration is reflected in new toponyms in Dnipropetrovsk and Dnipro named after Italian national hero Giuseppe Garibaldi, medieval Czech thinker Jan Hus and the 1968 Prague Spring, as well as more general street names such as European, Krakow, Belgian, Bratislava, and Croatian. Until 2015, *Horvatska* (Croatian) Street was named after Oleko Dundich, a Croat who had fought for the Bolsheviks.

History and Controversy

Another important feature of decommunisation was the return of historical toponyms. Modern Dnipropetrovsk grew out of several smaller settlements which had existed in the seventeenth to eighteenth centuries. Novyy Kodak, Polovytsya, and Samara (Bohoroditska Fortress) influenced the formation of the city's infrastructure. Diyivka, Sukhachivka, Taromske, Mandrykivka, Lotsmanska Kamyanka, Kamyanka Livoberezhna, Lomivka, Amur, Manuylivka, Nizhnedniprovsk, and Samarivka were absorbed into the city of Dnipropetrovsk during different periods of history. The urban history of the Dnipro is characterised by polycentrism.

Prior to decommunisation, the city's historical development had been poorly reflected in its toponymy, especially on the right bank of the city. In the twentieth century, when the city grew rapidly with the appearance of new micro-districts, architects (usually sent from Moscow) did not consider local names when planning the city's development and they imposed communist names which had no ties to the region. Thus, Dnipropetrovsk was depersonalised and resembled oblast centres in other regions of the Soviet Union.

Five districts on the right-bank of Dnipro were renamed. All of them had standard names associated with iconic figures from the Soviet Communist Party pantheon or landmark events and organisations. These included *Leninsky*, *Babushinsky* named after Bolshevik revolutionary Ivan Babushkin who died long before the creation of the Soviet Union, Sergei Kirov Avenue named after member of the Politburo Kirov, *Zhovtneviy* in honour of the Bolshevik October revolution; and *Chervonogvardiysky* (Red Guards). As a result of the renaming, *Zhovtnevy* became *Sobornyy* in the *rayon* (district) with *Soborna* Square. *Babushkinsky* became *Shevchenkivskyy* named after the Ukrainian bard Taras Shechenko. Kirovsky became *Tsentralna* because the district occupies the central part of the city where the city council and central post office are located. *Chervonogvardiysky* became *Chechelivsky* because this was the oldest residential area in the nineteenth–twentieth centuries. *Leninsky* became *Novokodatsky* because part of the district consists of the former settlement of New Kodaky, the Cossack forerunner of today's city of Dnipro.

On the left bank of the city, the residential area Frunzensky-1, named after one of the military leaders of the Bolshevik Party Mikhail Frunze, was renamed *Lomivsky* after a former settlement of that name where well-known Soviet Ukrainian writer Oles Honchar was born. Frunzensky-2 was renamed *Kamyanskyy* because part of the district covers the former *Kamyanka Livoberezhna*. Soviet party functionary Vorontsov Avenue was renamed *Manuylivskyy* after a former village of the same name. French Communist Maurice Thorez Street was renamed *Berezanivska* after a former district of the same name. These new toponyms reflected the multifaceted history of Dnipropetrovsk and Dnipro and the Prydniprovya region throughout Ukraine's history.

Removing Monuments

Work was carried out as to which monuments were to be removed. After the demolition of the large Lenin monument in the central square in February 2014, activists tore off a memorial plaque from the building of the Dnipropetrovsk oblast council which had immortalised head of the Cheka Soviet secret police Felix Dzerzhinsky. Another monument to Lenin, which stood near the Ilyich Palace in the Chervonohvardiyskyy *rayon*, was dismantled on 26 February 2014. On 27 June 2014, the National Defence Headquarters dismantled the bust of Lenin near the Dnipropetrovsk oblast State Administration. However, the stone plinth on which the bust stood with the inscription 'Victory of Communism is Inevitable' was dismantled only on 10 June 2016. In August 2014, activists removed a plaque in honour of Stanislaw Kosior, one of the organisers of the Holodomor, on the street named after him. In April 2015, two Lenin monuments in the Prydniprovsk and Pivnichnyy *rayons* were demolished.

The next steps to implement the law 'On Condemnation of the Communist and National Socialist Regimes' were taken by newly elected city mayor Filatov. In November 2015, the City Commission prepared a list of eighteen monuments, twenty-three plaques, two stella's and one obelisk which were to be dismantled. A proposal was put forward to create a 'Park of the totalitarian period' which would house these dismantled monuments;[12] however, the authorities were in no hurry to finance this.

On 29 January 2016, without waiting for a response from the authorities, public activists in Dnipropetrovsk dismantled the monument to Grigory I.

---

[12] Shrub Kostyantyn, 'Pamyatniki gotovyatsya k demontazhu,' Dniepr vechernij, 100, 24 November 2015.

Petrovsky on Station Square.[13] The monument had personified an entire era when Dnipropetrovsk was a closed city in the Soviet Union and Petrovsky closely connected the city with Soviet identity.

In February 2016, new members of the city council headed by Mayor Filatov issued another resolution to dismantle 46 objects which fell under the decommunisation law, a step which speeded up the dismantling of monuments and memorials throughout the oblast.[14] On 16 February 2016, a plaque dedicated to the leader of the Communist Party of Ukraine Volodymyr Shcherbytskyy, known for his ruthless repression of dissidents and Russification policies, was removed from the building of the Dnipropetrovsk oblast council. On 11 November 2016, memorial plaques to Leonid Brezhnev and Shcherbytskyy were removed from the Maxim Gorky Theatre.

On 3 March 2016, the bust of the Bolshevik Artem (Sergeev) was removed from the territory of the *Dniprovazhpapirmash* plant. On 9 March 2016, the bust of Bolshevik Mikhail Kalinin was dismantled in the Memory and Reconciliation Square (the new name of Mikhail Kalinin Square). On 16 March 2016 on Oleksander Pole Avenue a bust of Bolshevik Kirov was removed. On 5 May 2016, images of Bolsheviks Sergo Ordzhonikidze, Kalinin and Kliment Voroshilov were removed from the Gorky Theatre.

Renaming the City and Oblast

The city council also had to deal with the question of renaming the city and oblast which combined the name of the river (Dnipro) and a Bolshevik and co-founder of the Cheka secret police (Grigori Petrovsky). Prior to 2014, pro-Russian groups, such as the Russian Orthodox Church in Ukraine, and the Party of Regions had supported the return of the Tsarist Russian Empire's name of Ekaterinoslav. Ukrainian patriots pointed out that Empress Catherine II had destroyed the autonomous Ukrainian Cossack Hetmanate. In response, pro-Russian supporters of Ekaterinoslav resorted to manipulation by saying the city will be re-named after St. Catherine. After 2014, the implementation of this proposal became impossible. Another manipulation took place in 2014–2016 when the Opposition Bloc (consisting of former members of the Party of Regions) supported re-naming Dnipropetrovsk after St. Peter.[15] These

---

[13]   M. Skidanova, 'Petrovskogo bez nog – na sklad KP,' Vesti, 16, 1 February 2016.
[14]   Decision of the Dnipro City Council on removing Soviet monuments, 5 February 2016. https://dniprorada.gov.ua/uk/chapters/item/11232/u-dnipropetrovskij-merii-pidgotovleno-rishennja-schodo-demontazhu-pamjatnikiv-radjanskogo-rezhimu-oleksandr-sanzhara
[15]   A. Beliy 'Vilkul predlagaet ustanovit v Dnepropetrovske pamyatnik apostolu Petru: gorod mozhet nazyvatsya v chest svyatogo,' Dniepr vechernij, 59, 14 July 2015, and A.

different manipulations by opponents of the renaming of the city and oblast were aimed at keeping the city under the influence of the Russian World.

The growth of Ukrainian patriotism after 2014 increased the number of supporters of the idea of renaming the city to Sicheslav. This name had been first proposed by Yavornytskyy in 1918 at the congress of the Ekaterinoslav Ukrainian Teacher's Association which had been supported by Chairman of the Ukrainian Teacher's Association Eugene Vyrovyy. Supporters of this name change included representatives of the intelligentsia of Ekaterinoslav, such as writers Vasyl Chaplenko, Valerian Polishchuk, Vasyl Sokil and others. The change to Sicheslav was supported in the Ukrainian diaspora; for example, by the writer Yar Slavutych.[16] After 1991, Sicheslav's work was popularised in Ukraine with the reprinting of his work in the *Sicheslav* newspaper, the regional Writer's Union magazine, *Sicheslav Almanakh* published by the *Sicheslavshchyna* Dnipropetrovsk regional organisation of the National Union of Local Lore of Ukraine and other publications. Renaming Dnipropetrovsk to Sicheslav was especially popular among supporters of the Euromaidan Revolution and veterans and volunteers from the Russian-Ukrainian war.

The city commission considered Sicheslav as the new name for the city of Dnipropetrovsk and submitted it for approval to the city council. Among other proposals, the name Dniproslav enjoyed support among some members of the commission because it combined parts of the names of Dnipropetrovsk and Ekaterinoslav (Svitlenko 2016, 102). Other proposals included Dniprovsk, Dnipropol, and Novyy Kodak. In July 2015, eight names (Dniproslav, Dnipro, Sicheslav, Dnipropetrovsk, Dnipropol, Kodak, Novyy Kodak, Svyatoslav) were submitted for public vote via the city council's website.[17] Of these, Dnipro was chosen. The city stands on the Dnipro River, which divides and unites it at the same time, and is a famous place for many Ukrainian writers and poets. Besides, for many decades the city's residents had been accustomed to using the abbreviated name of Dnipro for the city. The Ukrainian parliament's Committee on State Building, Regional Policy and Local Self-Government supported the renaming of Dnipropetrovsk to Dnipro on 5 February 2016 and parliament adopted a resolution implementing the decision on 19 May 2016.[18]

On the same day, the head of the Dnipropetrovsk oblast State Administration Valentyn Reznichenko signed the order 'About the renaming of toponyms in

---

Beliy, 'Apostoly v pomosch,' Dniepr vechernij,65, 4 August 2015.

[16] Ivan I. Rovenchak, 'Sicheslav' mae zaminiti nazvu 'Dnipropetrovsk,' Visnyk geodezii ta kartografii, 4 (97), 2015, 21–23.

[17] Y. Kokoshko, 'Ulichnyie boi: Bandera protiv Lenina,' Dniepr vechernij, 64, 31 July 2015, 13.

[18] 'Postanova Verhovnoi Rady Ukrayiny pro pereymenuvannya mista Dnipropetrovsk i Dnipropetrovskoy oblasti,' 19 May 2016.https://zakon.rada.gov.ua/laws/show/1375-VIII

settlements in the region.' Besides changing the name of the city, it also changed the names of another 35 toponyms. The city council officially renamed the city to Dnipro on 7 September 2016. On the same day a second vote by the city's council abolished Dnipro's brotherhood with Russian cities.

From spring 2016, the power to rename toponyms within the decommunisation process transferred to the Dnipropetrovsk oblast State Administration. On 2 March 2016, a working group of historians, archival and museum staff, experts on monuments and government officials was established to control the implementation of the law 'On Condemnation of Communist and National Socialist (Nazi) Totalitarian Regimes' throughout the territory of Dnipropetrovsk oblast.[19] A group of experts focused on toponymic reform throughout the region.

Decommunisation Slows Down

The creation of a Park of the Totalitarian Period was discussed on 29 November 2016 during a round table which took place in the Dnipro city council.[20] On 31 March 2017, a conference on the 'Park of Totalitarian Periods as a Tool for Decommunisation of Dnipro' took place in the city council. Scholars from Dnipro, Kyiv, Zaporizhzhya, Lviv, and Kryvyy Rih discussed the scholarly and practical aspects of the idea of creating a park.[21] At the beginning of 2018, a location for the future park had been determined and project documentation completed.[22] However, because of subjective and objective circumstances, the realisation of the idea of creating a park slowed down.

A similar situation emerged with renaming Dnipropetrovsk oblast. In January 2018, Dnipro activists submitted a petition with a proposal to rename Dnipropetrovsk to Sicheslav oblast.[23] The explanatory note to the petition

---

[19] 'Rozporyadzhennya holovy Dnipropetrovskoyi oblasnoyi derzhavnoyi adminiastratsii,' no.R-91/0/3-16, 2 March 2016. https://adm.dp.gov.ua/npas/pro-vnesennya-zmin-do-rozporyadzhennya-golovi-oblderzhadministratsii-vid-22-lyutogo-2016-roku-r-6903-16-60e07119bcb40f78c2257f6c003e7d5a

[20] 'Istoriya maye nas taki navchit,' 13 November 2016. http://dda.dp.ua/2016/11/30/stvorennya-u-dnipri-istoriko-muzejnogo-kompleksu-park-totalitarnogo-periodu/

[21] 'U Dniprovskiy miskiy radi tryvae vseukrainska konferentsiya 'Park totalitarnyh periodiv yak instrument Decommunisation Dnipra,' 31 March 2017. https://dniprorada.gov.ua/uk/chapters/item/13133/2017-03-31-10-58-03

[22] 'U Dnipri vyznachyly misce roztashuvannya Parku totalitarnogo periodu,' 9 February 2018. https://dnipro.depo.ua/ukr/dnipro/u-dnipri-viznachili-de-bude-rozmischeniy-totalitarniy-park-20180209724106

[23] 'Dnipryany podaly petytsiyu pro pereymenuvannya Dnipropetrovskoyi oblasti,' 26 January 2018. https://www.pravda.com.ua/news/2018/01/26/7169584/

stated that the proposed name is specific to the historical and geographical area, corresponds to world and domestic practices of toponymic nomination and would positively affect the image, economic and socio-political situation in the city and region. In 2018, public hearings were held, and proposals were submitted to parliament where 240 deputies supported the renaming of Dnipropetrovsk oblast to Sicheslav on 7 February 2019 in Bill 9310-1. The bill was passed to the Constitutional Court of Ukraine which voted on 2 April 2019 in favour of renaming the region. The next step was to hold a vote in parliament to change the Constitution, but this was prevented by presidential and pre-term parliamentary elections leaving the renaming unresolved.

Conclusions

Toponymic reforms in 2015–2016 and the decommunisation process in 2014–2019 led to 300 changes in toponyms in the city of Dnipro. Dozens of monuments and memorials were dismantled. The urban toponymic landscape was fundamentally changed to names related to local history and Ukrainian symbolism. New toponyms reflect the complex and multifaceted history of the city which arose in Cossack times and formed by Ukrainians and other ethnic groups.

In Southern-Eastern Ukraine, the greatest decommunisation process took place in Dnipropetrovsk. Monuments and names linking the city and region to the Tsarist Russian Empire and Soviet Union have been nearly all removed. The change of name of Dnipropetrovsk to Sicheslav oblast remains on the table. Nevertheless, changing the consciousness of the city and region's inhabitants is a longer-term process which would require decommunisation to be succeeded by a process of decolonisation.

Figures

6.1. *'Afgantsi'* (veterans of the Soviet occupation of Afghanistan) ripping apart a Ukrainian national flag, Dnipropetrovsk, Taras Kuzio, 1990.

6.2. *'Afgantsi'* attacked Ivan Sokulskyy (pointing) and Ivan Shulyk (to his right), head of Dnipropetrovsk regional branch of *Rukh*, Dnipropetrovsk, Taras Kuzio, 1990.

Oliinyk, Anna and Kuzio, Taras. (2001). 'The Euromaidan Revolution, Reforms and Decommunisation in Ukraine,' *Europe-Asia Studies*, 73, 5: 807–836.

Portnov, Andriy. (2015). 'Pro dekomunizatsiyu, identychnist ta istorychni zakony deshcho inakshe,'*Krytyka*, May. https://m.krytyka.com/ua/articles/pro-dekomunizatsiyu-identychnist-ta-istorychni-zakony-deshcho-inakshe

Motyl, Alexander, J. (2015). 'Dekomunizatsiya Ukayny,' Krytyka, March. https://krytyka.com/ua/articles/dekomunizatsiya-ukrayiny

Svitlenko, Serhiy, I. (2016). 'Toponimichna reforma v misti Dnipropetrovsk 2015–2016: dosvid provedennya ta rezultati' In: *Prydniprovya: Istoriko-Kraeznavchi doclidzhennya*, Dnipro: Lira. http://www.dnu.dp.ua/zbirnik/fistor/21

Turchenko, Fedir, G. and Turchenko, Halyna, F. (2015). *Proekt «Novorossiya»: 1764–2014.* Zaporizhzhya: Zaporizhzhya National University.

Zhuk, Sergei I. (2010). *Rock and Roll in the Rocket City: The West, Identity, and Ideology in Soviet Dniepropetrovsk, 1960–1985.* Washington DC and Baltimore: Woodrow Wilson Center and Johns Hopkins University.

7

Do National and Geopolitical Identities Explain Attitudes to Decommunisation? A Comparison of Dnipro and Kharkiv

OLEKSIY MUSIYEZDOV

Dnipro and Kharkiv are cities that have much in common, but also some notable differences. In the Ukrainian media and public discourse, Dnipro, unlike Kharkiv, is frequently described as a bastion of civic nationalism. However, with very few exceptions (Buckholz 2019 Gentile 2020, Nitsova 2021), they have not been subject to explicit comparison in the scholarly literature. Decommunisation in both cities did not have mass support. It can be assumed that inhabitants of these cities whose peak of development is perceived to have been in the Soviet era should assess that period positively. Additionally, they should have pro-Soviet/pro-Russian and anti-Western geopolitical orientations, and this should be a predictor for their attitudes towards decommunisation. This chapter tests this notion empirically.

We start with a brief explanation of what decommunisation is and how to explain the difference in attitudes towards decommunisation via identity and geopolitical preferences in Ukraine. Then we will compare Dnipro and Kharkiv and will show and explain similarities and differences in assessment of decommunisation by inhabitants of these cities based on a survey undertaken in 2018.

What is Decommunisation?

Decommunisation is the process of removing Soviet symbols from public spaces. This process began after the disintegration of the USSR but accelerated significantly with the implementation of the decommunisation laws adopted in April 2015.[1] According to one of the laws, the utilisation and propaganda of symbols of communist and national-socialist (Nazi) totalitarian regimes is prohibited. Thus, communist monuments should be removed, and public places named after communist-related themes should be renamed. In 1991 Ukraine inherited more than 8,200 items of Soviet monumental art (Oleksandra Hayday 2018, 47) and approximately 5,500 monuments to Lenin (Serhii Hromenko 2019), of which about 3,750 had been dismantled before the 'laws of decommunisation' were adopted (Hayday 2018, 164).[2] According to Anton Drobovych, Head of Ukrainian institute of National Remembrance (UINP), more than 51,000 toponyms have been renamed – including about 2,500 monuments in the last five years.[3]

From the very beginning 'decommunisation laws' became a target of criticism. The main argument against the laws was that they politicise history, which leads to the prevention of academic study and debates by imposing certain assessments of historical persons and events as well as discrimination of people's political views, deepening social divisions and even prompting violence (Shevel 2016; Zhurzhenko 2017; Portnov 2015; Yavorskyy 2015). Despite the political will which was embodied in the laws, attitudes to decommunisation vary significantly across different social groups and regions in Ukraine. Predictably, public opinion pays more attention to renaming of toponyms and removal of monuments than academic freedom.

According to the Rating Sociological Group in November 2016, 35 per cent of Ukrainians supported the renaming of toponyms and 57 per cent were against.[4] The latest research at the time of writing (April 2020) by the Democratic Initiatives Foundation (DIF) shows that 32 per cent approve the ban on symbols and 30 per cent approve renaming toponyms while those

---

[1] See Law no. 2558 (April 2015) 'On Condemning the Communist and National Socialist (Nazi) Totalitarian Regimes and Prohibiting the Propagation of their Symbols', https://zakon.rada.gov.ua/laws/show/317-19#Text

[2] We thank Anna Olinyk and Taras Kuzio for this information.

[3] 'Za roky decommunizatsii v Ukrayini demontuvaly bilsh yak 1300 pamyatnykiv Leninu' *Ukrinform*, 16 July 2020. https://www.ukrinform.ua/rubric-society/3064494-za-roki-dekomunizacii-v-ukraini-demontuvali-bils-ak-1300-pamatnikiv-leninu.html

[4] 'Attitude toward certain historical figures and decommunisation process in Ukraine,' Sociological Group 'Rating', 17 November 2016. http://ratinggroup.ua/en/research/ukraine/otnoshenie_k_otdelnym_istoricheskim_lichnostyam_i_processu_dekommunizacii_v_ukraine.html

opposed are 34 per cent and 44 per cent, respectively. Approval is higher in Ukraine's Western and Central regions (up to 44 per cent) and is lower in Southern and Eastern regions (down to 22 per cent) and is higher among younger people and lower for older.[5]

How Do We Explain Attitudes Towards Decommunisation?

The main logic of the explanation is that people support historical, political, and geopolitical discourses due to successful attempts to impose them. 'Soviet' discourse has been imposed for many years, which is why older and Russian speaking people (which are the majority in Ukraine's East and South) support Soviet names and symbols more than younger and Ukrainian speakers. Using sociological language, this means a symbolic struggle for making a certain worldview dominant — the one according to which the position of a certain group is privileged (Bourdieu 1990). Psychologically it means that this position must provide positive self-esteem, and that any attempts to question such an interpretation will meet at least disapproval (Musiyezdov 2016b). That is why attitudes towards decommunisation cannot be reduced to political preferences only but affects *identities*.

The main problem is the question of what identity is and how to measure it? Despite some differences in disciplinary interpretations, in general we use this category to mark something that is at the core of people's self-understanding. Identity is a perception of 'who am I' and identity is something that can explain people's behaviour. But we must remember that identity is our instrument, which can be substituted by concepts such as 'values', 'interests', and 'needs' (Musiyezdov 2016a).

What Is Identity?

The concept of identity is used in different disciplines where it generally means that an object is the same as some other object or the same as this object. In the first case it is referring to a classification and in the second case to the 'inner essence' of the object. Many philosophers have attempted to interpret identity using both meanings. As an academic concept, identity has arisen due to Sigmund Freud and has been developing in psychology where it means the subject's (psychological) result of (usually subconscious) identification with another subject, a group, or a pattern.

---

[5] 'The sixth year of decommunisation: the attitude of Ukrainians toward prohibition of symbols of the totalitarian past,' Democratic Initiatives Foundation, 24 July 2020. https://dif.org.ua/en/article/the-sixth-year-of-decommunisation-the-attitude-of-ukrainians-toward-prohibition-of-symbols-of-the-totalitarian-past

Sociology emphasises that identity is socially determined; society offers and imposes positions to identify with and makes people conform. Modern theories (see Baumeister 1986; Giddens 1991, Castells 1997; Baumann 2001) explore the development of identity through the development of society and usually agree that, nowadays, identity is the result of personal choice in changing social circumstances.

For example, according to Anthony Giddens (1984) identity and self-identity are cultural phenomena in modern society which arise and perform in the daily life of a particular individual. Common identity is often an unconscious confidence of individuals belonging to a particular team, common feelings and ideas reflected in consciousness. Utilisation of the concept of identity means that researchers assume that people behave based on their perception about who they are. Researchers seek to explore these perceptions to be able to make predictions about future behaviour or at least interpret social dependencies.

In sociology, the measurement of identity is the answer to the question, 'who am I' given in terms of social groups. This means that societies offer people sets of social groups, and people must feel strong connections with one or some of them.[6] An important note should be made about groups with which people are asked to identify. In sociology one of the main questions is about what groups really exist and what does it mean for the group to exist? This question is highly debatable, and the answer can be given by taking specific circumstances into account. The existence of a group is highly dependent on its visibility in collective actions as well as in a prevalent worldview (Kachanov and Shmatko 1996) which is why symbolic struggle is so important and why sets and structures of groups are highly changeable. This means that talking about identities appealing to groups are not reliable enough indicators. When asking about self-description, researchers offer different *types* of people; and they are aware that these types could or could not be groups. This approach enables clarification about different dimensions of solidarity.

Geopolitical Orientations and Identities in Ukraine

In contemporary Ukraine one of the important dimensions is 'geopolitical'. By using the concept of 'geopolitical identity' we do not confine certain groups in the sense of 'groupism' (Brubaker, 2002). We emphasise that being a supporter of certain geopolitical preferences means that 1) this is important

---

[6] In the annual 'Ukrainian society' monitoring of public opinion since 1992 by the Institute of Sociology of the National Academy of Sciences of Ukraine, the question is formulated as 'Who do you consider yourself in the first place?' with the following options for answers (Vorona and Shulha 2018, 465).

for people and is connected to other important factors like values, visions of social justice, and interests and 2) it can predict their attitudes and behaviour towards other processes and events – such as decommunisation. Geopolitical preferences are demonstrated in Figure 7.1.

As we can see, the main changes in geopolitical attitudes took place in 2012–2014 during the Euromaidan Revolution and Russian-Ukrainian war: people began to assess the idea of Ukraine's accession to the union of Russia and Belarus more negatively and the idea of Ukraine's accession to NATO more positively (in both cases some supporters and opponents have changed approximately two times). Also, we can see corresponding changes in identities in Figure 7.1 (Vorona and Shulha 2018, 465) where the biggest changes are local (regional), 'Soviet' and especially civic identities. These changes are a product of stepping back from 'Soviet' (as an embodiment of dignity neglect and Russian politics towards Ukraine) and unity of Ukrainians in the face of a common threat.

Another predictable result is that geopolitical attitudes remain different in Ukrainian regions. In June 2019, joining the European Union is supported by 85 per cent of Ukrainians in the West and 34 per cent in the East of Ukraine, joining NATO – 80 per cent and 29 per cent respectively (Table 7.1).[7] This means that the place of the city on the map of Ukraine reflects these regional differences. Inhabitants of the Central Ukrainian region of Dnipro should have been more in favour of decommunisation than the Eastern Ukrainian region of Kharkiv. As we will see, most of the people in these two cities do not support decommunisation but the level of opposition is higher in Kharkiv than in Dnipro. What can explain these differences? Is this a regional factor only? Answering this question will lead to a deeper understanding of decommnunisation processes in Ukraine in general. This is the main aim of this chapter.

Dnipro and Kharkiv: Similarities and Differences

Scholarly literature has rarely compared Dnipropetrovsk and Dnipro and Kharkiv. Quentin Buckholz (2019) argues that the success or failure of separatist movements across Eastern Ukraine (especially in Kharkiv and Dnipro) is best understood with reference to the preferences and actions of local political and economic elites. Michael Gentile (2020) compares these cities in the dimensions of disinformation and nationalism, but not their attitudes towards decommunisation. Silviya Nitsova (2021) analyses

---

[7] 'Social and political moods of Ukrainians: IRI poll,' Sociological group 'Rating', 10 July 2019. http://ratinggroup.ua/en/research/ukraine/opros_iri_dinamika_obschestvenno-politicheskih_vzglyadov_v_ukraine_iyun_2019.html

differences between these cities on the one hand and Donetsk and Luhansk on the other hand from the point of view of explaining differences in their fate in 2014 and since. This chapter contributes to the discussion of decommunisation by comparing these two cities using a survey undertaken in 2018.

What do these cities have in common and what are the important differences between them? Both are large, Russian-speaking, highly industrialised with a developed high-technology sector in Soviet times. Moreover, both became important centres of resistance during the Russo-Ukrainian war.

The city of Dnipro is the fourth largest city in Ukraine. It is situated in the south-east of Ukraine on the Dnipro River. The city was officially established in 1776 as Yekaterinoslav and became an industrial centre at the beginning of the twenty-first century (Portnova 2012). From the 1950s the city Dnipropetrovsk became a large centre of science and technology after the opening of the *Pivdenmash (Yuzhmash)* Machine-Building Plant and Experimental Design Bureau OKB-586 and OKB Yuzhnoye which designed and produced space and military production (in particular - rockets). In 2019 the population of the city was about 998,000[8] people with an ethnic composition (2001 census) of 72.55 per cent Ukrainians, 23.51 per cent Russians, and 0.98 per cent Jews.[9]

The city of Kharkiv is the second largest city in Ukraine situated in the Eastern part of the country. The city was officially established in 1654. Like Dnipro it transformed into an industrial centre at the beginning of 20th century (Chornyy 2007). Since the 1930s, many research and development institutions were opened, and after the 1950s Kharkiv became one of the largest academic centres in the USSR. Plants such as the Kharkiv Tractor Plant, 'Turboatom' (turbines), Malyshev Factory (military machinery), Kharkiv Aircraft Manufacturing Company, Experimental Design Bureau's (OKB-692, KB *Electropryladobuduvannya*, NVO *Electroprylad* (space and rocket technology) and other high technology industry plants were situated in the city. In 2020 the population of the city was about 1,443,000[10] with an ethnic

---

[8] 'Chyselnist naiavnoho naselennia m.Dnipra na 1 serpnia 2020 roku,' Holovne upravlinnya statystyky Dnipropetrovskoi oblasti. http://www.dneprstat.gov.ua/expres/2020/09/21_09_2020/chis-nas-mDnipra.pdf

[9] 'Chyselnist naiavnoho naselennya m.Dnipra na 1 serpnya 2020 roku,' Databank of the State Statistics Service of Ukraine. http://database.ukrcensus.gov.ua/MULT/Database/Census/databasetree_uk.asp

[10] 'Chyselnist naselennya (za otsinkoyu) po mistakh oblasnoho znachennya ta rayonakh,' (shchomisyachna informatsiya). http://kh.ukrstat.gov.ua/chyselnist-naselennia-shchomisiachna-informatsiia

composition (2001 census) of 60.99 per cent Ukrainians, 34.25 per cent Russians, and 0.77 per cent Jews.[11]

Rivalry between Kharkiv and Dnipro of course existed. For both cities the peak of development was perceived to be between the 1960s and 1980s. Memory of Kharkiv as 'The First Capital' not only referred to 1918–1934, when Kharkiv was the capital of Soviet Ukraine, but also emphasised its economic, industrial, and academic development and potential (Musiyezdov 2016b). In 1959–1987, Dnipropetrovsk was a closed city for foreign citizens and had additional restrictions due to the existence of space and military industry and research; the positive side to this was it gave the inhabitants higher standards of living that was perceived as an elite privilege status (Portnova 2017; Zhuk 2010). These circumstances led to the situation when residents of both Kharkiv and Dnipropetrovsk looked down at other cities, especially working-class Donetsk.[12]

Historically Kharkiv and Dnipropetrovsk elites played noticeable role in Ukrainian politics. Thus Petro Shelest (from Kharkiv) who was the First Secretary of the Communist Party of Ukraine in 1963–1972 was replaced by Volodymyr Shcherbytskyy (from Dnipropetrovsk) who occupied this post until 1989. Soviet leader Leonid Brezhnev (1964–1982) was from Dnipropetrovsk as well as the second President of Ukraine Leonid Kuchma (1994–2004).

Andriy Portnov tells the Soviet Dnipropetrovsk joke about three periods of Russian history: 'pre-Petrine, Petrine, and Dnipro-petrine (dopetrovski – petrovski – dnipropetrovski, with the first two names relating to the first Russian emperor, Peter the Great)' (Portnov 2015b, 63). Dnipropetrovsk inhabitants and elites saw their city as 'neither the first nor the second' and did not see Kyiv as their capital. A similar situation existed in Kharkiv, which used to compare itself with Moscow and Leningrad and not with Kyiv (Musiyezdov 2016b).

There were few leaders from Kharkiv who had some impact on Ukrainian politics (Vladimir Grynyov, Yevgenii Kushnaryov, Boris Lozhkin). But the names of those from Dnipropetrovsk are much better known: Pavlo Lazarenko, Yulia Tymoshenko, Valery Pustovoytenko, Viktor Pinchuk and Ihor Kolomoyskyy (Denis Kazanskyy 2015). Both Kharkiv and Dnipropetrovsk elites were defeated in the struggle for Ukrainian power by the Donetsk elite in the 2000s.

---

[11] Databank of State Statistics Service of Ukraine. http://database.ukrcensus.gov.ua/MULT/Database/Census/databasetree_uk.asp

[12] This viewpoint is based on our personal observations living in Kharkiv and attending meetings of people from Kharkiv and Donetsk.

In 2014, Kharkiv and Dnipropetrovsk played important roles during the so-called 'Russian spring'. Andrii Portnov (2016), for example, expresses the popular idea that similar cities in the East of Ukraine experienced different fates due to accidental circumstances. Donetsk, Luhansk, Dnipropetrovsk and Kharkiv are relatively large, Russian-speaking, oblasts. In his opinion the 'Russian spring' failed in the latter two cities because of a specific constellation of local elites' interests and different impacts of policies by the central authorities. It is difficult to disagree with this, but additional arguments could be added. Cities in the Donbas are characterised by the predominance of mining and metallurgy and, consequently, a homogeneous composition of the population. This contrasts with a diverse population and a varied range of industries in Kharkiv and Dnipropetrovsk, including high-tech, which reduces the potential for monopolisation by one political force. Only in the Donbas was a monolithic party of power (Party of Regions) created; in Kharkiv and Dnipropetrovsk local elites never united. From the point of view of countering attempts to make the city a pro-Russian 'people's republic' the diversity found in Kharkiv and Dnipropetrovsk was a positive inhibiting factor (Musiyezdov 2015). During the Russian-Ukrainian war both cities became important logistical, medicine and military centres, both accepted large numbers of IDPs from the Donbas and Kharkiv (for Luhansk) and Dnipropetrovsk (for Donetsk) military hospitals for wounded soldiers.

General Attitudes Towards Decommunisation

To assess how inhabitants of Kharkiv and Dnipro assess decommunisation, we use the results of surveys carried out in these two cities in 2018.[13] As we can see from table 7.4, most of the people in these two cities do not support decommunisation but the level of opposition is higher in Kharkiv than in Dnipro. What can explain these differences?

The question about identities has already been discussed earlier in our chapter. We can compare not only total samples from Dnipro and Kharkiv but also groups of people who support decommunisation in both cities[14] (see

---

[13] This study is based on two sample surveys conducted among the adult (18+) population in Dnipro (n=1258) and Kharkiv (n=1254) in early and mid-2018, respectively. The surveys were designed by Michael Gentile and the fieldwork and sampling were conducted on a contractual basis by the Centre for Social Indicators (CSI), whose field resources and expertise are shared with the reputed Kyiv International Institute of Sociology (KIIS) polling agency. Funding from the Norwegian Research Council (NORRUSS project 287267, 'Ukrainian Geopolitical Fault-line Cities: Urban Identity, Geopolitics and Urban Policy') supported this work. The data collection effort was funded by the Department of Sociology and Human Geography at the University of Oslo via a Småforsk grant.

[14] People who 'absolutely support' or 'rather support' the renaming of streets. The question about the removal of Lenin monuments has a vague option ('they should be moved to another place') which could be interpreted for or against 'decommunisation' depending on the context.

Table 7.6). Let us note though that feeling affinity or even belonging to a certain group does not mean an impossibility of feeling affinity or belonging to other groups. That is why some researchers ask to what extent people consider themselves as representative of several groups (see Musiyezdov 2007). The same technique has been used in our research. The data provides several interesting observations:

1. Self-identification as European is the only identity that correlates with a positive assessment of decommunisation; in other words, the more people feel they are European, the more they support decommunisation (Spearman coefficient is 0.567 in Kharkiv and 0.370 in Dnipro for the question about streets renaming).
2. While self-identification as Russian could reflect the ethnic specifics of these cities, self-identification as European (which is more popular in Dnipro) is very divisive: 29 per cent answered 'yes' or 'rather yes' on this question in Dnipro while 22 per cent gave the same answer in Kharkiv.[15]
3. Feeling European does not correlate (positively or negatively) with other identities.
4. Supporters of decommunisation in Dnipro are a little bit more Ukrainian than the inhabitants of Dnipro in general (96 per cent vs. 90 per cent respectively).
5. Supporters of decommunisation in Kharkiv are a little bit more Soviet than supporters of decommunisation in Dnipro (34 per cent vs. 19 per cent respectively).

Did European identity exist before the 2014 crisis and was it at the same level as now? Table 7.8 shows that in both cities the majority of those who felt European now felt European before (69 per cent in Dnipro and 78 per cent in Kharkiv). But compared to them a significant part of the people who support decommunisation now did not feel European before (52 per cent in Dnipro and 61 per cent in Kharkiv). This means that support for decommunisation is a reaction to socio-political events rather than a result of previous identification with Europeans.

'Belonging' as well as feeling affinity to a certain group could have different meanings. For example, identification with a country can be based on different ideas of what a country is. Is it a state (political and legal unity), a 'Motherland' (historical unity with some ethnic connotation) or a unity of people who now have something in common (no matter why) (Musiyezdov, 2012)? Citizenship and nationality are often confused in Western democracies (for example, on customs declarations). Therefore, the clarification of the impact of feeling European on other attitudes must be studied in further research.

---

[15] Here and other emphasised differences are statistically significant at the 1%-level.

Let us now move on to geopolitical preferences (see Tables 7.8 and 7.9). Here we can see the following results:

1. Supporters of decommunisation are pro-Western.
2. Supporters of decommunisation in Kharkiv are less radical in their opinions than in Dnipro. While the general agreement or disagreement is the same in these groups in both cities, inhabitants of Kharkiv more often chose 'rather agree' than 'absolutely agree' than inhabitants of Dnipro.
3. People in Kharkiv are less pro-European than in Dnipro. 26 per cent in Kharkiv compared to 44 per cent in Dnipro agree that Ukraine must defend European values and 32 per cent in Kharkiv compared to 42 per cent in Dnipro agree that the influence of Western Europe on the Ukrainian way of life is positive. 55.7 per cent in Kharkiv compared to 36.6 per cent in Dnipro do not see benefits for Ukraine from becoming a member of NATO and the European Union while 28.2 per cent in Dnipro compared to 11.7 per cent in Kharkiv see such benefits.
4. Even pro-decommunisation groups generally do not deny their closeness to Slavic peoples in both cities with 74 per cent in Kharkiv and 76 per cent in Dnipro agreeing that Ukraine must defend Slavic values.
5. 81 per cent in Kharkiv compared to 69 per cent in Dnipro agree that Russians and Ukrainians are one people. On the one hand this statement can be treated as an example of Russian propaganda that refers to the idea that Ukrainians are an artificial construction produced by Western forces to weaken Russia. But on the other hand, it seems to reflect the Soviet narrative about *druzhba narodiv* (people's friendship) where cultural and ethnic differences should not play any significant role.

Differences in attitudes towards Slavic values and Russians between the inhabitants of Kharkiv and Dnipro are interesting, but we do not have good explanations for this. It can be assumed that appeals to 'Slavic values' and 'Slavianism', in any form, reflects the idea and Russian narrative that Russians and Ukrainians are very close nations (if not as Russian President Vladimir Putin always says, 'one people'). Perhaps it reflects the ethnic composition in these cities and/or the existence of long-term border cooperation with Russia in Kharkiv, but this assumption does not seem comprehensive enough. Again, it would be necessary to explore what people mean by NATO, European Union, Slavic values, Russians, and Ukrainians in future research.

We would assume that decommunisation would be supported by those who consider the Soviet period negatively. In Table 7.10 we can see that this assumption is correct with those in favour of decommunisation in both cities viewing the Soviet period more negatively than inhabitants in the two cities more generally. Inhabitants of Dnipro estimate the Soviet period more negatively than the inhabitants of Kharkiv among the population in general and those in favour of decommunisation.

Explanations of the differences between Dnipro and Kharkiv

General opinions about decommunisation, geopolitical orientations, identities, and assessment of Soviet history have quite similar trends in Dnipro and Kharkiv. But despite this closeness there are crucial differences between two cities: Dnipro appears to be much more pro-Western/pro-European and pro-Ukrainian as well as less pro-Soviet than Kharkiv. This is not a new phenomenon. 'The views and opinions of South-Eastern regions residents of Ukraine: April 2014' conducted by the Kyiv International Institute of Sociology discovered similar differences which decisively impact upon attitudes towards decommunisation.[16]

People in both cities are aware of their differences (Table 7.11) with 38 per cent in Dnipro agreeing that their city is more pro-Ukrainian than Kharkiv (28 per cent disagree) and 40 per cent in Kharkiv agreeing with this statement (12 per cent disagree). How do we explain the gap in pro-Ukrainian 'self-confidence' among Dniprovians versus Kharkovians? There could be at least three assumptions.

First, it can be assumed that these differences are partly based on geography because Kharkiv is a border city and has a greater number of ties with Russia than Dnipro from which it is difficult to escape. It refers to economic connections (Buckholz 2019), identities (Zhurzhenko 2015) and susceptibility to Russian propaganda (Stebelsky 2018; Tomazs Piechal 2015). Since 1991, Kharkiv was forced to compare itself with Kyiv, not with Moscow and Leningrad as it used to do before (Musiyezdov 2016b). Comparison with Kyiv was perceived as new and quite unfair (Kravchenko 2019). And it led to the enforcement of Soviet nostalgia – the reference to the Soviet period as to something like a 'Golden age' that has been embodied by the myth of 'The First capital', which was a reference to the late Soviet era – not the 1920–1930s. Also, Kharkiv lost its status as the 'capital of the East of Ukraine' with the rise of Donetsk clan in the 2000s which may have increased frustration and prevented a decline in Soviet nostalgia in the city.

Second, the local history and heritage of the Jewish community in Dnipro might matter. According to the last (2001) census the proportion of Jews is 0.98 per cent (10,503) and 0.77 per cent (11,176) in Dnipro and Kharkiv

---

[16] 'The views and opinions of south-eastern regions residents of Ukraine: April 2014,' Kyiv International Institute of Sociology, April 2014. http://www.kiis.com.ua/?lang=eng&cat=reports&id=302&y=2014&m=4&page=1

respectively.[17] In both cities the number and proportion of Jews decreased during the Soviet era. According to some resources, the Jewish populations of both cities were almost equal and declined from about 8 per cent in 1959 to about 3 per cent in 1989.[18] This makes researchers question Soviet census figures about the number of Jews. Some of them say that the proportion of Jews should be about 10 per cent (Bystriakov 2015). It is difficult to prove this statement, but we could agree that the real figures are larger than official ones.

We can see the proportions of Jews in Dnipro and Kharkiv were very similar since 1939. But in 1926 the difference was noticeable; in the 1897 census, there were 34.77 per cent of Jews in Dnipro[19] and 5.66 per cent in Kharkiv[20] showing a big difference between them. This can be explained by the fact that until 1914–1917 Dnipro (then Yekaterinoslav) was a part of the Pale of Settlement – the Western territory of Russia Empire where Jews were allowed to settle, but Kharkiv was not (Yannay Spitzer 2012).

This means that Jews in Dnipro could live and maintain their traditional culture. Jews in Kharkiv were so called 'useful Jews' – those who have higher education (usually doctors or engineers) or were successful entrepreneurs (having certain amount of capital). So, they should feel lesser connection to Jewish traditional culture living apart from the Jewish community. After 1914, many Jews fled to Kharkiv. Usually, they were refugees from World War One or quite poor people who sought prosperity outside traditional communities. This process increased in the beginning of Soviet era when many Jews who supported Soviet power came to Kharkiv as the capital of Soviet Ukraine. This raised the number and proportion of Jews in Kharkiv to levels comparable to those of Dnipropetrovsk. But the connection to Jewish tradition was different in these cities: quite strong in Dnipropetrovsk[21] and quite weak in Kharkiv.

---

[17] Databank of State Statistics Service of Ukraine. http://database.ukrcensus.gov.ua/MULT/Database/Census/databasetree_uk.asp

[18] 'Elektronnaya yevreyskaya enciklopediya,' Dnipro. https://eleven.co.il/diaspora/communities/11444/; Kharkiv. *Elektronnaya yevreyskaya enciklopediya*. https://eleven.co.il/diaspora/communities/14456/. See also *Demoscope Weekly*. http://www.demoscope.ru/weekly/pril.php

[19] 'The First General Census of the Russian Empire of 1897. Breakdown of population by mother tongue and districts in 50 Gubernia of European Russia. Yekaterinislav district – the city of Yekaterinislav,' *Demoscope Weekly*. http://www.demoscope.ru/weekly/ssp/rus_lan_97_uezd_eng.php?reg=426

[20] 'The First General Census of the Russian Empire of 1897. Breakdown of population by mother tongue and districts in 50 Gubernia of European Russia. Kharkov district – the city of Kharkov,' *Demoscope Weekly*. http://www.demoscope.ru/weekly/ssp/rus_lan_97_uezd_eng.php?reg=1604

[21] In particular, the Seventh Lubavitcher Rebbe, Menachem Mendel Schneerson (1902–1994), grew up in Dnipropetrovsk which is why the city was especially important for the Hasidic tradition. See the chapter by Ishchenko.

That is why the Holocaust and Soviet anti-Semitism had greater impact on Jews in Dnipropetrovsk than in Kharkiv and formed the situation where Jews in Dnipro 'hold no nostalgia for the USSR' (see Chapter three) while Jews in Kharkiv exhibited such a nostalgia.

Third, the role of local elites should be taken into consideration. The number of leaders from Dnipropetrovsk who rose to prominence nationally (Leolid Kuchma, Pavlo Lazarenko, Yulia Tymoshenko, Valery Pustovoytenko) could give the impression that Ukraine 'belongs to them,' meaning that they have their political and economic interests tied with Ukraine. The Kharkiv authorities, on the other hand, were less involved in Ukrainian politics and more connected with Russia, at least economically. Dnipro elites saw the events of 2013–2014 and the Russo-Ukrainian war as an opportunity to regain their control of Ukraine after years of 'Donetsk clan' dominance (Buckholz 2019; Kuzio 2019, Portnov 2015b).

Also, Jewish oligarchs from Dnipro (Viktor Pinchuk, Ihor Kolomoyskyy) are more closely associated with Jewish traditions and to the anti-Soviet attitude of Jews in Dnipro than are Kharkiv's elites who have Jewish ancestry (Gennadii Kernes, Mykhaylo Dobkin).[22] This factor influences policies in these cities, including their attitudes towards decommunisation.

Some General Assumptions

First, we can assume there are five different 'dimensions' of perceiving Soviet identity:

1. Political: correspondence to certain political views (communist, socialist, left-wing).
2. Economic: correspondence to certain economic views ('fair' distribution system and the level of its embodiment in the USSR).
3. Cultural: correspondence to Russian or Russian-speaking literature.
4. Historical: correspondence to certain interpretation(s) of history,
5. Biographical: correspondence to the fact of the one's birth in the USSR or acknowledgement of habits and attitudes as Soviet.

---

[22] For example, Gennadii Kernes considered himself an Orthodox Christian and his funeral service took place in an Orthodox Church. See 'U Kharkovi poproschalysya z Kernesom: usi podrobytsi,' *Obozrevatel*. https://news.obozrevatel.com/ukr/politics/u-harkovi-proschayutsya-z-kernesom-vsi-podrobitsi-onlajn.htm). Mykhailo Dobkin is a founder of the Party of Christian Socialists. See 'Dobkin Mykhaylo Markovych. *Vidkrytyi reyiestr natsionalnyh publichnyh diyiachiv Ukrayiny*.' https://pep.org.ua/uk/person/388.

Perhaps it is possible to add some other dimensions; each of them could have different interpretations. But all of them are 'doctrinal', 'cognitive', 'discursive' ones which means they relate to some rational and conscious statements while in many cases the emotional element is much more important. In this context, the concept of nostalgia seems productive because it covers attitudes towards the past through the prism of collective memory and personal experience, and is connected to identities, values and interpretations of the present, which all include an emotional component.

In the case of Soviet nostalgia, it would be useful to use the distinction on 'soft' and 'hard' nostalgia. 'Hard nostalgia' is espoused by Russian President Vladimir Putin, who said: 'The collapse of the USSR was the greatest geopolitical catastrophe of the 20th century'. 'Soft nostalgia' is evident in Socialist Party of Ukraine leader Oleksandr Moroz's statement: 'You have no heart if you don't regret the loss of the USSR, but you have no head if you want the USSR revived.'[23] This statement stems from the late 1990s and was made to mark the difference between the Socialist Party and the Communist Party. Nowadays 'soft nostalgia' might be present among those with Ukrainian and European identities, but 'hard nostalgia' (probably) is not. 'Soft nostalgia' could explain some of the rather passive opposition to decommunisation (which we can observe) while 'hard nostalgia' likely motivates anti-decommunisation activists.

This distinction echoes Svetlana Boym's (2002) distinction between 'restorative' and 'reflective' nostalgia. For her, 'restorative' nostalgia involves the idealisation of the object of nostalgia, whereas 'reflective' nostalgia enables some interpretation of and feelings for the past and its relation to the present – without the expectation or desire of going back.

Conclusions

Identities and geopolitical orientations do explain attitudes towards decommunisation. Decommunisation is aimed at removing visual Soviet legacies which are interpreted as something that prevents the development of Ukraine, which is why it could be argued that the most connected identities would be Ukrainian and Soviet. But European identity has the closest collection to attitudes towards decommunisation. Also, geopolitical orientations play a significant role here because higher support for pro-Western attitudes translates into higher support for decommunisation. We therefore argue that the concept of values can be as useful as the concept of identity (perhaps even more so). Feeling European does not correlate positively or negatively with other identities, and the pro-European mindset is

---

[23] 'Politychna biografiya Oleksandra Moroza,' *Radio Svoboda*. https://www.radiosvoboda.org/a/947905.html

most likely distinct, possibly being an outgrowth of the Euromaidan Revolution.

Despite holding pro-Western/pro-European positions and a negative view of Soviet history, supporters of decommunisation do not deny their Soviet past completely; indeed, many of them continue to feel Soviet, consider Russians and Ukrainians to be one people and tend to support Slavic values. On the other hand, disapproval of decommunisation could be explained by pragmatic reasons rather than by ideological factors.

Differences between Dnipro and Kharkiv are sometimes quite significant. In general, inhabitants of Dnipro support decommunisation more, are more pro-Western/pro-European and more pro-Ukrainian and are less pro-Soviet. These differences do not deny similar opinions in both cities, but they do nevertheless matter. It can be assumed that these differences are based on geography and whether the city is a border city, which impacts economic ties, identities and susceptibilities to Russian disinformation. Two other factors are the role and local history of the Jewish community in Dnipro (see above) and the role of local elites in Ukrainian politics and economy.

Since identification is extremely sensitive to the meanings which are involved in the processes[24] a thorough study of these meanings should be part of any research into Ukrainian identity. This chapter contributes to the study of decommunisation and identities by providing new ground in comparing Kharkiv and Dnipro and by pointing to the need for further research.

---

[24] What groups or other patterns are? Why they are what they are? How are they interpreted and by whom? What are the similarities and differences between their positions?

Acknowledgments

We thank Taras Kuzio for his valuable comments on earlier drafts of this chapter. Funding from the Norwegian Research Council (NORRUSS project 287267, 'Ukrainian Geopolitical Fault-line Cities: Urban Identity, Geopolitics and Urban Policy') supported this work. The survey was funded by the Department of Sociology and Human Geography at the University of Oslo via a Småforsk grant given to Michael Gentile. The survey fieldwork was conducted by the Kyiv-based Centre for Social Indicators (CSI).

Figures and Tables

7.1. Geopolitical Attitudes in Ukraine

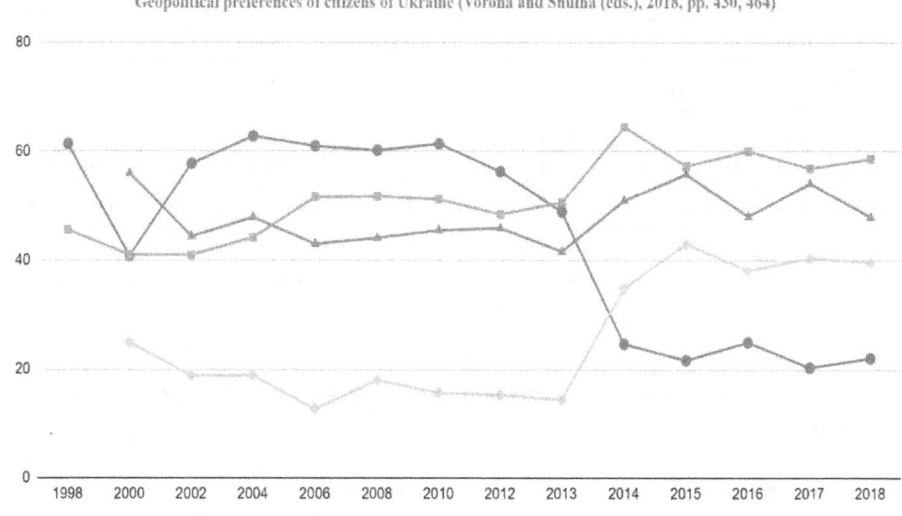

7.2. 'If Ukraine could only enter one international economic union, which of the following should it be?'

	West	Centre	South	East
EU	85	60	46	34
CIS Customs Union	3	14	32	41
Other	6	12	10	13
Difficult to answer/ No answer	6	12	10	13

7.3. 'If a referendum were held today on Ukraine joining NATO, how would you vote?'

	West	Centre	South	East
Would vote for Ukraine to join NATO	80	54	36	29
Would vote against Ukraine joining the NATO	7	23	47	57
Would not vote	3	4	5	5
Difficult to answer/No answer	10	19	12	10

7.4. Was it necessary to demolish the monuments to Lenin, starting in 2014? (valid %)'

	Dnipro	Kharkiv
No	50	59
They should be moved to another place	27	23
Yes	15	9
Difficult to answer	8	9

7.5. 'Do you personally support or oppose the renaming of streets with Soviet names (valid %)'

	Dnipro	Kharkiv
Absolutely oppose	45	55
Rather oppose	21	26
Rather support	14	9
Absolutely support	12	4
Difficult to answer	7	6

7.6. 'Do you feel like... (valid %)' *Table continues overleaf.*

	Dnipro (total)	Dnipro (pro-decommunisation group, N=296)	Kharkiv (total)	Kharkiv (pro-decommunisation group, N=161)
... Ukrainian				
Absolutely yes	67.1	75.7	63.6	61.5
Rather yes	22.8	20.6	25.3	23.6
Rather not	3.8	2.0	4.7	9.9
Absolutely not	4.5	1.4	5.1	4.3
Difficult to answer	1.5	0.3	1.3	0.6
... Russian				
Absolutely yes	7.8	2.7	11.0	8.7
Rather yes	11.1	6.8	14.2	22.4
Rather not	28.2	25.0	24.2	23.0
Absolutely not	47.5	63.5	47.9	42.9
Difficult to answer	5.0	2.0	2.7	2.5
... Soviet				
Absolutely yes	17.0	6.8	14.6	10.6
Rather yes	18,8	12.5	21.7	23.6
Rather not	20.4	18.2	18.2	28.0
Absolutely not	38.4	58.1	40.9	34.2
Difficult to answer	5.0	4.4	4.5	3.7
... European				
Absolutely yes	9.6	21.3	4,4	9.9
Rather yes	19.1	32.4	18.0	31.7
Rather not	26.9	24.7	20.0	35.4
Absolutely not	36.0	16.6	52.0	17.4
Difficult to answer	8.3	5.1	5.5	5.6
... Dniprovian / Kharkovite				
Absolutely yes	83.0	79.4	76.7	69.6
Rather yes	12.0	13.5	19.5	23.6

Rather not	2.2	3.7	2.4	4.3
Absolutely not	1.4	2.0	0.7	0.6
Difficult to answer	1.3	1.4	0.6	1.9

7.7. 'Who did you feel like 4–5 years ago, before the events of the Maidan, the annexation of Crimea and the war in the East? At that time, did you feel European (valid %)'

	Dnipro (pro-decommun-isation group, N=296)	Dnipro ('Europeans', N=340)	Kharkiv (pro-decommun-isation group, N=161)	Kharkiv ('Europeans', N=254)
Absolutely yes	20.3	28.8	8.1	15.0
Rather yes	22.6	40.6	25.5	62.6
Rather no	28.4	18.5	42.9	16.5
Absolutely no	24.0	7.1	18.0	3.1
Difficult to answer	4.7	5.0	5.6	2.8

7.8. 'Do you think is it beneficial for Ukraine to become a member of NATO or of the European Union? (valid %)'

	Dnipro	Kharkiv
Yes, both NATO and European Union	28.2	11.7
Yes, NATO only	5.1	4.4
Yes, European Union only	12.1	14.8
No	36.6	55.7
Difficult to answer	17.4	13.4

7.9. To what extent do you agree or disagree with the following statements: ('Absolutely agree' + 'Rather agree', valid %)

	Dnipro (total)	Dnipro (pro-decommun-isation group, N=296)	Kharkiv (total)	Kharkiv (pro-decommun-isation group, N=161)
Ukraine must defend European values	43.6	72.3	26.4	72.0
Ukraine must defend Slavic values	83.9	76.4	80.4	74.4
The influence of Western Europe on Ukrainian culture is negative	39.5	16.9	44.1	29.8
The influence of Western Europe on Ukrainian way of life is positive	42.4	72.3	32.2	777
Russians and Ukrainians are one people	68.5	39.2	70.9	41.6

7.10. 'In general, the Soviet period was… ('Absolutely positive' + 'Rather positive', valid %)'

	Dnipro (total)	Dnipro (pro-Decommunisation group, N=296)	Kharkiv (total)	Kharkiv (pro-Decommunisation group, N=161)
For Dnipro / Kharkiv	64.0	53.7	66.7	50.3
For Ukraine	58.5	44.3	66.2	49.1
For Baltic countries	28.0	19.6	41.1	29.8

7.11. 'Opinion on the relative 'pro-Ukrainianness' of the residents of the neighbouring major cities, among Dniprovians and Kharkovians, respectively'

	The city of Dnipro is more pro-Ukrainian than Kharkiv or Zaporizhzhya (statement presented to Dnipro respondents)	The city of Kharkiv is more pro-Ukrainian than Dnipro (statement presented to Kharkiv respondents)
Absolutely yes	13.2	5.5
Rather yes	25.2	7.3
Rather no	21.0	20.3
Absolutely no	7.2	19.4
Difficult to answer	32.9	47.0

7.12. 'Percentage of Jews in Kharkiv and Dnipro [then Dnipropetrovsk] (%)'

Year	Kharkiv	Dnipropetrovsk
1926	19.45[25]	26.62[26]
1939	15.64[27]	17.88[28]

---

[25] 'Vsesiyuznaya perepis' naseleniya 1926 goda. Natsional'nyi sostav naseleniya po regionam respublik SSSR. Ukrainskaya SSR – Khar'kovskiy okrug – Gorodskiye poseleniya,' *Demoscope Weekly.* http://www.demoscope.ru/weekly/ssp/sng_nac_26.php?reg=2051

[26] 'Vsesiyuznaya perepis' naseleniya 1926 goda. Natsional'nyi sostav naseleniya po regionam respublik SSSR. Ukrainskaya SSR – Dnepropetrovskiy okrug – Gorodskiye poseleniya,' *Demoscope Weekly.* http://www.demoscope.ru/weekly/ssp/sng_nac_26.php?reg=2181

[27] 'Vsesiyuznaya perepis' naseleniya 1939 goda. Natsional'nyi sostav naseleniya rayonov, gorodov i krupnyh sel coyuznyh respublik SSSR. Khar'kovskaya oblast – Gorod Kharkov,' *Demoscope Weekly.* http://www.demoscope.ru/weekly/ssp/ussr_nac_39_ra.php?reg=480

[28] 'Vsesuyuznaya perepis naseleniya 1939 goda. Natsionalnyi sostav naseleniya rayonov, gorodov i krupnyh sel coyuznyh respublik SSSR. Dnepropetrovskaya oblast – Gorod, Dnepropetrovsk,' *Demoscope Weekly.* http://www.demoscope.ru/weekly/ssp/ussr_nac_39_ra.php?reg=80

References

Abramov, Roman. (2014). 'Vremia i prostranstvo nostalgii'. *Sotsiologicheskiy Zhurnal*, 4: 5–23.

Baumann, Zygmunt (2001) *The Individualized Society.* Cambridge: Polity Press.

Baumeister, Roy. (1986). *Identity. Cultural Change and Struggle for Self.* N. Y., Oxford.

Boiko, Natalia *et al.,* (1998). *Pravliacha elita Ukrainy. Analitychna dopovid N10* (Kyiv: Instytut sotsiolohii NAN Ukrayiny).

Bourdieu, Pierre. (1990). *In Other Words: Essays toward a Reflective Sociology* Stanford University Press.

Boym, Svetlana. (2002). *The Future of Nostalgia.* New York: Basic Books.

Brubaker, Rogers. (2002). 'Ethnicity without groups,' *European Journal of Sociology / Archives Européennes De Sociologie / Europäisches Archiv Für Soziologie,* 43, 2: 163–189.

Bystriakov, Aleksandr (2015). 'Khronika zhyzni evreiev Yekaterinoslava – Dnepropetrovska' In: *Almanac 'Yevreiskaya starina,'* 2 (85). http://berkovich-zametki.com/2015/Starina/Nomer2/Bystrjakov1.php

Buckholz, Quentin. (2019). 'The Dogs That Didn't Bark. Elite Preferences and the Failure of Separatism in Kharkiv and Dnipropetrovsk,' *Problems of Post-Communism*, 66, 3: 151–160.

Castells, Manuel. (1997). *The Power of Identity, The Information Age: Economy, Society and Culture, Vol. II* Cambridge, MA; Oxford, UK: Blackwell.

Chornyy, Dmytro. (2007). *Po livyy bik Dnipra: problem modernizatsii mist Ukrayiny (kinets XIX – pochatok XX st.).* Kharkiv: Kharkiv National University.

Gentile, Michael (2020) 'Diabolical Suggestions: Disinformation and the Curious Scale of Nationalism in Ukrainian Geopolitical Fault-line Cities,' *Geopolitics*, DOI: 10.1080/14650045.2020.1830766.

Giddens, Antony. (1991). *Modernity and Self-Identity. Self and Society in the Late Modern Age*. Cambridge: Polity Press.

Giddens, Antony. (1984). *The Constitution of Society. Outline of the Theory of Structuration* Cambridge: Polity Press.

Hayday, Oleksandra. (2018) *Kamyanyy hist. Pamyatnyky Leninu v Tsentralniy Ukrayini*. Kyiv, K.I.S.

Hromenko, Serhii. (2019) 'Dekomunizatsiya. Deradyanizatsiya? Dekolonizatsiya!' *Lokalna Istoriya*, 11 December. http://localhistory.org.ua/dekomunizatsiya-deradyanizatsiya-dekolonizatsiya-5-rokiv-pereosmyslennya-radyanskoyi-symvoliky/

Kachanov, Yuri and Shmatko, Natalia. (1996). 'Kak vozmozhna sotsial'naya gruppa? (k probleme real'nosti v sotsiologii),' *Sotsiologicheskiye Issledovaniya*, 12, 90–105.

Kazanskyy, Denys. (2015). 'Susidski viyny,' *Ukrayinsky Tyzhden*, 11 October 2015. https://tyzhden.ua/Politics/147621

Kravchenko, Volodymyr. (2019). 'Kharkiv: The Past Lives On', *The Soviet and Post-Soviet Review*, 46, 3: 324–351.

Kurina, Aksiniia. (2016). 'Istoryk Georgii Kasianov: Sposoby zdiysnennia dekomunizatsii nagaduiut' komunistychni praktyky,' *Ukrayinska Pravda. Zhyttya*, 7 May. https://life.pravda.com.ua/society/2016/05/7/211912/

Kuzio, Taras. (2019). *Viyna Putina Proty Ukrayiny. Revolutsiya, Natsionalism, i Kriminalitet*. Kyiv: Dukh i litera.

Marples, David. (2015). 'Open Letter from Scholars and Experts on Ukraine Re. the So-Called 'Anti-Communist Law,' *Krytyka*, April. https://krytyka.com/en/articles/open-letter-scholars-and-experts-ukraine-re-so-called-anti-communist-law

Musiyezdov, Oleksiy. (2007). 'V poshukah regionalnoi identychnosti (na prykladi doslidzhen studentiv-pershokursnykiv kharkivskyh vnz),'*Visnyk Lvivskoho Universytetu. Seriya Sotsiologichna*, 1, 11–21.

Musiyezdov, Oleksiy. (2012). 'Uyavlennia pro krayinu yak osnova hromadyanskoi identychnosti' In: Arbenina, Vera and Sokurianska, Ludmyla eds. *Ukrainske studentstvo u poshukah identychnosti*. Kharkiv: Kharkiv National University, 69–80.

Musiyezdov, Oleksiy. (2015). 'Multikulturnost goroda v globalnom obschestve: Primer Kharkova,' In: *Metodologiya, teoriya ta praktyka sotsiologichnogo analizu suchasnoho suspilstva: Zbirnyk naukovyh prats*. Kharkiv: Kharkiv National University, 167–173.

Musiyezdov, Oleksiy. (2016a). 'Identychnosti vs. Tsinnosti: Scho naspravdi poyasnuye Yevromaidan,' *Ukrayina Moderna*, 2 March. http://uamoderna.com/blogy/oleksi-musiezdov/identychnosti-vs-cinnosti

Musiyezdov, Oleksiy. (2016b). *Miska identicnist u (post)suchasnomu suspilstvi: ukrayinskyy dosvid*. Kharkiv: Kharkiv National University.

Nitsova, Silviya (2021) 'Why the Difference? Donbas, Kharkiv and Dnipropetrovsk After Ukraine's Euromaidan Revolution,' *Europe-Asia Studies*, 73, 10: 1832–1856.

Piechal, Tomasz. (2015). 'The Kharkiv oblast: a fragile stability,' *OSW Commentary*, 6 September. https://www.osw.waw.pl/en/publikacje/osw-commentary/2015-06-09/kharkiv-oblast-a-fragile-stability

Portnov, Andriy. (2015a). 'On Decommunisation, Identity, and Legislating History, From a Slightly Different Angle,' *Krytyka*, May. https://krytyka.com/en/solutions/opinions/decommunisation-identity-and-legislating-history-slightly-different-angle

Portnov, Andriy. (2015b). 'The Heart of Ukraine'? Dnipropetrovsk and the Ukrainian Revolution' In: Wilson, Andrew ed. *What does Ukraine think*. London: European Council on Foreign Relations, 62–70.

Portnov, Andriy. (2016). 'How 'eastern Ukraine' was lost,' *OpenDemocracy*, 14 January. https://www.opendemocracy.net/en/odr/how-eastern-ukraine-was-lost/

Portnova, Tetiana. (2012). 'Evolutsiya miskoho seredovyscha Katerynoslava kintsya XIX – pochatku XX st.,' *Historians.in.ua*, 20 February 2012. http://www.historians.in.ua/index.php/en/doslidzhennya/144-tetiana-portnova-evolyutsiya-miskoho-ser

Portnova, Tetiana. (2017). 'Tema 'zakrytoho mista v istorii radyanskoho Dniproprtrovska 1950-80-h rokiv,' *Historians.in.ua*, 11 December. http://www.historians.in.ua/index.php/en/doslidzhennya/2351-tetyana-portnova-tema-zakritogo-mista-v-istoriji-radyanskogo-dnipropetrovska-1950-80-kh-rokiv

Shevel, Oxana. (2016). 'Decommunisation in Post-Euromaidan Ukraine. Law and practice,' *PONARS Eurasia Policy Memos*, 411. http://www.ponarseurasia.org/memo/decommunisation-post-euromaidan-ukraine-law-and-practice

Solodko, Pavlo. (2012). 'Dnipropetrovsk. Yak opovisty istoriyu mista bez istorii,' *Istorychna Pravda*, 26 January. https://www.istpravda.com.ua/articles/2012/01/26/70102/

Stebelsky, Ihor. (2018). 'A tale of two regions: geopolitics, identities, narratives, and conflict in Kharkiv and the Donbas,' *Eurasian Geography and Economics*, 59, 1: 28–50.

Spitzer, Yannay. (2012). 'A New Map of Jewish Communities in the Russian Empire,' *Yannay Spitzer. Bits and Pieces of My Work and Interests*. 22 July. https://yannayspitzer.net/2012/07/22/a-new-map-of-jewish-communities-in-the-russian-empire/

Ukrainian Parliament. (2015). 'Law On Condemning the Communist and National Socialist (Nazi) Totalitarian Regimes and Prohibiting the Propagation of their Symbols.' https://zakon.rada.gov.ua/laws/show/317-19#Text

Vorona, Valerii and Shulha, Mykola eds. (2018). *Ukrayinske suspilstvo: monitorynh sotsiyalnykh zmin*, 6 (20). Kyiv: Instytut sotsiolohii NAN Ukrainy.

Yavorskyy, Volodymyr. (2015). 'Analiz zakonu pro zaboronu komunistychnyh symvoliv,' *Prava ludyny v Ukrayini. Informatsiynyy portal Kharkivskoi pravozahysnoyi hrupy*, 1 May. http://khpg.org/index.php?id=1430493970

Zhuk, Sergei, (2010). *Rock and Roll in the Rocket City: The West, Identity, and Ideology in Soviet Dniepropetrovsk, 1960–1985.* Washington DC and Baltimore, ML: Woodrow Wilson Centre Press and Johns Hopkins University Press.

Zhurzhenko, Tatiana. (2015). 'Ukraine's Eastern Borderlands: The end of ambiguity?' In: Andrew Wilson ed. *What does Ukraine think*. London: European Council on Foreign Relations, 45–52.

Zhurzhenko, T. (2017). 'The making and unmaking of revolutions. What 1917 means for Ukraine, in light of the Maidan,' *Eurozine*, 30 November. https://www.eurozine.com/the-making-and-unmaking-of-revolutions/

8

IDPs and the Media: What Shapes the Narratives on Internally Displaced People in Dnipro Media?

KOSTYANTYN MEZENTSEV AND EUGENIA KUZNETSOVA

Long thought of as unthinkable in Ukraine, the issue of IDPs suddenly appeared on the agenda during the 2014 crisis. Scholarly literature and the media firstly looked on their lives and problems through the lens of temporariness. However, when displacement lasts longer than five years, it is worth looking deeper into this issue through the perspective of protracted displacement, not only through issues of survival and coping strategies, but considering the refusal to return and (forced or conscious) integration with a view to a long-term coexistence in their new environment. Although like Georgia (Brun, 2016), which suffered from two internal wars in South Ossetia and Abkhazia, Ukrainian society strives to maintain people with their IDP status because their existence and possible return to the Donbas symbolises the hope of regaining control over occupied territories.

'The problem of internal displacement in Ukraine cannot be explained in pure numbers' and 'should not be understood in terms of a simplistic model of positive-negative attitudes towards the IDPs in host communities' (Ivashchenko-Stadnik 2017, 42). This is a much more complicated and confusing problem. Although most displaced people are of the same ethnicity and religion as the host society, at the same time, some IDPs and media represent them as a specific, different group of 'Donbas people' who have their own 'Donetsk character', 'Donbas spirit' and even dialect. Moreover, IDPs from the Donbas are not homogeneous, but a rather diverse group demographically, economically, and in their geopolitical attitudes.

Media play an essential role in the construction and reproduction of the refugees' (as well as IDPs) narratives (Kwansah-Aidoo and Mapedzahama 2015), and shape attitudes and responsibilities towards IDPs (Šarić 2019). Using frames with a set of framing devices (metaphors, catchphrases, visual images, lexical choices, selection of sources, graphics, stereotypes, and dramatic character) (Van Gorp 2005), mass media select some aspects of IDPs' issues and make them more salient (Entman 1993). These IDPs' media representations are not consensual, but rather contested and not mutually independent, sharing a common hostility and hospitality themes (Leudar, Hayes, Nekvapil, and Turner Baker 2008). Several studies have proven the feasibility of using the concept of frames to analyse the representation of forced migrants' issues. While using the concept of agenda-setting one could answer the question of what is represented in the media about IDPs by the framing concept going beyond answering this question which may shed light on audience perceptions of a certain group (Kwansah-Aidoo 2005; Kwansah-Aidoo and Mapedzahama 2015; Pan and Kosicki 1993). This leads us to discuss the representation of IDPs in Dnipro media through the lens of frames.

Internal displacement is directed mainly to urban areas where there is a so-called 'flight to the cities' of 'crisis migrants' (Fagen 2014). This trend actualises the problem of rethinking urban policy and its revision in terms of considering the new urban actor. At the same time, it significantly complicates the profiling of IDPs because they are not readily identifiable in new urban settings (Davies and Jacobsen 2010). The actual number of IDPs in urban areas is extremely difficult to ascertain (Guterres 2010), making it difficult to understand their problems beyond those circulating in the media, such as housing, employment, and state support.

While national media receive a bigger audience, local media gain more weight during crises when communities feel their daily life is affected by the decisions of local authorities. The ongoing coronavirus pandemic illustrates this trend where communities want to know local developments and therefore tend to consume local media (Media Development Foundation 2020). Moreover, national media are less interested in portraying the lived experiences of the displaced (Rimpiläinen 2020). The IDPs' crisis affected certain regions more than others, including Dnipro, where local media covered IDP issues more actively.

Local television channels and online media are the most trusted types of regional media (41 per cent and 44 per cent respectively), while local printed media are only trusted by 20 per cent of respondents. Every third Ukrainian watches regional television news. Participants of focus-groups conducted in

2019 found regional and national media to be equally important (USAID 2019). Thus, our chapter seeks to define the narratives in reporting on IDPs by local television channels in Dnipro and identify the media frames which are used for selecting and emphasising issues faced by IDPs.

IDPs in Dnipro

More than 45 per cent of all IDPs in Dnipropetrovsk oblast are concentrated in the city of Dnipro — 32.5 thousand (as of early 2020). Compared to residents, their share is insignificant at 33 IDPs per 1,000 inhabitants. Almost a third of IDPs in Dnipro (32 per cent) are retirees and another 17 per cent are children.

There are two places of collective residence of IDPs in the city which include a 'transit town' (fully inhabited) and a reconstructed building of the Regional Dermatological and Venereological Dispensary (less than half inhabited) with a total capacity of over 400 places. Three more reconstructed buildings were previously planned for IDPs accommodation, but there was no demand for them.

Slightly more than 1 per cent of all IDPs live in collective centres (362 inhabitants, 30 per cent of these are children). That is, almost 99 per cent of the IDPs are scattered throughout the city of Dnipro. Their distribution roughly corresponds to the distribution of the overall population of the city, according to the Ministry for Reintegration of the Temporary Occupied Territories.

IDPs in the Local Media: Salience and Silence

Involving selection and salience (Entman 1993), media framing affects populations by stressing certain aspects of reality and pushing others into the background (Lecheler and de Vreese 2012). This generates public support in favour of or condemnation of the related policy (Van Gorp 2005) and makes some of IDPs issues more accessible, visible, or salient to the public (Joris and De Cock 2019). Moreover, the media not only select some of the topics they report on, but also define the way they cover them when it comes to news angle and tones (Joris and De Cock 2019). Media can influence the importance people attach to important issues (Iyengar 2013).

Greg Philo (2013) identified several key themes (or frames) in the media coverage which are pursued in the news when covering asylum seekers in the United Kingdom. These include (1) conflation of forced and economic migration; (2) numbers and exaggeration; (3) burden on welfare and job market; (4) criminality; (5) threats; (6) deportation and human rights; (7) need for 'immigration control;' (8) benefits of immigration; (9) problems facing asylum seekers; (10) global capitalism; and (11) imperialism and Western responsibility (Philo 2013, 56–57). To some extent these frames explain the representation of IDPs in the media. However, we propose talking about three groups of frames in terms of reflecting upon IDP issues.

The first group are of ordinary frames of commonplace issues; that is, the issues discussed in any city where forced migrants appear, including IDPs. Firstly, these frames represent housing, employment, and state support. The second group is one of contrasting frames of IDPs stigmatisation, victimisation or even heroisation, which represent them either as victims or as threats and encourage either hostility or hospitality of the local community towards IDPs. The third is peripheral frames of hidden, latent, and overlooked IDPs' issues. These frames represent IDPs' personal experiences and aspirations, individual problems, dreams, and intentions. They are peripheral in relation to the occasional, vague, or imperceptible appearances in the media on the backdrop of more pronounced and more covered issues.

Earlier reports on media coverage of IDPs in Ukraine showed a range of problematic issues related to their media framing which included statistical narration, lack of comprehensive material for the audience, identification of issues, but not addressing them (Spilnyy Prostir 2015). While the media used correct terminology and the tone of publications was mostly neutral, the reports about IDPs lacked long-term vision and an analytical approach (Spilnyy Prostir 2016). Mass media, when covering IDPs, tend to focus on statistical data and politicise the issue with instances of spreading stereotypes and prejudices (Buromensky et al 2016, 43). Monitoring reports from other contexts show that the media tend to avoid negative content related to IDPs (for instance, abuses at the camps for IDPs in Nigeria (Isola and Yusuf 2019) and recommended that journalists devote a greater amount of space to IDPs to voice their problems, not just flagging the hardships they experience (Journalists for Christ 2019).

Ordinary Frames: Housing, Jobs and Social Support

IDPs moving to new locations primarily face the problems of searching for housing, jobs and social support, problems which are understandable to policymakers and journalists. Therefore, these receive a greater amount of attention in the media. Media headlines related to IDPs' housing, employment and state support are commonplace and sporadically appear in the local media. Such news is usually focused on temporary housing for IDPs, high cost of housing rents, difficulties in obtaining jobs and social assistance. As

Bulakh (2017) noted, the areas that were the first in portraying a negative image of IDPs were in the real estate and labour markets (Bulakh 2017).

A World Bank report on IDPs in Georgia concluded there are no significant differences in poverty levels between IDPs and non-IDPs; however, differences persist in unemployment and income security for IDPs. Poor housing conditions are the main source of vulnerability for IDPs, and IDPs are more acutely affected by unemployment than non-IDPs living in the same area (World Bank 2015).

Media reports more often focus on collective centres accommodating IDPs which are the most visible form of their dwellings (Brun 2016). A shortage of housing and job prospects has kept them in these 'long-term temporary' housing (Dean 2017). To a certain degree, public attitudes to IDPs and their behaviour and memories are affected by these official narratives, including those voiced by the media (Toria 2015).

Karine Torosyan et al (2018) noted that although labour market outcomes for IDPs are discussed in many policy papers, these are largely descriptive in nature and there are relatively few academic papers on this topic (Torosyan, Pignatti, and Obrizan 2018). However, there are significant disadvantages in the labour market outcomes for IDPs because sometimes they stay unemployed longer compared to locals with similar characteristics even after many years of being displaced (Kondylis 2010; Torosyan et al 2018).

IDPs rely on the assistance of governmental and non-governmental organisations in obtaining social assistance. The social capital of IDPs primarily depends on their relatives or kin and their network of relationships rather than on governmental and non-governmental organisations (Collado 2019). In addition to the socio-economic problems of housing, employment and state support, academic literature and media raise other issues, such as finding that civil conflicts and displacement significantly reduced school attendance and grade completion and affected the mental and physical health of IDPs (Minoiu and Shemyakina 2012; Shemyakina 2006; Siriwardhana and Stewart 2013).

Contrasting Frames: Stigma versus Victims

Another strand of media reports concerns stigmatisation of displaced people, their 'criminalising', presenting them as undesirable, a social threat (Bulakh 2017) or 'failed citizens' (Diken and Laustsen 2005), or alternatively, as victims and heroes (Scarabicchi 2019). Media reports mostly contrast positive and negative attitudes towards IDPs in a 'black versus white' (Joris and De

Cock 2019) and victim-frame versus the intruder-frame (Van Gorp 2005). They rarely represent IDPs simultaneously as victims and perpetrators (Ivashchenko-Stadnik 2017) or threats, and victims (d'Haenens, Willem, and Heinderyckx 2019).

The phenomenon of the shaping and reinforcing of negative attitude to IDPs in the mass media and the production of multiple forms of anxiety and anger have received significant attention in scholarly literature (see Horton and Kraftl 2014). IDPs living in collective centres, stigmatised to some extent (Brun 2016), have received particular attention from the media. They are mostly represented as dwellers of sub-standard housing situated in 'non-places' on the city's edge, as 'failed citizens' or even 'enemies' (Diken and Laustsen 2005). Moreover, this type of media coverage further isolates and stigmatises them (Philo 2013).

If IDPs appear, they are traditionally viewed in terms of the threat of conflict and are linked to a growth in crime and even the risk of foreign invasion. Bulakh (2017) emphasises that prejudiced and stereotyped categorisation of IDPs from the Donbas as a social threat is a growing tendency in Ukrainian media. This is based on a deep stereotype of 'an industrial, underprivileged, and criminal environment' and a widely circulated myth in the media that crime from the Donbas has 'followed IDPs to other regions' (Bulakh 2017). IDPs may inadvertently, directly, or indirectly contribute as both victims and agents to the spreading of conflict to other 'peaceful' regions (Bohnet, Cottier, and Hug 2018; Muggah 2010). They are an easy target because they are concentrated and vulnerable (Lischer 2008).

But in other cases, positive media coverage of IDPs evoke emotion and sympathy, activating private individuals to assist them (Tyyskä, Blower, Deboer, Kawai, and Walcott 2018). To prevent negative associations and stigmatisation, and not to be in the 'media spotlight', IDPs who can afford to move not to the temporary collective centres (such as the so-called transit towns in Ukrainian cities), but to gated communities within city limits and in suburbia. Thus, the polarisation of IDPs can be observed between two different types of gated camps.

Peripheral Frames: Temporariness, Social Networking and Trauma

Visible problems of officially registered IDPs who receive state support in housing, employment and social assistance appear frequently in the media. However, a significant 'multi-layered pie' of the problems of invisible IDPs who solve their own problems are often overlooked. These 'layers' include 'permanent temporariness' and 'double temporariness' (Brun, 2000 2016), their 'hybridity' and 'shuttling' displacement (Ivashchenko-Stadnik 2017), self-generated social networking, and everyday emotional-affective impact of the trauma they experienced (Horton and Kraftl 2014).

Naohiko Omata (2019) describes selection bias concerning research on IDPs who did not receive sufficient and adequate attention from academics, domestic and international aid organisations, students, and journalists. While the 'over-researched' IDPs are increasingly distrustful and decline to participate in further studies because they have not seen any improvement in their life, the 'under-researched' IDPs remain under the media radar and their voices are less audible in the global (and especially urban) arena (Omata 2019).

Less visible self-settled IDPs who live with relatives and friends or rent dwellings (so called 'privately accommodated IDPs') have less access to social assistance and protection and they represent a heterogeneous group about whom we know very little (Brun 2016). Moving reluctantly from dwelling to dwelling, they have experienced a 'double temporariness' with temporary status as IDPs and temporary lives in the dwellings they occupy (Brun 2016). Moreover, protracted displacement or 'permanent temporariness' (Brun 2000 2016) of IDPs can be understood as a kind of 'normal abnormality' (Mcintyre 2002) at a time when public interest in their problems is decreasing. Meanwhile, temporary displaced dwellers increasingly solve problems on their own.

It is difficult to unambiguously assess the social impact and attitudes to 'shuttling IDPs' who are registered as displaced persons to receive social assistance, but at the same time have no will power to rent accommodation, search for jobs in their new locations or to leave Russian-controlled territories in the Donbas (Ivashchenko-Stadnik 2017). Therefore, the media sometimes prefer to not raise these issues. It is difficult to understand IDPs' 'hybridity' of both being displaced without gaining an official status and having an official status but not being displaced (Ivashchenko-Stadnik 2017).

Social networks, being underrepresented in public media, play a key role in the daily life of IDPs and solve a range of their problems. On the one hand, several studies have emphasised the more important role of mutual assistance of IDPs through internal social networks, especially relatives and friends, as a coping strategy (Collado 2019; Ivashchenko-Stadnik 2017). On the other hand, the loss of established connections and to some extent the closeness and inaccessibility of local networks for (unwanted) newcomers, forces them to rely only on themselves or to disguise their IDP status. Some of them prefer to not be recognised as IDPs, suggesting that such a status excludes them from full membership in the hosting community as temporary stayers (Brun 2016). This invisibility may be not only an obstacle but also an alternative coping strategy (Montemurro and Walicki 2010).

To some extent, the media pay more attention to the problems of female IDPs who often experience violence and mental health problems, such as traumatic stress disorder and depression (Roberts, Ocaka, Browne, Oyok, and Sondorp 2008). Research findings show that employment and poverty affect men and women equally. Moreover, Peter Kabachnik et al (2013) highlights the issue of 'traumatic masculinities'. Studies of IDPs from Georgia's Abkhazian region emphasised that men experienced trauma through their inability to improve their poor living conditions and to provide prospects for a better life in the future, and as consequently they would lose their privileged status as the head of the household (Kabachnik et al 2013). The same can be seen for male displaced persons from the Donbas. Traditionally, men who work hard in coal mines and industrial plants are unquestionably perceived as breadwinners. Women are becoming more active in addressing family issues and more present in official and unofficial media while men are losing their visibility (Brun, 2000; Kabachnik et al 2013).

Urban Turn

Even though displaced people tend to concentrate in urban areas (Christensen and Harild 2009) 'the question of IDPs' is largely considered as a nationwide question, and responsibility for resolving it therefore belongs to the national government (Albuja & Ceballos 2010; Su 2010). As a result of this, local media represent IDPs as a nationwide phenomenon who are temporarily affecting their city. However, urban displacement has clearly localised effects and municipal administrations have become front-line actors (Guterres 2010). Paraphrasing Rick Su (2010), IDPs issues matter to urban policymakers and urban issues matter to IDPs policymakers. Therefore, an 'urban turn' in media analysis can lead to an understanding of IDPs issues more adequately and be helpful for all stakeholders in urban development.

Most of Dnipro's residents have limited contacts with IDPs, both because of their small share in the city population and because they do not to want to stand out among others and attract too much attention. Media are the main source of information on IDPs for locals (Joris and De Cock 2019) and local media play an important role in 'projecting' IDPs' issues to the city.

The media use their influence on the interpretation of some processes and problems by emphasising specific frames and downplaying others (Gamson and Modigliani 1989; Joris and De Cock 2019). At the city level this is more visible when media emphasise frames to interpret these problems according to desirable (for certain political forces) urban policy. This allows for an understanding of opposition to or cooperation with various urban development actors, not only on IDPs but more broadly on the public opinion about the effectiveness of resolving urban problems.

Methods

To analyse the media coverage of IDPs in Dnipro we selected three local television channels controlled by Ukrainian oligarchs (IMI 2017). Channel 9 is tied with the Privat group controlled by former governor of Dnipro Ihor Kolomoyskyy (Forbes 2020a) and Hennadiy Boholyubov; channel 11 is owned by Viktor Pinchuk's Star Light Media (Forbes 2020c); and Rinat Akhmetov's Systems Capital Management has a majority (68 per cent) stake in Channel 34 (Forbes 2020b). The three television channels have traditionally been considered the most influential in Dnipropetrovsk oblast (Kurbatov 2018).

For our analysis, we collected a total of 168 reports which included 52 from channel 9, 19 from channel 11 and 95 from channel 34. Our sample includes both video material and texts published by the websites of the three channels between December 2016 and July 2020 and containing the lexeme 'IDPs' in plural referring to IDPs as a group. The lexeme is identical in the Ukrainian and Russian language as *'переселенц'*. Search tools allowed us to ignore endings which were different in Ukrainian (*переселенці*) and Russian (*переселенцы*) enabling us to collect publications mentioning IDPs in both languages. We used integrated search tools on the websites of the three television channels.

For encoding the collected content, a codebook was developed (see Annex 1). Apart from its basic characteristics (headline, link, dates) a coder had to define the topic of a news item choosing between seven available options: (1) accommodation and housing; (2) employment: (3) state support; (4) human rights; (5) charity; (6) personal stories; and (7) others. A coder also had to indicate whether the news story included direct quotes by IDPs (yes or no) and define whether IDPs were represented as a proactive group, or they lacked agency (yes or no).

Intercoder reliability was measured based on the formula and procedure proposed by Stephen Lacy and Daniel Riffe (1996). For 95 per cent level of probability and the sample size of 64 units, the coder agreement was 95.3 per cent higher than the assumed level of agreement of 90 per cent.

IDPs in the Local Media: Key Topics

The largest share of publications about IDPs concerned charity efforts (28 per cent) provided by international support, local initiatives, concerts, food, or supply of medicines. This share was greatest at Channel 34 where 40 per cent of publications mentioned Akhmetov's charity fund. The oligarch's name was mostly mentioned in quotes by IDPs who thanked him for medicine, housing or covering other needs. Interestingly, the IDPs thanked 'Rinat Leonidovich' personally, not the fund in general. Such news stories normally followed a certain structure of the description of a problem faced by an IDP which Akhmetov's fund had assisted in resolving followed by a direct quote by an IDP who thanked Akhmetov. Akhmetov's fund is sometimes mentioned in the headlines and the fund's visibility are featured in photos and videos. The other two channels did not mention charity initiatives by their oligarch beneficiaries.

Other leading topics were housing, employment, and state support for the IDPs which comprised half of all the publications in the sample. Housing (19 per cent) was the most pressing issue with media attention higher when it came to large-scale construction projects in the region. The topic of employment (13 per cent) was mostly represented by announcements or media reports about courses for IDPs aimed at improving their chances to find employment. The topic of state support (18 per cent) gave instructions on how to apply for social allowances for IDPs or provided details of local budgets. Several publications also provided stories about fraud committed by IDPs who did not have the right to receive social allowances. Channels 9 and 11 paid greater attention to the topics of housing, employment, and state support (e.g., every fourth publication about IDPs on channel 9 dealt with state support) compared to channel 34 which was more focused on charity efforts, especially those funded by Akhmetov.

The least reported topic in local media was human and citizen's rights (4 per cent), including their right to vote, rights of disabled people, children's rights, integration in local communities and other related issues. Personal stories of IDPs who escaped the war (11 per cent) also did not receive enough media attention.

Overall, the distribution of topics clearly showed the lack of empowering stories related to IDPs which concurred with previous reports of media coverage of IDPs in Ukraine. While there are instances of human-based stories, the media mostly analyse statistics and describe the issues without addressing them.

Representation of IDPs

More than a half of the publications in the sample (52 per cent) had no quotes by IDPs. This meant the materials did not directly quote representatives of IDPs or mention their interests or problems in general. Without quotes from individuals the stories did not have a 'face' and were impersonalised. IDPs are mainly mentioned as a faceless group accepting a helping hand. Based on media representations, they do not demand anything and passively accept what they are offered by donors, charity funds and the local authorities. Earlier monitoring of Ukrainian media also highlighted the problem of not quoting IDPs in their reports, documenting that while the coverage itself was presented neutrally, the IDPs or other sources were never quoted. Instead, the reports focused on official statements (Spilnyi Prostir 2015).

Journalists tend to cover certain topics related to IDPs almost without giving voice to the group. For instance, 81 per cent of the publications dealing with state support did not quote IDPs. In a video material aired on channel 11 about the regional forum 'Headline: Problems of IDPs were discussed at a regional forum at Regional State Administration' (Channel 11 2016a), IDPs were mentioned as a group and their problems were commented on by a local official and the Head of the Council of Europe office in Ukraine. The IDPs themselves, despite being present at the forum, did not voice their problems and remained faceless. Instead, officials discussed how to 'improve the life of IDPs and defend their rights.' Channel 34 demonstrated a similar approach when it reported that the State Regional Administration and the University of the Ministry of Internal Affairs 'will work together on the problems of IDPs,' seeking to emphasise how donors care about IDPs while at the same time ignoring the voice of the group.

Only 14 per cent of the publications mentioned IDPs as proactive people who were making efforts to improve their situation. The remainder of the publications (86 per cent) represented IDPs as supplicants who received state support and sought assistance. Obviously, most of the news stories (58 per cent) representing IDPs as a proactive group dealt with their personal stories. At the same time, 98 per cent of news stories covering charity initiatives represented IDPs as passive receivers of assistance. The local media probably do not view IDPs as headline stories of interest to their viewers and therefore they mainly covered charity initiatives.

IDPs were often mentioned along with other vulnerable groups or people in need. A typical news story about IDPs and charity initiatives stated that someone donated assistance to IDPs, such as along the lines of children of IDPs, orphans and students at a Sunday school received presents from the

Ukrainian Perspective Fund (Channel 34 2016). There were no stories and there was no background given about these children. The approach of channel 34 to charity materials was more sophisticated with IDPs given a voice and more background provided about their life story. Even when it came to employment and educational opportunities created for IDPs, students are still represented as receiving assistance. They remain passive even in the rare publications where IDPs are represented as a proactive group, such as 'active IDPs are taught how to start a business' (Channel 11 2016b). In publications where IDPs are represented as lacking agency, their passivity is even more common, with 'IDPs are left on their own' and 'IDP-teenagers will be sent to a summer camp' (Channel 34 2019).

The distribution of topics showed that local Dnipro media do not invest enough effort and resources into telling personal stories of IDPs or by humanising news reports with statistics and official events. IDPs often remain voiceless and faceless in media reports concerning their problems. Even when the news reports contain quotes by IDPs they still often represent them as a passive group in need of assistance.

Local media in Dnipro primarily represent IDPs as a vulnerable social group in need of housing, jobs, and state support. The contrasting frames of stigmatisation and 'heroisation', hostility and hospitality towards IDPs are less clearly traced. Finally, in the local media, peripheral frames are almost absent. Instead, the problems faced by IDPs are represented through the lens of they can be solved with the help of 'wealthy patrons' (i.e., oligarchs) who care about the city and newcomers to emphasise the importance of the principle 'we don't leave our people behind.'

Media coverage plays a key role in the construction of socially shared understandings and dominant representations (Tyyskä et al 2018) of IDPs in Dnipro. Based on media representation analysis, we identified four aspects of the imposition of the perception of IDPs to the city's residents. These included:

1. Attempting to persuade locals to perceive IDPs as a group of forced migrants as in any other city which faces typical problems of housing, employment, and social assistance.
2. Encouraging the city's residents to think about IDPs with gratitude towards a 'true lord of the city' who took care of solving their problems so that locals do not need to worry about them.
3. Exerting influence on locals to shift their focus from the IDPs as a part of their city and their neighbours to routine problems by emphasising this was not a specific issue for this city, there are already those who care about IDPs, or that the city has more urgent problems.

Encouraging residents to perceive IDPs collectively not as individuals with their own aspirations, intentions, dreams, and desires, but rather to perceive them within the framework of victim-threat which reduced them to a (temporarily) suffering, anonymous population (Smets, Mazzocchetti, Gerstmans, and Mostmans 2019), who could threaten the life of the city through greater risks of crime. The capabilities and future of IDPs with skills, ambitions, and dreams of their own (d'Haenens, Willem, and Heinderyckx 2019; Smets et al 2019) are thus ignored.

Conclusions

While media did not openly discriminate against IDPs and they use neutral language, our analysis mostly focused on pressing issues in a descriptive way, not by trying to address them. Among the leading local media topics are housing, employment, and state support for the IDPs while exaggerated attention is paid to charity efforts. Local media are biased and provide a bigger stage for oligarchs than for ordinary people. They cover IDP issues as a group receiving benefits, largely ignoring deeper issues such as their human rights, adaptation and trauma and the question of a sense of belonging. More than half of the analysed publications did not give voice to IDPs in any form and reports did not directly quote representatives of the group while mentioning their interests or problems.

The local media in Dnipro overwhelmingly use ordinary frames, while the contrasting frames are less clearly traced and peripheral frames are overlooked. Instead, the frame of charity is widely used by local media and abused by media owners. Media reports demonstrate that the analysed television channels are biased and dependant on (local) political elites, especially when it comes to Channel 34. They do not look for solutions to the urgent and hidden problems of IDPs. Thus, local media in Dnipro represent IDPs in more traditional ways as lacking deeper insight into their hidden problems and not providing outlets for the voices of invisible displaced persons. If they are proactive enough, they could act on a do-it-yourself basis, otherwise, their integration into their new home will remain a spontaneous process with unknown consequences and unforeseeable results.

Further research should focus upon the assessment of the impact of media frames on city residents' opinions about IDPs and their issues. Television reports bring attention to some aspects while obscuring others and may lead to different reactions among audiences (Entman 1993), sometimes unexpected. While identifying these reactions could deepen understanding of their problems.

In the city of Dnipro, one can find graffiti devoted to IDPs with the words: 'Home is not where you live, but where you are understood.' Do the local media aim to hear the voices of IDPs and understand them? Not very much. By and large, they stay within the predefined frames of IDPs' coverage. What will home mean to them in the future? Where will they be understood? This depends not only on geopolitical intrigues and national policy, but also on the reports in local media targeted at host communities.

Figures

8.1 Topic distribution of publications about IDPs in the three television channels

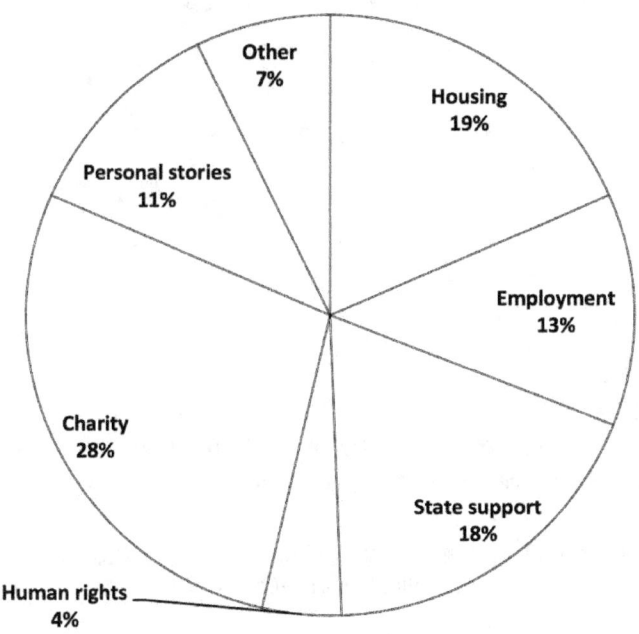

8.2. Topic distribution by television channels

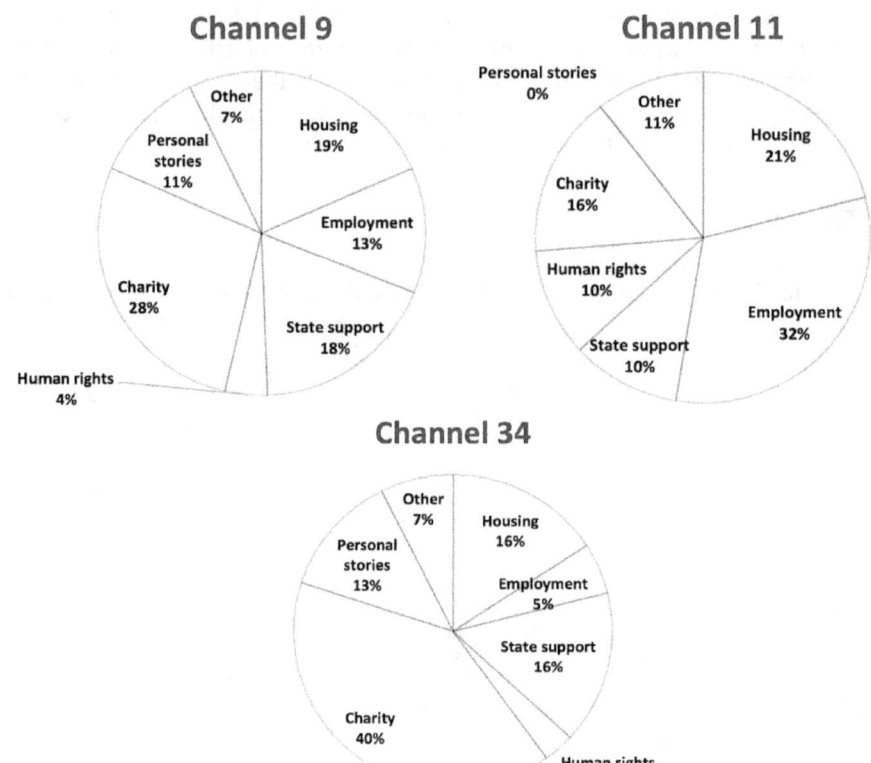

References

Albuja, Sebastion., & Ceballos, Marcela. (2010). 'Urban displacement and migration in Colombia.' *Forced Migration Review*, 34, 10–11.

Bohnet, Heidrun., Cottier, Fabien., & Hug, Simon. (2018). 'Conflict-induced IDPs and the Spread of Conflict.' *Journal of Conflict Resolution*, 62, 4: 691–716.

Brun, Cathrine. (2000). 'Spatial practices of integration and segregation among internally displaced persons and their hosts in Sri Lanka.' *Norsk Geografisk Tidsskrift*, 54, 3: 96–101.

Brun, Cathrine. (2016). 'Dwelling in The Temporary: The involuntary mobility of displaced Georgians in rented accommodation.' *Cultural Studies*, 30, 3: 421–440.

Bulakh, Tania. (2017). "Strangers Among Ours': State and Civil Responses to the Phenomenon of Internal Displacement in Ukraine' In: Agnieszka Pikulicka-Wilczewska & Greta Uehling eds., *Migration, and the Ukraine Crisis. E-International Relations Publishing*. Bristol, England: E-International Relations Publishing, 49–61.

Buromensky, Mykhaylo, Shturkhetsky, Serhiy, Beals, Emma, Kazanji, Zoya, Betz, Michelle, and Schuepp, Chris. (2016). *Conflict sensitive journalism: best practices and recommendations*. Oxford: Refugee Studies Centre. https://www.osce.org/files/f/documents/8/b/254526.pdf

Channel 11. (2016a). 'Na regionalnomu forumi v ODA obhovoriuvaly probleny pereselentsiv'. https://11tv.dp.ua/news/dp/20160714-26964.html, 14 July.

Channel 11. (2016b). 'U Dnipropetrovsku aktyvnykh pereselentsiv vchat, iak vidkryty svii bisness'. https://11tv.dp.ua/news/dp/20160105-26339.html, 5 January.

Channel 34. (2016). 'Na Dnepropetrovshchine podarki ot Fonda 'Ukrainskaia perspektiva' ko Dniu Sviatogo Nikolaia poluchili vospitanniki voskresnoi shkoly, deti-siroty i deti iz semei pereselentsev, 20 December. https://34.ua/na-dnepropetrovshchine-podarki-ot-fonda-ukrainskaya-perspektiva-ko-dnyu-svyatogo-nikolaya-poluchili-vospitanniki-voskresnoj-shkoly-deti-siroty-i-deti-iz-semej-pereselencev_n53436

Channel 34. (2019). 'Sotniu podrostkov-pereselentsev besplatno otpraviat na otdukh v ozdorovitelnyi lager,' 17 May. https://34.ua/sotnyu-podrostkov-pereselencev-besplatno-otpravyat-na-otdyh-v-ozdorovitelnyj-lager_n77126

Christensen, Asger, & Harild, Niels. (2009). *Forced displacement: the development challenge. Conflict, crime, and violence issue note*. Washington, DC: World Bank. https://openknowledge.worldbank.org/handle/10986/27717?locale-attribute=es

Collado, Zaldy, C. (2019). 'Living in displacement context: Coping strategies, changing attitudes and family dynamics among Internally Displaced Persons (IDPs) in Mindanao, Philippines.' *Journal of Human Behavior in the Social Environment*, 29, 4: 484–498.

Davies, Anne, & Jacobsen, Karen. (2010). 'Profiling urban IDPs.' *Forced Migration Review*, 34: 13–15. https://www.alnap.org/system/files/content/resource/files/main/davies-profiling-urban-idps-.pdf

Dean, Laura, A. (2017). 'Repurposing shelter for displaced people in Ukraine.' *Forced Migration Review*, 55: 49–55. https://www.fmreview.org/shelter/dean

Diken, Bulent, & Laustsen, Carsten, B. (2005). *The culture of exception: Sociology facing the camp. The Culture of Exception: Sociology Facing the Camp*. London: Routledge.

Entman, Robert, M. (1993). 'Framing: Toward Clarification of a Fractured Paradigm.' *Journal of Communication*, 43, 4: 51–58.

Fagen, Patricia, W. (2014). 'Flight to the cities.' *Forced Migration Review*, 45: 14–17. https://www.fmreview.org/crisis/weissfagen

Forbes. (2020a). 'Ihor Kolomoyskyy,' September. https://www.forbes.com/profile/ihor-kolomoyskyy/#1ef0df9f51dc

Forbes. (2020b). 'Rinat Akhmetov,' September. https://www.forbes.com/profile/rinat-akhmetov/#6333e88424fa

Forbes. (2020c). 'Victor Pinchuk,' September. https://www.forbes.com/profile/victor-pinchuk/

Gamson, William, A., and Modigliani, Andre. (1989). 'Media discourse and public opinion on nuclear power. A constructionist approach.' *American Journal of Sociology*, 95, 1: 1–37.

Guterres, Antonio. (2010). 'Protection challenges for persons of concern in urban settings.' *Forced Migration Review*, 34: 8–9.

Horton, John, & Kraftl, Peter. (2014). *Cultural Geographies: An Introduction*. New York: Routledge.

IMI. (2017). *Khto vplyvaye na ZMI Dnipra*, 27 April. https://imi.org.ua/articles/hto-vplivae-na-zmi-dnipra-i147

Isola, Olusola and Yusuf, Toba. (2019). 'Assessment of Media Coverage of Human Rights Abuses in Internally Displaced Peoples' Camps' In: Ibrahim Seaga and Senth Selvarajah eds., *Reporting Human Rights, Conflicts, and Peacebuilding*. Basel: Springer International Publishing, 137–152.

Ivashchenko-Stadnik, Kateryna. (2017). 'The Social Challenge of Internal Displacement in Ukraine: The Host Community's Perspective' In: A. Pikulicka-Wilczewska and G. Uehling eds., *Migration, and the Ukraine Crisis*. Bristol, England: E-International Relations Publishing, 25–48. https://www.e-ir.info/publication/migration-and-the-ukraine-crisis-a-two-country-perspective/

Iyengar, Shanto. (2013). *Is Anyone Responsible? How Television Frames Political Issues*. Chicago: University of Chicago Press.

Joris, W. and De Cock, Rozane. (2019). 'The Effects of Dominant versus Peripheral News Frames on Attitudes toward Refugees and News Story Credibility' In: L. D'Haenens, W. Joris, and F. Heinderyckx eds., *Images of Immigrants and Refugees in Western Europe. Media Representations, Public Opinion and Refugees' Experiences*. Leuven: Leuven University, 159–174.

Journalists for Christ. (2019). *Monitoring media reportage and portrayal of Internally Displaced Persons (IDPs) in Africa*. https://new.waccglobal.org/wp-content/uploads/wacc-global/Images/Articles/2019/08aug/MonitoringMediaReportageandPortrayalofIDPSin Africa.pdf

Kabachnik, Peter, Grabowska, Magdalena, Regulska, Joanna, Mitchneck, Beth, and Mayorova, Olga V. (2013). 'Traumatic masculinities: the gendered geographies of Georgian IDPs from Abkhazia.' *Gender, Place and Culture*, 20, 6: 773–793.

Kondylis, Florence. (2010). 'Conflict displacement and labor market outcomes in post-war Bosnia and Herzegovina.' *Journal of Development Economics*, 93, 2: 235–248.

Kurbatov, Oleksandr. (2018). 'Televiziina revoliutsiia u Dnipri: novi kanaly ta stari interesy,' *Detektor Media*, 12 November. https://detector.media/rinok/article/142512/2018-11-12-televiziina-revolyutsiya-u-dnipri-novi-kanali-ta-stari-interesi/

Kwansah-Aidoo, Kwamena. (2005). 'Prospects for agenda-setting research in the 21st century' In: K. Kwansah-Aidoo ed., *Topical issues in communications and media research*. Huntington, NY: Nova Science, 35–60.

Kwansah-Aidoo, K., and Mapedzahama, Virginia. (2015). 'Media Event, Racial Ramblings, or Both? An Analysis of Media Coverage of the Tamworth Council Sudanese Refugees Resettlement Case (2006),' *SAGE Open*, 5 (4). https://doi.org/10.1177/2158244015621600

Lacy, Stephen, and Riffe, Daniel. (1996). 'Sampling Error and Selecting Intercoder Reliability Samples for Nominal Content Categories.' *Journalism & Mass Communication Quarterly*, 73, 4: 963–973.

Lecheler, Sophie, and de Vreese, Claes, H. (2012). 'News Framing and Public Opinion: A Mediation Analysis of Framing Effects on Political Attitudes.' *Journalism & Mass Communication Quarterly*, 89, 2: 185–204.

d'Haenens, Leen, Joris, Willem and Heinderyckx, Francois eds. (2019). *Images of Immigrants and Refugees in Western Europe. Media Representations, Public Opinion and Refugees' Experiences*. Leuven: Leuven University Press, 199–202.

Leudar, Ivan, Hayes, Jacqueline, Nekvapil, Jiri, and Turner Baker, Johanna (2008). 'Hostility themes in media, community and refugee narratives.' *Discourse & Society*, 19, 2: 187–221.

Lischer, Sarah, K. (2008). 'Security and displacement in Iraq: Responding to the forced migration crisis.' *International Security*, 33, 2: 95–119.

Mcintyre, Alice. (2002). 'Women researching their lives: exploring violence and identity in Belfast, the North of Ireland.' *Qualitative Research*, 2, 3: 387–409.

Media Development Foundation. (2020). *Independent regional media in Ukraine: how to go ahead and plan*. http://mdfresearch2020.tilda.ws/ua

Minoiu, Camelia, and Shemyakina, Olga. (2012). 'Child health and conflict in Côte d'Ivoire.' *American Economic Review,* 102, 3: 294–299

Montemurro, Marzia, and Walicki, Nadine. (2010). 'Invisibility of urban IDPs in Europe.' *Forced Migration Review*, 34: 11–12. https://www.alnap.org/system/files/content/resource/files/main/montemurro-invisibility-of-urban-idps-in-europe.pdf

Muggah, Robert. (2010). 'Once We Were Warriors: Refugee Militarization In Africa' In: Alice Edwards and Carla Ferstman eds., *Human Security and Non-Citizens*. Cambridge: Cambridge University Press, 166–194.

Omata, Naohiko. (2019). ''Over-researched' and 'under-researched' refugees.' *Forced Migration Review*, 61: 15–18.

Pan, Zhongdang, and Kosicki, Gerald M. (1993). 'Framing analysis: An approach to news discourse.' *Political Communication*, 10, 1: 55–75.

Philo, Greg, Briant, Emma, and Donald, Pauline. (2013). *Bad News for Refugees*. London: Pluto Press.

Pruitt, Lesley J. (2019). 'Closed due to 'flooding'? UK media representations of refugees and migrants in 2015–2016 – creating a crisis of borders.' *The British Journal of Politics and International Relations*, 21, 2: 383–402.

Rimpiläinen, Emma. (2020). 'Victims, Villains, or Geopolitical Tools? Representations of Donbas Displacement in Ukrainian and Russian Government Media.' *Europe-Asia Studies*, 72 (3), 481–504.

Roberts, Bayard, Ocaka, Kaducu F., Browne, John, Oyok, Thomas, and Sondorp, Egbert. (2008). 'Factors associated with post-traumatic stress disorder and depression amongst internally displaced persons in northern Uganda.' *BMC Psychiatry*, 8, 1: 38.

Šarić, Ljiljana. (2019).'Visual Presentation of Refugees During the 'Refugee Crisis' of 2015–2016 on the Online Portal of the Croatian Public Broadcaster.' *International Journal of Communication*, 13: 991–1015.

Scarabicchi, Caterina. (2019). 'Borrowed voices: narrating the migrant's story in contemporary European literature between advocacy, silence and ventriloquism.' *Journal for Cultural Research*, 23, 2: 173–186.

Shemyakina, Olga. (2006). 'The effect of armed conflict on accumulation of schooling: Results from Tajikistan.' *Journal of Development Economics*, 95, 2: 186–200.

Siriwardhana, Chesmal, & Stewart, Robert. (2013). 'Forced migration and mental health: Prolonged internal displacement, return migration and resilience.' *International Health*, 5, 1: 19–23.

Smets, Kevin, Mazzocchetti, Jacinthe, Gerstmans, Lorraine, and Mostmans, Lien. (2019). 'Beyond Victimhood: Reflecting on Migrant-Victim Representations with Afghan, Iraqi, and Syrian Asylum Seekers and Refugees In Belgium'. In: Leen d'Haenens, Willem, Joris and Heinderyckx, Francois eds. (2019). *Images of Immigrants and Refugees in Western Europe. Media Representations, Public Opinion and Refugees' Experiences*. Leuven: Leuven University Press, 177–197.

Spilnyy Prostir. (2015). *Media coverage of IDPs in Ukraine (South)*. http://memo98.sk/www/uploads/_media/Ukraine_media coverage of IDPs_SOUTH__FINAL_161115.pdf

Spilnyy Prostir. (2016). *Media Monitoring Summary Report (East, North-Centre, South, West of Ukraine). Media coverage of Internally Displaced Persons in the Ukrainian mass media*. http://www.prostir-monitor.org/upload/reports/final-reports-wave-3/Summary_W3-en.pdf

Su, Rick. (2010). 'Immigration as Urban Policy.' *Fordham Urban Law Journal*, 38, 1: 363–391.

Toria, Malkhaz. (2015). 'Remembering Homeland in Exile: Recollections of IDPs from the Abkhazia Region of Georgia.' *Journal on Ethnopolitics and Minority Issues in Europe*, 14, 1: 48–70.

Torosyan, Karine, Pignatti, Norberto, and Obrizan, Maksym. (2018). 'Job market outcomes for IDPs: The case of Georgia.' *Journal of Comparative Economics*, 46, 3: 800–820.

Tyyskä, Appu., Blower, Jenna, Deboer, Samantha, Kawai, Shunya, and Walcott, Ashley. (2018). 'Canadian media coverage of the Syrian refugee crisis: Representation, response, and resettlement.' *Geopolitics, History, and International Relations*, 10, 1: 148–166.

USAID. (2019). 'Media Consumption Survey.' https://drive.google.com/file/d/1Oi2Edvl5Srk4hS-D2KoxoKkamCarUX7f/view

World Bank. (2015). 'Georgia Transitioning from Status to Needs Based Assistance for IDPs. A Poverty and Social Impact Analysis,' https://openknowledge.worldbank.org/handle/10986/24412

Acknowledgment

Funding from the Norwegian Research Council (NORRUSS project 287267, 'Ukrainian Geopolitical Fault-line Cities: Urban Identity, Geopolitics and Urban Policy') supported this work.

Note on Indexing

Our books do not have indexes due to the prohibitive cost of assembling them. If you are reading this book in paperback and want to find a particular word or phrase you can do so by downloading a free PDF version of this book from the E-International Relations website. View the e-book in any standard PDF reader and enter your search terms in the search box. You can then navigate through the search results and find what you are looking for. If you are using apps (or devices) to read our e-books, you should also find word search functionality in those.

You can find all of our books here: http://www.e-ir.info/publications

www.ingramcontent.com/pod-product-compliance
Lightning Source LLC
Chambersburg PA
CBHW071610080526
44588CB00010B/1089